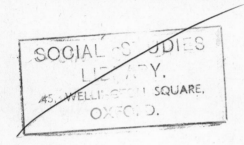

Care of the child facing death

Care of the child facing death

Edited by
Dr Lindy Burton

Nuffield Department of Child Health,
The Queen's University of Belfast

Foreword by

I. J. Carré, M.A., M.D., F.R.C.P., D.C.H.

Professor of Child Health,
The Queen's University of Belfast

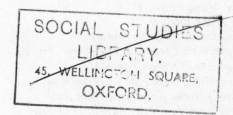

Routledge & Kegan Paul
London and Boston

First published in 1974
by Routledge & Kegan Paul Ltd
Broadway House, 68-74 Carter Lane,
London EC4V 5EL and
9 Park Street,
Boston, Mass. 02108, USA
Set in 10/11 English
and printed in Great Britain by
The Lavenham Press Ltd, Lavenham, Suffolk.
© Routledge & Kegan Paul 1974

ISBN 0 7100 7863 3
Library of Congress Catalog Card No. 74-80749

Contents

Part III **Helping the child**

Part IV **Helping the family**

Contributors

Margaret Atkin, Head of the Social Work Department, The Hospital for Sick Children, Great Ormond Street, London.

Lindy Burton, Research Psychologist, Nuffield Department of Child Health, The Queen's University of Belfast.

Yvonne Craig, J.P.

John A. Dodge, Department of Paediatrics, Welsh National School of Medicine, Cardiff.

Janet Duberley, Sister-in-Charge, Children's Ward, St Thomas's Hospital, London.

George A. Edelstyn, Consultant Oncologist, Hume Street Hospital, Dublin, and Northern Ireland Radiotherapy Centre, Belfast.

Pamela Gibbons, Casework Consultant, Invalid Children's Aid Association, London.

Bianca Gordon, Consultant Psychotherapist, Hampstead Child Therapy Clinic, London.

Roy Howarth, Consultant in Psychiatric Medicine, The Hospital for Sick Children, Great Ormond Street, London.

Mary Lindsay, Consultant Child Psychiatrist, Aylesbury and Bletchley Child Guidance Clinics, and Department of Paediatrics, Stoke Mandeville Hospital, Aylesbury.

Dermod MacCarthy, Consultant Paediatrician, Stoke Mandeville Hospital, Aylesbury.

Audrey T. McCollum, Research Associate in Social Work, Department of Pediatrics, Yale University School of Medicine, Connecticut.

Alexander T. Mennie, Consultant, Pain Research unit, Royal Marsden Hospital, London.

CONTRIBUTORS

Maureen Oswin, Hospital Teacher, London.

Mary Patten, Lecturer in Sociology, Department of Extra-Mural Studies, The Queen's University of Belfast.

Michael B. Rothenberg, formerly Departments of Pediatrics and Psychiatry, Albert Einstein College of Medicine, and the Bronx Municipal Hospital Center, New York.

Rev. Simon Stephens, Founder of the Society of Compassionate Friends.

Foreword

Professor I. J. Carré

During the past half-century social changes embodying improvements in domestic hygiene, nutrition and living standards, together with advances in medical knowledge, have brought about a dramatic reduction in infant and childhood mortality. Whereas former generations of parents expected, and to some extent were prepared, to lose at least one child during his early years, such an eventuality is now beyond contemplation. Whilst this situation is a cause for satisfaction, the fact that some childhood mortality is no longer considered inevitable tends to accentuate the difficulties of families who have to contend with a potentially fatal childhood illness.

Not only has the general improvement in life expectancy made it more difficult for parents to accept the diagnosis and prognosis of their child's illness, but it has also removed a great deal of community support. As a generation we are inexperienced in dealing with the problem of death. The ceremonial aspect of death has declined, if not largely disappeared, and in an increasingly secular society traditional sources of religious support are no longer so widely valued. With greater geographical and social mobility near relatives are not so readily available, and families faced with supporting a potentially dying child are often at a loss to know where to turn for help.

Such difficulties are not confined to parents. Many of those whose professional task it is to care for the sick and the dying are equally ill-prepared and insufficiently supported for their role. Present-day medicine demands mastery of increasingly complex diagnostic procedures and therapeutic regimes which tends to leave little time for the non-physical management of disease. Equally, the still prevailing attitude of equating medical success with patient survival results in insufficient emphasis being accorded to the supportive aspects of patient care. A patient's death challenges professional competence and so is subconsciously resented and denied. Such denial is mirrored in the failure of medical and nurse training programmes to accord the care of the terminally ill adequate significance in their curricula. A new perspective is needed. We must depose physical recovery as the sole criterion of medical effectiveness and replace it by the challenge of providing a patient with as normal and complete a life as possible. Instead of viewing the patient solely as a repository of challenging symptoms, greater attention must be focused on him as a whole and unique person, with complex emotions, social and intellectual needs.

Such an approach may in itself do much to counteract his physical distress. It is argued in this book that pain can be potentiated by an adverse emotional and social environment, and that an unhappy child is ill-equipped either to combat disease or participate actively in treatment. It is now widely recognised that a child's personality can be adversely affected by inadequately supported illness and hospitalisation. This fact is not only of significance to the child with a reversible disorder. Improvements in therapy which today can only prolong life, may tomorrow effect a cure, and should a child's physical survival be the sole cause of concern he may ultimately emerge physically intact but emotionally scarred. Equally, whether he lives or dies, the experiences which his family have to sustain during his illness may in turn have a profound effect—either positive or negative—both upon their own physical and mental health, and upon the emotional integrity of their other children.

The emotional problems posed by illness are not unique to children. Fear of separation, pain, mutilation and death are common to everyone irrespective of age. Moreover, whilst medical advances have extended life they have also made it harder to die so that children with a potentially fatal illness may live for months or even years in a limbo of expected demise. The resultant stresses and strains imposed on a family can therefore be of harrowing intensity and duration.

Family strength rather than weakness in the face of adversity is accorded particular emphasis in this book. Dr Burton, as a child psychologist, experienced in working with sick children and their parents, has endeavoured in her own contributions to evaluate the factors which make for positive adaptation to the situation. As such, much valuable information is provided about the ways in which family members face up to, and overcome, threats to their domestic and emotional stability. Methods of coping with a potentially fatal disease are not dissimilar to those used by families to overcome other social and economic threats. The experience and knowledge gained from dealing with an illness situation may thus be usefully applied to other social dilemmas.

This book is therefore concerned with pinpointing the problems which exist for parents and those involved in the care of sick children, both in terms of accepting the facts of a child's illness, and in loving, supporting, and stimulating him to maximum functioning within the limits of his condition. As well as general problems, more specific difficulties are considered such as those of the child in pain and the child and his family who have to shoulder the burden of an exacting treatment régime. The vexed question of what, and how much, to say to a sick child about his illness is also fully discussed. But perhaps the strength of this book lies not so much in highlighting the problems, but rather in enumerating the many sources of help available within the community for the sick child and his family. Full use of such resources can do much to alleviate the feelings of isolation and hopelessness which can so often prove to be the most damaging and wide-ranging aspect of this situation.

Part I   General problems

1 The size and nature of the problem

John A. Dodge

Thirty years ago it was not uncommon to find groups of small children scaring each other with tales of pneumonia, diphtheria, or tuberculosis. Similarly, a century earlier cholera and scarlet fever were childhood bogies. Today's children are scarcely aware of such diseases, and certainly their existence presents them with no threat. Social development and advances in medical knowledge since the mid-nineteenth century have virtually eliminated these sources of fear. Equally, the sweeping social changes of the last century, and the improvements in living standards and domestic hygiene, have meant that it is no longer a matter for favourable comment when a mother of a large family successfully rears all her children: this is what we have come to expect. Now, not only the fittest survive, but death, when it comes to a child, is the more bitter for being stealthy, unexpected and selective.

Today, childhood deaths are relatively infrequent (Table 1 summarises details for the United Kingdom), the most numerous being in the immediate newborn period, from disorders associated with prematurity and the birth process. Infant deaths are often sudden and unexplained ('cot death'), and throughout childhood accidental death figures prominently in the mortality statistics. Such children die after a very short illness, or none at all, and are not therefore the subjects of this chapter.

In contrast to the last century, death from infections such as pneumonia is uncommon, unless it occurs in a child who is already chronically ill or congenitally malformed, when it is simply a terminal event. Malnutrition—a major underlying factor which predisposes children to die with an infection—has largely been removed from our community, though its presence in developing countries contributes to high mortality rates and continues to cause concern.

3

Table 1   *England and Wales 1970**

Deaths, all causes 0—14 years	18,997
Tuberculosis	26
Poliomyelitis	5
Diphtheria	0
Neoplasms (including leukaemia)	844
Respiratory diseases	3,210
Cystic fibrosis	132
Accidents, poisoning and violence	2,042
Congenital anomalies	3,526

*From the Registrar General's Report.

Despite all this, from time to time the paediatrician, surgeon or family doctor finds himself telling parents that their child has a deadly disease. It may be a malignant process, such as leukaemia or a brain tumour, or it may be an inherited progressive disorder of the nervous system or muscles. Other conditions such as cystic fibrosis have a variable but not inevitably downward course, so that the prognosis, although statistically gloomy, must be given very cautiously. The fact is that we can rarely predict with any degree of accuracy the duration, or severity of course, which any individual child's illness will take. Nevertheless, analysis of records from different centres enables us to obtain a clear picture of average survival times from diagnosis, and current trends towards more effective treatment.

Childhood malignancy

In the field of childhood malignancy, tumours of the brain are the most numerous (Table 2). They are of various types and found in several different sites, and although all present problems of diagnosis and treatment, some carry a relatively good outlook. The onset is usually insidious. Fits, a common presenting symptom of cerebral tumours in adults, are much less frequent, and occur later, when a child is the victim. This is probably due to the fact that most childhood tumours lie in the brainstem, whereas in adults the majority of growths occur in the cerebral hemispheres. The occurrence of persistent headaches, often accompanied by vomiting, may indicate that the intra-cranial pressure is raised, but occurs whether the cause is a tumour, an abscess, meningitis or hydrocephalus, and is in no way specific. Highly malignant tumours of the brainstem are

4

inoperable and rapidly fatal, with sometimes a limited response to radiotherapy. Tumours in the cerebellum may disturb balance and limb movements, but are sometimes slowly growing, relatively benign, and susceptible to complete removal leaving varying degrees of handicap. An unusual variety of tumour, the craniopharyngioma, arises from an embryological remnant in the region of the pituitary gland, and by local pressure produces impairment of the hormonal regulation of growth and sexual development, as well as interfering with vision. Although it is not usually malignant, it can be extremely difficult to remove because its situation is almost inaccessible without serious damage to vital structures. Pineal gland tumours are rare, but may present as precocious puberty, also due to a disturbance of the endocrine system.

Table 2 *Approximate annual incidence of certain childhood illnesses in Great Britain**

Cerebral tumours	700
Other tumours (kidney, adrenal, embryonic, etc.)	600
Leukaemia, lymphatic	320
Leukaemia, myeloid	80
Cystic fibrosis	600
Degenerative diseases of the brain and nervous system	< 100
Measles	300,000
Spina bifida	3,000

*Sources: Registrar General's Survey, 1967-71 and personal communications from the Cystic Fibrosis Research Trust, the Leukaemia Society, and the Hospital for Sick Children, Great Ormond Street, London.

With the exception of some tumours which are associated with rare inherited disorders of the nervous system and skin (neurofibromatosis, tuberose sclerosis), the aetiology of brain tumours is quite unknown. The prognosis is bad, death usually occurring within months of diagnosis in the case of brainstem tumours. In the more benign, well defined tumours of the cerebellum or cerebral hemispheres, cystic changes may occur and even when complete surgical removal is not possible a fatal outcome may sometimes be postponed for many years by simple drainage. Similarly, relief of pressure can sometimes be brought about by inserting a drainage tube into the ventricles of the brain with the other end passing into the circulation. In this way worthwhile palliation may be provided particularly when a slowly growing tumour is situated in such a way that it obstructs the flow of cerebro-spinal fluid. It must be emphasised, however, that the brain tumours most frequently encountered in children are not really amenable to any of the treatments currently available.

Near to the brain, the retinoblastoma is a highly malignant tumour of the eye. It has an hereditary basis. Removal of the eye may be curative, along with drug treatment. When, as sometimes occurs, the tumours are bilateral, the more severely affected eye is removed and a suitable drug can be injected into the artery supplying the other. Like most very malignant tumours, it is very sensitive to radiation and to chemical agents, so that in the absence of widespread secondary deposits a favourable outcome may follow if the tumour has been detected in time.

Abdominal tumours are next in order of frequency to those of the brain. Within the abdomen, neuroblastomas arising from the adrenal glands are slightly more common than nephroblastomas arising from the kidneys. Both of these tumours are only found during childhood. The neuroblastoma is actually derived from the adrenal medulla, the part of the gland which originated in the embryo from the primitive nervous system. Neuroblastomas are very malignant, and tend to produce secondary deposits at distant sites such as the long bones of the limbs, and, characteristically, in the orbit behind the eye. They are unusual tumours in that they occasionally undergo spontaneous regression, so that evaluation of treatment is not always easy. It was this fact which led to a vogue for treating neuroblastomas with injections of vitamin B12 but later trials failed to confirm its usefulness. With a combination of agressive surgery and radiotherapy, three-year survival rates of up to 60 per cent are being reported, and a large proportion of these children will probably be completely cured. Neuroblastomas of infancy have a decidedly better prognosis than those occurring in older children. Following appropriate treatment, it is possible to test the urine at intervals for specific products of the tumour, and by this means recurrences can be detected.

Nephroblastomas are also known as Wilm's tumours. They occur in the kidney and may come to light when the child passes blood in his urine, or on feeling a large hard mass in his abdomen. In recent years treatment has been directed along several lines: complete surgical excision of the tumour followed by radiotherapy. Distant secondary deposits often respond to chemotherapy with agents such as actinomycin D, and sometimes surgical removal of secondaries is also worthwhile.

Current opinion is that whenever possible treatment of childhood malignancies should be centralised on a regional basis, so that an experienced team of physicians, surgeons, radiotherapists and pathologists may bring to each young patient the necessary expertise.

The same requirements obtain for leukaemias which are essentially a form of malignancy which affects the white blood cells. The peak incidence in children is between the ages of two and four years. The most common variety is acute lymphatic leukaemia where microscopic examination of a blood film characteristically shows a greatly enlarged number of primitive lymphocytes. The lymphatic glands of the body are enlarged, and superficial ones in the neck, groins and armpits can be easily felt. (It must be remembered that there are very many other causes of glandular enlargement, most of which are benign. Much unnecessary anxiety is produced by the mere discovery of a few enlarged glands in the neck in children suffering from nothing more serious than a mild respiratory infection.)

Acute myeloid leukaemia is less frequently encountered in children, and is distinguished by the presence of large numbers of leucocytes of a different variety in the circulating blood. Some of the important symptoms in both types include lassitude, pallor, shortness of breath, throat and mouth infections, bleeding gums, spontaneous bruising and proneness to infection. The onset is abrupt and symptoms at the time of diagnosis rarely extend back more than a few weeks. Deposits of abnormal blood cells may be found in the liver and spleen, and also in the bones where they may give rise to severe pain. Diagnosis is made by examination of the blood and also of a small sample of bone marrow which is obtained with a needle. The marrow puncture is repeated at intervals to determine the efficacy of the treatment: relapse will be detected earlier than by waiting for the abnormal cells to reappear in the peripheral blood. Sometimes deposits appear in the meninges which cover the brain and spinal cord, giving rise to a type of meningitis, but fortunately this complication usually responds well to local injection of a drug by a lumbar puncture.

The basic cause of leukaemia is unknown. Much research is in progress to determine the factors which cause white blood cells to multiply and invade. The leukaemic cells are abnormal and despite their large numbers are ineffective in combating infection. Leukaemic changes can be induced in the blood of certain strains of mouse by exposing them to irradiation by X-rays, and by some viruses, but the relationship between mouse and human leukaemias is not very clear. In humans, it is sometimes observed that a number of children in one locality may develop leukaemia within a short time of each other, suggesting an infective origin, but the incidence is so low that additional factors must operate to make individual children especially susceptible. Neither the identity of the hypothetical viral agent nor the nature of the predisposing factors in the child have been ascertained, and apart from the observation that leukaemia is commoner than expected in mongol children, little evidence exists that there is any genetic predisposition. The increased risk to brothers and sisters of affected children is very slight.

Treatment is aimed at suppressing production of the abnormal cells, a process known as inducing a remission. In complete remission, a child should be in good general health with no evidence either clinically, or on bone marrow examination, that he is suffering from leukaemia. Such a remission is obtainable in the great majority of children with acute lymphatic leukaemia, and about half of those with the acute myeloid variety. Treatment must be continued to prevent a relapse, and different drugs are used for maintenance than those employed for inducing a remission. The maintenance drugs may be given in an alternating, cyclical fashion, or in one long course of the same drug.

First remissions of up to three years are now quite common, but after relapse has occurred subsequent remissions are usually of shorter duration, the disease responding less well even though heroic treatment is employed. It is therefore essential to make the initial attack as effective as possible, with full dosage of appropriate drugs while the disease is responsive. The drugs used to induce remission in lymphatic leukaemia include prednisone (a synthetic hormone) and vincristine (a plant extract). Prednisone may produce a moon-like facial appearance, but its short-term use as an induction agent is unlikely to cause any serious side effects. Similarly, although vincristine can have severe unwanted effects if used for a prolonged period, it is unlikely to cause more than a relatively mild bowel upset when used for induction. The maintenance drugs, such as cyclophosphamide, 6-mercaptopurine and methotrexate may cause a variety of toxic effects, including mouth ulcers, diarrhoea, alopecia and liver damage. In standard dosage these may not be troublesome. Acute myeloid leukaemia responds best to daunorubicin and cytosine arabinoside, but unfortunately these drugs have a marked effect on production of normal as well as abnormal blood cells so that correct dosage levels can be difficult to achieve. A completely different approach to treatment is one which stimulates the patient's own defence mechanisms to destroy the malignant cells. Following reduction of the leukaemia cell population by intensive standard chemotherapy, antibody production is stimulated by injections of BCG (a tuberculosis vaccine), irradiated leukaemic cells, or both. Early results of this therapy have been encouraging and extensive trials are in progress, particularly in France. Clearly, the care given to leukaemic children and their families must be undertaken with great skill and sensitivity, and with all the facilities of a large medical centre.

Inherited disorders

Not all the prolonged fatal illnesses of childhood are due to malignant processes. There are a number of inherited disorders of the nervous system which run a variable but relentless course before a fatal termination (the psycho-social implications of which are dealt with in chapter 5 p. 60). One such disorder, Werdnig-Hoffman disease, affects primarily the spinal cord, leading to generalised paralysis. The course is more rapid when the onset is early in infancy, and such infants usually die before their first birthday. The milder nature of the disease in older children suggests that it may be a different, though similar, condition, and indeed there are a number of disorders formerly included in this diagnostic category which are now clearly demarcated. It is important to make an accurate diagnosis, after electromyographic studies, muscle biopsies and enzyme estimations, because true Werdnig-Hoffman disease progresses inexorably, whereas some superficially similar children will make a partial or complete recovery. No curative treatment is available at the present time.

Degenerative disorders of the brain are many and varied. They are frequently known by eponyms such as Tay Sachs disease, Krabbe's disease, Batten's disease and Pelizaeus-Merzbacher disease. The symptoms and signs differ according to the age of onset, the rapidity of progress and the structures involved within the brain. The clinical picture of one of them, metachromatic leucodystrophy, will serve as an example for the group. Typically, the patient is a child of three to four years of age whose early development was entirely normal. Gradually he develops difficulty in walking and is noted to be clumsy and rather unsteady on his feet, particularly when he tries to run. Within a year mental deterioration is apparent, and the child tends to be withdrawn and to play more and more by himself. He later loses control over his bladder and bowels, and his speech becomes indistinct and incoherent. By this stage he is unable to understand much more than simple commands. Further deterioration occurs in both his mental state and his limb movements, until he finally becomes bedridden. His paralysed state and inability to clear his chest of inhaled secretions makes him prone to pneumonia, which may prove to be the final event. The whole course of metachromatic leucodystrophy is usually about three years, but longer survival is not uncommon.

Post-mortem examination may be necessary before an accurate diagnosis can be made although in the case of metachromatic leucodystrophy examination of the nerve cells seen in a biopsy taken from the rectum or from a peripheral nerve is usually sufficient. Clinical and microscopic examination of these cells will reveal the presence of an abnormal deposit with characteristic staining properties. Such deposits which differ in their nature from one disease to another are found in a number of these degenerative diseases. The substances are accumulated because a particular enzyme responsible for their normal chemical breakdown is missing from the patient's cells. The capacity to manufacture a particular enzyme is inherited from the parents, and understanding of basic genetics is necessary in order to appreciate the way in which certain types of disease may occur in families where no previous generations appear to have been afflicted.

Within the nucleus of each cell in the body there are structures known as chromosomes. These have a rod-like shape and in man they number 46. They can be distinguished from each other by their length and other characteristics so that they may be set in pairs of identical chromosomes numbered from 1 to 22, the twenty-third pair being made up of the sex chromosomes. In females there are two sex chromosomes of equal length which are known as X chromosomes, while in the male there is only one X chromosome, the other member of the pair being smaller and known as a Y chromosome. The information required to pass on characteristics from one generation to another is contained within the genes which are arranged in sequence along each chromosome. Each gene will have its counterpart on the corresponding chromosome of any twin pair, except in the case of the male sex chromosomes where part of the X has no equivalent on the Y. There is therefore only one representative of certain genes in the male. The chromosomes and their genes have been inherited one from each parent, and they determine many of our characteristics, including such things as hair and eye colour. Where conflicting characteristics are transmitted, for example inheritance of a gene for blue eyes from one parent and that for brown eyes from the other, only one of these will operate in the child, (in this case the gene for brown eyes). This will be known as the dominant gene, and the other is termed recessive. Faulty genes are usually recessive so that the inheritance of a normal dominant from one parent will suffice to ensure that the offspring is normal. The carrier of a faulty gene may however transmit it to his own children just as readily as the normal gene. When two faulty genes are inherited, the capacity to manufacture the enzymes for which they are responsible is lost. Various types of disease may result from such an enzyme deficiency including most of the group of neurological degenerative disorders. Each disease is due to the lack of a specific enzyme with which a specific gene is connected. The marriage of two carriers of a recessive condition implies a risk that one child in four will be affected and this risk remains the same each time the mother becomes pregnant. Clearly the fact that the parents have produced one abnormal child does not mean that the next three will be normal. The chances of a further combination of two abnormal genes remains one in four.

A well-known example of a recessively inherited condition is cystic fibrosis. The specific defect in this condition has not yet been established but it appears to be connected with transport of certain materials across cell walls. It is a relatively common condition, occurring approximately once in every two thousand live births, and the gene is carried by about one person in every twenty-five. It may present in several ways. At birth the child may be found to have an obstruction to his bowels produced by excessively sticky and tenacious meconium. Later in infancy he is likely to suffer from repeated chest infections and these may progress until extensive and severe lung damage has occurred. The digestive juices produced by the pancreas are deficient so that the child's food is not properly absorbed and stools become large, greasy and foul smelling. The sweat of these children is excessively salty, and this is the basis of the diagnostic test which is used.

With modern treatment children with cystic fibrosis are living longer and sometimes grow up to adult life but a large proportion still die in childhood from intractable respiratory disease. A diagnosis of cystic fibrosis is not therefore synonymous with a death sentence although for some children it does not prove possible to maintain life for more than a few years. Treatment is aimed both at controlling the digestive disorder and keeping the chest free from infection. The addition of extracts of animal pancreas to the food can be an effective replacement for the digestive enzymes but unfortunately all the preparations in present use are more or less unpalatable and sometimes children refuse to take them. Reduction of the amount of fat in the diet is another useful approach. Additional vitamins are also necessary in the majority of cases. It is the chest disease which is most serious and is the usual cause of death. Physiotherapy can play a great part in clearing mucus from the chest but it needs to be carried out at least twice a day, and is very time-consuming especially when there are several affected children in the family. (Chapter 6 deals in greater detail with the social problems involved.) During physiotherapy the child is kept in a rather uncomfortable position, and some parents find it quite impossible to carry out at home. Antibiotic treatment is given for every chest infection, and in some children is kept up continuously. In North America, and, to a lesser extent, in Britain children with cystic fibrosis sleep in mist tents in which the air is fully saturated. This means that a noisy compressor is kept running all night in their bedrooms, and the children wake up with wet bedclothes and pillows. Obviously this can be most inconvenient particularly when the family live in crowded circumstances. Frequent hospital admissions are likely to be necessary for intensive physiotherapy and management of severe chest infections.

A different type of inheritance pattern is known as X-linked in-heritance. The gene responsible for an X-linked characteristic is carried on the X-chromosome. In male children the X-chromosome has been derived from the mother, and the Y from the father. A defective gene on the unpaired region of the X-chromosome has no complementary normal dominant gene to mitigate its effects: hence the child will suffer from the effects of the abnormal gene. Female children, on the other hand, will derive a normal gene from the father which will be present on their second X-chromosome, and will not show any clinical evidence of the disease. The best-known example of this type of X-linked inheritance where apparently normal females transmit an abnormality to some of their male off-spring is haemophilia, which so devastated the royal families of Europe during the last century. Haemophilia is now rarely fatal, although its effects may be crippling.

An X-linked disease which is unfortunately still inexorable in its progress, and fatal in outcome, is the Duchenne type of muscular dystrophy. As with metachromatic leucodystrophy, the affected boy appears normal in early infancy but develops weakness in his legs when he is perhaps three or four years old. He has particular difficulty in rising from a recumbent position, characteristically 'climbing up his legs' with his hands. His calf muscles appear bulky, giving rise to the name 'pseudohypertrophic' muscular dystrophy, but microscopic examination reveals that the muscle cells have largely been replaced by fat. Over a period of one to two decades the weakness increases, ultimately affecting the upper limbs. The child requires braces on his legs to keep him upright, but later takes to a wheelchair existence and finally to his bed. His intelligence is only slightly impaired, if at all, and he is well aware of both the nature and outcome of his disease, especially if he has had similarly afflicted older brothers. Blood tests performed on his female relatives can sometimes, but not always, predict which of them are carriers. Half the male offspring of carrier females are likely to develop muscular dystrophy. There are other less common varieties of muscle disease also called dystrophies, which can affect females as well as males. Their course is much more benign, and full life-span is possible.

Congenital malformation

An example of a congenital malformation which may cause death shortly after birth, or after a variable passage of time, is spina bifida. Minor degrees of spina bifida are compatible with a normal life, but in the most severe cases infants are born with an open sac in the lumbar area of the back, and concomitant paralysis and deformity of the legs, incontinence, and severe hydrocephalus. Survival in these instances may not be more than a few months or, at best, a few years. Between these extremes it becomes a matter of judgement as to whether the quality and duration of life to be achieved justifies a lengthy series of operations designed to close the lesion on the back, control the hydrocephalus which is usually present, provide an alternative bladder with an outlet to an external bag, and to help the patient stand and perhaps walk after various orthopaedic procedures. The alternative approach, to do nothing but wait for the child to die from meningitis or pneumonia, is justifiable in practical terms only if it succeeds; and everyone involved in this field knows only too well that this sequel is not predictable. The result may be a live child suffering even greater handicaps following medical neglect, but nevertheless likely to live for a number of years. Current trends are towards accurate assessment of the problems shortly after birth, with careful selection of those who will benefit from treatment. Unfortunately it is extremely difficult to establish criteria for selection. Some workers hold the view that all children with spina bifida should be subjected to the whole gamut of techniques which may be required to keep them alive and make them mobile, but it is questionable whether the misery of the child, and the prolonged anxiety of the parents, may not outweigh the possible moral and professional satisfaction to be gained. Others, equally sincere, feel that virtually all these children should be 'left to die' and that limited medical resources should be deployed elsewhere: but it is fair to state that this is usually an armchair view taken in the abstract by persons not directly involved in the care of these children. For most paediatricians and surgeons the therapeutic choice in spina bifida is a recurring dilemma for which reliable guidelines are urgently needed. Hope is appearing that the basic cause of spina bifida may be discovered, and ultimately that it may be preventable. At present we are aware that mothers who have given birth to an affected child have an increased risk of repeating the experience; but the statistics do not fit a predictable genetic pattern. It may be that some factor in the uterine environment is responsible, possibly some substance in the mother's diet which has a harmful effect on the developing fetus.

Other congenital malformations may shorten life without being fatal in the newborn period. Some varieties of congenital heart disease may be inoperable, so that the child gradually goes downhill over a period of months or occasionally years. He is short of breath, has difficulty feeding, may look blue, and may at times experience chest pain. With the great progress in surgical techniques in recent years, more and more children with heart disease can be treated, either in a palliative fashion, or by complete correction of their defect, but there remains a number for whom nothing worthwhile can be done.

Chronic kidney disease also occurs from time to time, either as a result of a congenital malformation, or from progressive changes following infection. Children in chronic renal failure may live for a number of years, with dietary restriction and drug therapy. It is possible to keep them alive in the same way as adults, by regular use of a dialysis machine, in the hope that a suitable donor will be found to allow transplantation of a kidney. In Great Britain, few transplants have been performed on children, but it is estimated that 250 a year have chronic renal failure, and might be suitable for this procedure.

The future

Research in various fields is opening up possibilities for prevention and treatment of some of the disorders which have been mentioned. It is possible to directly visualise the fetus in the uterus at an early stage of pregnancy using a special fine probe like a periscope. If a major malformation such as spina bifida is present, the mother may be offered a termination of pregnancy. The sex of the child can be detected either directly or by microscopic examination of some superficial cells, and in the case of an X-linked disease, carrier mothers reassured that the child is a girl or offered termination in the case of a boy. Estimation of specific enzyme activity in the cells is also a possibility, and has been used to successfully predict the outcome in pregnancies where there is a risk of certain genetic defects. Some of these enzyme defects may be correctable, either by replacement of the missing enzyme using human plasma infusions, or actually 'grafting' the enzyme into cells using a virus as the transfer agent. These techniques are in early stages of development but offer some hope for the future. With some conditions, such as cystic fibrosis, early diagnosis and adequate treatment seem to greatly improve the survival rate, and attempts are being made to establish a reliable screening test which can be applied to *all* newborn infants. An aggressive approach, using surgery, chemotherapy and radiotherapy is likely to be rewarding in some varieties of childhood malignancy, and further improved survival and a higher percentage of complete cures can be expected in this area. The management of leukaemic children in the best centres is also allowing a little guarded optimism that the long-sought 'breakthough' in treatment may not be too far away.

2 Tolerating the intolerable— the problems facing parents and children following diagnosis*

Lindy Burton

The parents

Little is worse for parents than learning that their child has a life-threatening illness. The diagnosis itself implies pain and hopelessness, and seems to preclude all joyful expectations for a normal, satisfying life together. As such, it is responded to not just as a threat for the future but as a real and actual loss, beginning at the moment the news is broken.[8,23]

The way in which parents respond to this loss will vary considerably, depending on a wide range of background factors, some of them in existence even prior to the establishment of the family. In this respect some researchers[21,31,35] believe social class membership, cultural background, religious affiliation and financial status to be significant factors. Others[24,45,66,77] emphasise the importance of psychodynamic factors such as the parents' mode of coping with past crises, their previous experience with illness and death, the previous losses they have sustained, and the special meaning the sick child has for them. The support given by family members to each other is of prime significance. Indeed 'at no other times does the previous integration of the personality and of the family unit reflect itself so clearly'.[66]

The child's actual physical condition, and his response to being sick, will also influence his parents' reactions to the diagnosis. If the child accepts his illness bravely, fights against incapacity, and is relatively free from pain, parental adaptation will be facilitated. In addition, the sex, birth order, and age of the child at the onset of

*For convenience, problems facing parents and children are dealt with separately in this chapter, but it cannot be emphasised too strongly that parents and children always interact, and the responses of one to the situation influence the responses of the other.

16

symptoms may influence parental adaptation to diagnosis.[77] The conditions of treatment—whether home or hospital based—will also be of significance, parents most usually responding best where the child remains close to them.

Whilst emphasising the vast individual differences displayed by parents in both short and long term adaptation to diagnosis, clinical observation has shown that most respond initially as if already bereaved, exhibiting a syndrome of anticipatory mourning, not unlike the classical mourning syndrome described first by Lindemann.[43] The diagnosis may be experienced as a physical blow or injury to the self, following which parents may feel stunned or in a state of shock. This is especially apparent where the child's prediagnostic medical history was insufficient to warn them of the severity of his condition. Sometimes, upon being told the prognosis, a sense of numbness or unreality is experienced, serving to defend the individual from a full appreciation—especially an emotional appreciation—of the unwanted news.[14,49] Such numbing may enable parents to function adequately in the stressful situation, though some sensitive parents may detect this apparent lack of affect in themselves, and become disturbed by what they take to be a sudden loss of feeling for the child.

Denial of either the diagnosis or prognosis is not uncommon at this stage, and serves as an additional defence against excessively painful emotions. In this way denial may temporarily subserve a useful purpose—making an intolerable situation partially tolerable.[17]

Where early symptoms were slight, or apparently non-existent, some parents may seek a second opinion, themselves comb the relevant medical literature in search of loopholes through which the child may escape;[10] or take the child to a faith healer. Where previous symptoms were severe enough to preclude denial of the severity of the condition 'it was the hopelessness of the prognosis that mothers were compelled to deny or fight'.[8] Denial is probably reduced when parents are immediately involved in the child's treatment, and Knudson and Natterson[36] found that allowing parents to participate in their child's hospital care is especially valuable in this context.

Inevitably, with time, and continuing disease manifestations, denial is replaced by an acknowledgment of the child's condition, and parents commence to grieve for the anticipated loss. Many clinicians have noted somatic disturbances indicative of grief, such as loss of appetite and feelings of nausea and nervousness,[8,14] sleep disturbances[59] and feelings of weakness, sighing, crying, depression and preoccupation with the child.[23,39,47,79] In this context, Orbach,[59]

17

using a projective personality test (the Thematic Appreciation Test) with mothers of leukaemic children, found evidence to suggest that such anticipatory mourning was taking place at an unconscious level long before treatment procedures were exhausted.

For parents 'the capacity to produce unimpaired offspring is psychologically and culturally important';[2] and, when the diagnosis becomes known, parents may experience a sense of personal inadequacy, seeing it as a slur on their own child-rearing abilities. Cummings[15] has described how mothers of chronically ill children show a higher level of psychological discomfort and social alienation than mothers of normal children, and probably all parents of children with a life-threatening illness repeatedly question the reasons for its occurrence. In the extreme, such questionings lead to agonising self appraisals. Some clinicians[8,17,36] feel that such appraisals mirror parental feelings of guilt and responsibility, whilst others[14,24] view them as part of the parents' attempt to understand the causation of the disease. This search to understand the origins of the illness may further defend the parents from a full appreciation of the situation, for it enables them to concentrate on details, thereby avoiding 'the more general, but also the more tragic and threatening aspects of the case'.[25]

Inevitably emotional acceptance of the severity of the child's condition is accompanied by an alteration in parental hopes for the child. Whereas previously the child 'was the embodiment of a promise', after diagnosis 'the promise is either gone or at least reduced in value'.[77] Diminished hopes produce bitterness and anger, and the feeling of being unjustly singled out by an ironic fate. Such feelings are accentuated where physicians seem unable to arrest or reverse the course of the disease. Whilst some parents may attempt to choke down such anger, others express it, either directly against the disease[8] or against the doctor[71] because he seems impotent to act.

Occasionally parents find themselves becoming angry with the sick child. Such a response is normal and understandable, for 'If a human being has been meaningful to his family, they feel angry because he is leaving them, or is being taken from them. His dying deprives them of a relationship that had emotional importance'.[17]

Such anger may be expressed indirectly, for example Tropauer[79] writing of children with cystic fibrosis, found that parental hostility was conveyed to the child by the strength of the mother's pounding during necessary physiotherapy sessions. But open expression of such resentment is rarely possible—for who could be angry with a dying child?—so there is a need to displace this emotion on to other family members and even well children may be used as scapegoats for expression of pent-up feelings. Bozemann[8] noted such hostility, and one mother of a nine-year-old girl dying of a brain tumour told me:

'When I come back from the hospital I can't bear the other children near me. It seems such an insult to her to be cuddling them. I hate to see other children in the street too, being happy. I keep thinking, "why couldn't it have been an unwanted child, not her".'

Such changes in wider relationships are characteristic of the bereaved. Lindemann[43] observed, 'There is a disconcerting loss of warmth in relation to other people and a tendency to respond with irritability and anger—a wish not to be bothered with others'.

Inevitably such hostility produces resentment in well children who do not understand its origins. They may also resent the attention given to the sick child.[6,68] Behaviour disorders and depression may result, further stressing the parents.

Green and Solnit[28] have described the processes whereby parents attempt to conceal and compensate for the latent hostility occasioned by their sense of impending loss by becoming over-protective towards their children. With well children, such over-protectiveness may take the form of fearful curbing of normal physical activities. One father of a leukaemic child wrote to me: 'One thing I have noticed is that we take more care of the other children. It's as if we are afraid somehow that the same thing may happen to them', and a mother of a four-year-old cystic girl confided: 'We keep them in now, close to the house. You wouldn't want an accident, would you?' In terms of the ill child, overprotectiveness may develop into a pattern of pampering and overindulgence,[25,28] many parents over-looking even the elementary rules of child upbringing.[22] In this context one paediatrician warned: 'To shower a child with gifts, to look at him and weep, to whisper behind his back, to single him out as different is to threaten his world and his happiness'.[32]

Overprotection may be accentuated following hospitalisation, and in addition such hospitalisation may accentuate parental separation anxiety, the parents experiencing acute anxiety at being separated from the child. Mothers of leukaemic children may defend themselves against this fear by 'insistence on close bodily contact' with their children.[8,42,45] Because of this some clinicians feel it essential to involve parents in the physical care of their child whenever hospitalisation becomes essential.[66]

The conflicting emotions produced by the threatened loss of a child may lead some parents to fear for their sanity.[8,24,49] In such circumstances parents become extremely concerned with maintaining self control. For this reason they may increasingly prefer not to speak of the illness, and their spouses, sensing this, may similarly refrain from discussing the topic. This mechanism may explain Turk's[80] finding that some families coping with cystic fibrosis are locked in a 'web of silence'—the silence assisting family members to function without breakdown. Even normal discussions and decisions with regard to the rest of the family may seem impossible.[8]

In most instances such a congealing of interest and enthusiasm is characteristic only of the initial period after diagnosis, though it may recur from time to time when the child's symptoms exacerbate or his condition becomes more critical. Like massive denial of the diagnosis, it tends to be a disruptive defence mechanism. Other defences—such as an initial blunting of feeling, and a compensatory indulgence in activity—may be more productive, a factor noted by Chodoff[14] who stated 'Life without defences would be intolerable', and by Lourie[45] who wrote 'The healthier defences of the individual can be very useful—if properly deployed'. Chodoff[14] has assessed the defence mechanisms or coping strategies of the individual to be effective in so far as they (1) enable the individual to carry on, fulfilling his caring functions, and (2) protect the individual against disruptive degrees of anxiety. Visotsky,[82] working with young polio victims, has defined adequate coping behaviour as that which keeps 'distress within manageable limits, mobilizing hope, maintaining a sense of personal worth, restoring relations with significant other people, enhancing prospects for recovery'. In this respect parents have to maintain a very delicate balance. Too much care for the child may prejudice their own emotional equilibrium, too much protection of themselves may be prejudicial to the child.[25]

Whilst parental ability to cope is obviously crucial in the management of a short term life-threatening illness, it becomes imperative when the child's condition permits the expectation of several years of valuable life. In such circumstances, unless parents can control their own basic emotions, the child's days may be clouded by the shadow of death, rather than spent in a normal joyful manner, even though medical science has arrested or controlled the physical symptoms, and the pattern and quality of the child's physical life could be indistinguishable from normal.

Probably the most essential problem therefore challenging parents is the problem of maintaining a sense of normality in the home. Any weakness on their part, or attempt to compensate for the illness may be resented by their well children, and played upon by the sick child, producing disciplinary problems.[1,68,79] Such problems will be increased where parents are imbued with the sense that the child is no longer completely theirs 'but only on a tenuous loan'.[28] In such instances their resulting overprotectiveness may be noted by the child, who in turn 'may correctly interpret pandering by parents as of ominous import and draw his own conclusions. In so doing, he becomes increasingly dispirited and disconsolate thus endangering his will to persevere with the vital programme of therapy'.[64] Understandably, therefore, many clinicians[9,16,24,25,45,58,79,85] have emphasised the enromous importance of parental attitude for therapeutic effectiveness. In this context Haller[29] has commented: 'If the child is permitted to focus on his disease or his deformity, so that the image dominates him, he will remain chronically ill despite excellent clinical care... If a child can become convinced that his disability is only relative, half of the therapeutic battle is won'.

Parental attitude is therefore essential for optimal physical functioning, and is also of immense significance in terms of the child's overall development. If he is to remain happy and positive he must be challenged to maximum achievement within the limitations of his illness state. This is not an easy task for parents—it involves rethinking their objectives and expectations for the child, inevitably relinquishing some of the fantasies and goals which were attached to him when he was healthy.

Parents may be handicapped in this and other child-orientated tasks, by the very nature of the grief work, which takes place despite any conscious effort on their part. Lindemann[43] has defined such grief work as an 'emancipation from the bondage to the deceased, readjustment to the environment in which the deceased is missing, and the formation of new relationships'. As such, anticipatory mourning tends to remove the parents emotionally from the child so that sometimes they have 'completely separated emotionally from the patient before the patient is dead'.[17] Friedman[24] quotes a parent as saying, 'I love him as much but we are more separate', and the mother of an eight-year-old cystic girl told me:

> 'It took a long time to adjust myself to the idea that I might lose her. I find it harder to love her in case I lose her... I'm scared of getting too close to her. I don't think I've drawn away—but it just hasn't developed. I could be closer to her. I have a guilt complex about her and that is the cause of it'.

Whilst such feelings of separation can be useful in allowing parents to handle the child more objectively, realistically appreciating and meeting his demands, some parents are frightened by these feelings. They sense the emotional distance between themselves and the child, and unconscious of its causation, blame themselves for being abnormal, and attempt to make even greater restitution.

Deciding what to tell the child about the diagnosis can also be a problem. Clinicians vary as to the advice they offer. Some [23,25,27] advocate that the child should be told, and emphasise the relief experienced by children with whom the diagnosis was discussed.[81] They argue that mothers who decide not to tell use all their available emotional energy in the negative, and largely unsuccessful, pursuit of hiding the diagnosis, rather than in the more positive task of supporting the child. Naturally, this militates against the development of any real supportive parent-child relationship. As a result, 'the child becomes mute, outwardly accepting the adult's benign words of falsehood but inwardly feeling abandoned. He is left to cope with his fears and anxieties by himself at the very time when he needs and seeks all the strength and support available'.[81] Children in such circumstances rarely ask what is going to happen to them.[27,45,57,66] This is not because they do not know, or are uninterested. More properly it is because the child knows 'it is a forbidden subject or because he is fearful of the answer'.[86] Yudkin also comments, 'I am sure that some avoid the subject altogether to spare both their parents and the doctors acute embarrassment and pain'.

Many adults—parents and medical personnel alike—tend to deny that young children are aware of the implications of their illness. Such denial may be an extension of the 'classic adult defence against coping with death anxiety',[84] representing part of the adult's defence against his own fears of extinction. Equally, it may result from an understandable unwillingness to accept the fact that the child must cope not only with the physical aspects of his illness, but also with all the concomitant emotional distress.

Parents may be helped to cope with the pain that such thoughts occasion by being challenged 'to protect their child from the knowledge that his lifespan is limited'.[32] The child should be surrounded by a sense of security.[40,70] As Saunders[70] has noted, security enables the child to 'face unsafety', unsafety being either 'the knowledge of their approaching death... apprehensions concerning investigations or treatment, changes in the situation, hospital admissions, or the acceptance of increasing weakness'. In addition, she believes 'security does what deceptions or denial cannot do—it protects from that isolation that accentuates all suffering'.

Certain medical conditions may require the mastering of a complex and time-consuming therapeutic régime. Not only does this involve the parents directly in the illness outcome (a factor discussed at greater length in chapter 6) but also it may prejudice the well-being of all family members. Social, recreational, and educational needs of all family members may be seriously compromised as a result.[37,49,80] Normal household routines are disrupted by the need for treatment, and even where medical treatment and drugs are free, special diets, parental accompanying of the child to outpatient clinics, and hospital visiting during his inpatient treatment can seriously prejudice some family budgets.[12] Understandably, it would seem that the stresses imposed on the family are accentuated when the family is already stressed for other reasons—be they financial, marital, or due to poor housing and unemployment. Such families, without any basic security, find it especially difficult to maintain optimism and treatment. As one mother of eight, with a total weekly income of £24, told me: 'It all comes down to money. If you've got enough, you can manage anything, even this old illness. When you haven't enough, you're always worrying and it makes everything worse.'

In families where the illness has a genetic basis, the question of further reproduction may assume significance, with 'the wish to plan a baby to replace the child who might die being opposed by the wish to avoid bearing more afflicted children'.[47] Families who, for religious or personal reasons, will not use contraception, or couples who are divided in their attitude to further family limitation, may find tensions developing in their marital relationship which further diminish their ability to cope with the sick child.[39,68,80] This is especially true if the marital relationship was poor before the advent of the child's illness.

Even where the problems are not great, temporary marital stresses may arise from time to time, for example, if the child is unwell. The mother of a six-year-old cystic child told me that, at such times, when she hears the child coughing in the next room, she turns away from her husband, 'I'm so worried I can't be with it—and then I don't seem to be treating him right either'. Divided loyalties, feelings of sexual tension and strain, all make for greater difficulty in coping with treatment and maintaining a necessary aura of optimism.

Undoubtedly the support that parents can offer each other is of crucial importance in determining their long-term adjustment to the child's illness.[8,77] Indeed, on the basis of stories made up by fathers of leukaemic children in response to a projective personality test (the Thematic Apperception Test), Murstein[54] concluded that the father's expectation of happiness was less dependent on the health of the child, and more dependent on his relationship with the mother. Parents may also be sustained if they are able to maintain good relationships with their healthy children,[48] and a greater integration of the family unit may develop if the problem is shared with them.[66]

Not all family relationships are sustaining, however. Some parents dread their hospitalised child's remission and return home because it presents relatives with a chance to deny the reality of the child's condition. Because of their own death fears, friends, relatives and especially grandparents may display 'denial processes of a prying and provocative nature'.[14] In some instances such denial processes may be so exaggerated as to leave the parents without any real social support, having to proclaim their child's illness in the face of what Friedman[25] has termed 'concentric circles of disbelief'. In these circumstances parents may well feel like executioners actually condemning their child.[10] Even where family members are supportive, parents may be stressed by the sick child's return home during remission. They may show fear of leaving the protective hospital facilities, and assuming major responsibility for the child's welfare.[25,45] In addition, their fear and confusion may be reinforced by the gratuitous advice of 'well-meaning neighbours, members of various sects, and quacks, each sponsoring their own brand of magic cure or plan of management'.[45]

Generally, people cope best with continuous stresses when they are occasionally permitted to escape from or temporarily forget them, but parents of children whose treatment is essentially home based and of long duration may experience problems in obtaining temporary relief. Either they may feel too guilty or responsible to leave the sick child, or friends and neighbours may be unwilling to assume sole charge in their absence. Even a temporary escape may meet with disapproval, for in some subsections of society, parents of sick children are not expected to participate in social events.[25]

The possibility of family disintegration due to the profound emotional stresses imposed by a life-threatening illness has been emphasised in most studies. None the less, the alternative of effective parental functioning has also been realised and many writers [12,14,30,31,79] have gained the impression of family strength rather than weakness in the face of adversity. Indeed, some studies have gone further in suggesting that illness—albeit chronic—can improve parent-child relationships, making for better personality functioning on both sides [4,33] and producing a 'deepening and consolidation of intra-familial relationships'.[48]

What makes for parental strength? As yet we do not fully know.

The degree to which the parents are able to defend themselves against the more painful emotions involved, and the love, respect and trust they have for each other are relevant considerations. In addition, the pleasure they have in their other children, the strength of their social contacts and religious beliefs, and their economic and social security must be considered. Openness and mutual support are imperative.[79] Tropauer noted 'little disruptive impact on the family unit' in open and supportive families. Interestingly, he found that the child's method of coping with the illness exactly mirrored that of his parents: 'Patterns of deception and avoidance practised by the parents became the child's style of coping with the experience themselves'.

One further essential factor noted by many clinicians [5,8,14,25,32,51] is the presence of hope, and Friedman[25] has commented that 'unlike massive denial, hope does not interfere with effective behaviour, and was entirely compatible with an intellectual acceptance of reality'. He added that, 'Hope actually helped the parents accept "bad news"'. Eventually, if anticipatory mourning has progressed satisfactorily, the parents may find this hope extending beyond their own child.[36] They begin to hope for sick children generally and may decide to join organisations devoted to raising funds for research into their child's illness, or to offer services to parents of other afflicted children [10,25] (both points are considered in greater detail in chapter 14, p. 166).

Where the child dies, and anticipatory mourning has not progressed satisfactorily, or where parents are markedly disparate in the degree of mourning which has been accomplished, [14,20,24] they may need long-term care and guidance. [46,62] Unfortunately, most such families lose their close contact with hospital personnel at this time, and consequently their specific needs in the situation are as yet unknown. Further research is therefore needed to ascertain the depth and extent of these problems.

The child

In order to understand the way in which children respond to a life-threatening illness, one must first understand something of the nature of childhood, and the meaning of the illness to the child who is experiencing it.

Basically, childhood is a time in which the child finds out about himself. It is a time in which he attempts, and normally masters, the innumerable mental, physical, social and emotional skills which enable him to relinquish his infant dependency and become a complete and separate person able to take his own independent place in the world.

The struggle to attain complete adulthood is not an easy one. Myriad obstacles to progress present themselves—some environmental, some due to the child's own immaturity, or inherent limitations. In overcoming these the child needs courage, determination, and the support and encouragement of all those around him, most especially of those whom he loves and trusts. In addition he needs the constant provision of opportunities to try out new skills commensurate with his ability, and protection from such trauma as may diminish his courage and congeal his strivings for self-expression.

Illness, which so frequently implies loss or curtailment of independence,[17,22,63] unfamiliarity,[73] anonymity,[63] loneliness, boredom[60,76] and pain,[6,17,22,27] cuts across such strivings for self-expression. As such it is inevitably resented and feared.

That it need not always destroy the child's self-confidence and bid for self-determination, is seen from the writings of parents,[50] sociologists[63] and psychoanalysts.[4] Some children not only emerge from their experiences emotionally unscathed but actually appear strengthened as a result. Jessner,[13] commenting on the integrative processes that can take place as a result of childhood illness, said 'illness may not only spur maturation but also widen the horizon, heighten sensitivity, bring forth a greater depth of feeling, capacity for empathy and for sublimation'. Because of this any assessment of the way in which children face up to their illness must consider both the situations which threaten the child's psychological well-being, and the ways in which he attempts to overcome these threats.

The child's response to hospitalisation is perhaps the most well documented aspect of the problem. Since the pioneer work of Bawkin[3] and Spitz[74] many observant clinicians and psychoanalysts[5,6,7,36,65,67] have noted how even short-term hospitalisation for young children—especially the one to five-year-olds can cause actual physical wasting and deterioration. Encompassing, as it does, crippling feelings of inadequacy, strangeness, and loneliness, hospitalisation can accentuate pain[17] and prejudice both immediate and long-term personality growth. The root cause of such anguish would seem to be the removal of the young child from the mother upon whom he depends for emotional and social support. Where a mother is allowed to remain close to her hospitalised child, traumatic effects are minimised.[65]

Providing mother substitutes in the form of good and devoted nurses does little with this younger age group to compensate for the loss of the mother, for many young children will not accept substitute mothers, their sense of abandonment being heightened by any usurpation of maternal comforting.[4,7] For this reason some paediatricians[5,73] advocate either a programme of parental participation in hospital nursing care, or the child's attendance on an outpatient basis.[36] This need is especially pressing if the child is in the terminal stage of his illness, giving parents and child a chance to experience each other as fully as possible before the final separation.[10]

Loneliness and a sense of isolation and abandonment are not conducive to emotional growth at any age, and yet such feelings are not solely confined to the very young hospitalised child, nor are they merely a figment of the older child's imagination. Many clinicians[14, 17,25,69,70,81,86] have described the way in which dying children receive less attention than other ill children. (Rothenberg describes one such case in chapter 3.) Waechter[83] also found that the dying child received significantly less nursing attention than other chronically ill children.

Failure to answer questions, or to be aware of the child's need to talk of his condition, may further heighten his sense of isolation. Vernick[81] quotes one leukaemic child as saying 'nobody really talked to me. It was like they were getting ready for me to die'. Children in such circumstances become imbued with the feeling that no one else is aware of what they are experiencing.[25] They believe that the disease is 'too awful' for them to be allowed to talk of it. Such feelings result in depression, withdrawal, and apprehension[8,72] and may be conveyed unconsciously in children's hospital diaries and compositions, or in response to enigmatic pictures (chosen from the Thematic Apperception Test). For example, one fifteen-year-old cystic boy recounted the following stories, all indicative of loneliness and inadequacy.

(13B) 'In this picture the young boy is lonely and its an old shack that he lives in. His parents is not rich. He is not well-dressed and he has no shoes or stockings on. The house in which he lives in looks bare and empty. I think he would be thinking that he would like to live with other people so that he could have friends to play with, to talk with.'

(3GF) 'In this picture you see a woman who looks to be in sorrow. She looks to be a worried person. If she is worried then she would be nervous. She's standing there as if she doesn't know what is the matter with her. She looks very weary and tired looking. She would like to have someone to talk to, to have friends to go out with and enjoy themselves—go to parties and try to get rid of most of the worries, or even to the pictures with a boyfriend.'

(16)'In this picture you see an old man fishing—the place he is fishing is in a large lake—the reason why he is fishing is because he is lonely or he has no one to talk to in the home. He could be living by himself. Fishing is a great sport. It helps you to concentrate on your work and it could take your mind off your worries—because old people do have a lot of worries. Old people live by themselves and they would be afraid of intruders, that they could not stand up against them, and they could be afraid they would be badly hurt and if they live by themselves and if they were sick they could not send for the doctor and they would have to do everything by themselves—do the housework by themselves and the shopping.'

Hospitalisation may prejudice the child in other ways. For example, it may threaten his nascent sense of independence. Unlike the adult who chooses hospital treatment for himself, the child is 'taken to the doctors by his parents and has had no control over the process that finally brought him to hospital'.[63] Once there, he is frequently turned—without explanation, preparation, or any weaning process—from a mobile, active, assertive child, whose opinions, for example about food or play, are considered and respected, into a passive recipient of treatment. Not only does the child resent passivity because it implies loss of identity and status, but also because it diminishes his chances of mastering basic skills, and is therefore contrary to the very nature of childhood. Whilst children of all ages protest against such curtailment of freedom, teenagers—so newly emancipated—may become especially disturbed, viewing restrictions as punishment for some wrong-doing.[17]

Enforced immobility may hinder normal discharge of negative emotions through movement[6] and produce considerable feelings of frustration and animosity[4] which may spill over whenever additional and unexpected treatment procedures are imposed on the child. Conversely, unexpressed feelings of animosity and frustration may produce feelings of apathy and resignation, and to combat this it is necessary to provide the child with an active role or some sense of choice in treatment.[27,78]

As early as 1947, Spence[73] emphasised the huge differences between the average home and the usual children's ward. More recently, Pill[63] commented that hospitalisation represents the child's first contact with a 'large scale bureaucratic organisation'. Not only does this necessitate his learning a new role—that of child-patient—

but also, by virtue of its very difference from his democratic home, it may undermine his self-confidence, making him more apprehensive subsequently in other social situations. The younger the child, the less well-developed his social skills and sense of self-confidence, the more permissive his background, the greater will be the damage to his personality.[76]

Obviously the child's physical condition will affect his response to the illness. Where illness manifestations are very obvious he may respond with shame.[47] Pain may evoke feelings of anger and resentment, or, alternatively, masochistic submission tinged with guilt and depression. All these feelings may be accentuated because the child is often 'unable to distinguish between feelings of suffering caused by the disease inside the body and suffering imposed on him from outside for the sake of curing the disease'.[22] Where he responds to the situation with rage, such feelings may further accentuate his physical pain.[17] Where discomfort is long-lasting he may respond more strongly than usual to even the most trivial setbacks or changes of environment.[27]

Treatment may evoke fear of pain, and negatively colour the child's relationship with the adult who is administering treatment. Whilst girls may respond to this with depression,[53] boys—especially in the six to ten year age group—may become suspicious, anxious[36] and actively rebel against it. Many children display an 'escalating sense of protest at the unfairness of it all'.[64] Treatment may be misconstrued as punishment by the child,[6] restrictions in diet being viewed as evidence of rejection, medicine being seen as an attack on the body, and the illness itself being thought of as a mysterious and frightening 'enemy within'.[22] Where treatment produces changes in a child's appetite mothers may feel threatened[8] and their expressed anxiety may reinforce the child's own apprehensions. Such apprehensions may explain the 'heightened anxiety about bodily intactness'[47] and the 'feelings of inadequacy'[79] observed in some seriously ill children. It is essential for us all to feel that our bodies are adequate and acceptable[58] and anxiety is engendered in children with illnesses which make them feel that their bodily image is lacking or unacceptable.[75,79] Such fears may find expression in children's drawings, for example, some children I have observed, who were receiving barrier treatment for leukaemia, reached a stage in which they could only visualise themselves as monsters, hideously and permanently deformed. Their attempts at self-portraits invariably turned into robot or monster shapes.[11] In Sweden, similar self-portraits have been produced by very severely affected cystic children.

Fears of mutilation and permanent damage may be accentuated where the child needs surgery, a factor noted by analysts and clinicians.[6,22,41,52,61] Such fears are compounded of the child's meagre knowledge of his own body, the confusion produced by the scraps of information—often erroneous—he picks up from other children, and the weird ideas he may have formed about operations from comics and television shows. Narcosis may heighten fears of mutilation, and Levy[41] noting 'manifest emotional sequalae' following operation, in twenty-five of the 124 children he studied, felt that such fears might underlie subsequent night terrors and fear of the dark. He deemed such fears greatest in younger children (under three years) because of 'their keener response to pain, poor comprehension of the experience and less facility in handling anxiety'. Where parental maladjustment, or neurotic trends in the patient, were already present, even uncomplicated surgery may have traumatic effects lasting into adult life.[52,61]

As with treatment procedures, surgical manipulations may change the child's image of himself, a factor noted by Calef[13] who observed 'the image of the self changes into "bad egg", rotten, a piece of garbage'. As a consequence the child may see himself as worthless, and become dispirited. In addition, he may be influenced by his parents' changed perception of himself. As Green and Solnit[28] point out, once the mother knows the child will die,

Doom, failure, and disappointment are built into the anticipation by both mother and child [and] although seemingly unrecognised by parents the child regularly senses his mother's expectation of his vulnerability and accepts his mother's distorted mental image of himself. This is communicated in many subtle ways but mainly through the mother's moods and in her way of granting him autonomy and independence with fearful inhibiting reservations.

Not only does this increase his 'feeling of precariousness'[27] but also it diminishes his trust in his parents[36,81] for 'The parents' helplessness, anxiety and incapacity to protect the child becomes painfully clear'.[13] At the time when the child needs them most, the parents may seem to have failed him.

Such feelings may become exaggerated when the child begins to understand the prognosis. He may glean such knowledge from a correct interpretation of his parent's feeling tone,[64] or from the cruel taunts of other children.[47,81] Equally, his knowledge may develop gradually from an appreciation of the significance of the medical care and attention lavished upon him. The earlier the development of his illness, and the more extensive his therapy, the more sophisticated he will become in matters of life and death, and children with a life-threatening illness are often more truly aware of the nature of death than are their more fortunate peers. Equally, they come to such knowledge at an earlier age. Wahl[84] observed death fears 'as early as the third year', Morrisey[53] found that thirteen out of fifty children (mean age 7·2 years), hospitalised for cancer and leukaemia were afraid to die, one of these being only three-and-a-half years old, and Green[27] described four-year-old Larry who asked his doctor for reassurance because of his fear of death. (His parents were unaware that he knew the prognosis.) Describing their own experiences in telling leukaemic children about their diagnosis, Vernick and Karon[81] wrote, 'every child who is lying in bed gravely ill is worrying about dying, and is eager to have someone to help him talk about it'. In this context, Waechter[83] has shown that fatally ill children tell significantly more stories indicative of threat to bodily integrity than do children hospitalised for chronic or brief illness.

But whilst many children under the age of five may talk of death, most usually regard it as a reversible process,[55,56] or a temporary separation. What they require in the situation is reassurance that they will not be abandoned.

Later, between ages five and ten, the child's fantasy life expands, and death may be seen as a removal to another state of physical existence, for example, a life in heaven, or it may be personified, for example as a bogey man coming to carry children away. Either notion, implying unfamiliarity and the possibility of loneliness and pain, may be actively feared, and such fears may become more disturbing than any loss of energy or health. In addition, such fears may be too terrible to verbalise directly, and may find expression only in play, or in an accentuation of negative behaviour, such as depression, apathy and unprovoked anger and resentment.[86] Denial of physical symptoms, and the flat refusal to continue or permit treatment may also symbolise a fear of death. Death fears may be expressed in dreams,[36] and in stories made up to enigmatic pictures. One six-year-old boy with cystic fibrosis told me in response to standard Thematic Apperception Test cards:

(3BM) 'He's dead. The man's dead, and he's up there, down in the bunks, that one, He has boots. He's dead. When you're dead you're deaf, you're blind, your brain dies. The rest is all right. He's wee trousers and black hair. He's not thinking of anything. He's just dead and that's that'.

(8BM) 'There's a boy and that's a man and he's dead. A rifle.
He's deaf. He's blind and he's bare skin. His moustache.
His nose. A knife and it cut into there. And a rifle and a boy.
He's going to be dead'.

A ten-year-old cystic boy endeavoured to control his fears through laughter.

(8BM) 'Looks as if they're having fun (laughs). I don't know.
Looks as if he's got something wrong with him. Something wrong
inside or he's been poisoned and they're going to do an operation
and that boy can't stand the sight of blood. He's not looking.
I think it's got something to do with the fish he ate. So they took
him to his cabin to start the operation and when they'd just
finished the operation he died—that's the end of that' (laughs).

Occasionally, such fears will be expressed directly in conversation, in some instances the child asking for reassurance, at other times, stating a fact. For example, one eight-year-old girl needing further operations for a brain tumour protested, 'But if they cut my head open and touch my brain, they'll kill me'.

Deaths of other children—either on the ward, or known through the outpatient clinic—may accentuate fears,[10,86] especially if hastily denied.[81] One paediatrician has emphasised how the present 'ugly and obscene' handling of death on a children's ward can 'open the way to endless fantasies', helping to 'characterise death as something secretive and fearful'.[86]

Teenage patients are perhaps the most sensitive to death fears. They do fully comprehend the irreversibility of death, and many are quickly able to deduce the severity of their condition. Not only does it represent the curtailment of their freedom, and the possibility of untimely extinction, but for some it also represents a dreadful adult retaliation against their strivings for independence. As such it may engender intense anger[23] and guilt, and may produce a total denial of all that is happening.

To some extent the child in a terminal state may be protected from a full realisation of the implication of his condition because of his altered physical state. Several clinicians[45,72] suggest that diminution of energy and eventual stupor produce a condition in which the child can best be described as 'living beside, not in the world'.

However such protection can basically only be expected towards the end of the terminal stage, and improvements in medical care mean that most children with life-threatening illnesses can now expect months—or even years—of fully sensate existence. Normality is therefore of essence in combating fears and in this context schooling becomes even more essential than usual, for as Bierman[5] observed, 'To abandon purposeful learning was in effect telling the parent and child that there was no future, no hope and only irresolute, useless time'. In addition, schooling combats destructive boredom,[60,76] and provides an answer to understandable fears of school failure due to absence.[18,34] Whilst clinicians[37,47] have noted school problems such as restlessness and failure to achieve in children with a life-threatening illness, it is possible that some individual children strive extra hard[50] to excel in this sphere as a compensation for their physical inadequacy. Equally, anxiety over bodily intactness may be met by a positive attempt to be more verbal and socially acceptable, and a tendency to take extra care about dress and hairstyle.[79]

Very little objective study has so far been made of the mechanisms which enable the child to tolerate his illness and the anxiety occasioned by it. Langsley[38] suggests the usefulness of the classic defence triad—denial, repression and regression. Morrisey[53] observed that 70 per cent of the fifty children he studied made a good overall adjustment to their hospitalisation for leukaemia, despite severe or noticeable anxiety. He noted three factors which were of significance in attaining this adjustment—the child's previous character structure, the quality of the parent-child relationships, and the actual medical circumstances of the child. He concluded: 'Two children may have similar levels of anxiety but the anxiety may operate differently in the two individuals, one child may be emotionally paralyzed and the other use resources constructively to keep anxiety under control'. In this respect, he agrees with Tropauer[79] who, observing cystic children, commented 'It is not the existence of anxiety *per se* that handicaps the sick child and intensifies his invalidism, but rather its degree and his methods of dealing with it'.

Some children undoubtedly protect themselves from anxiety concerning disease manifestations by developing a heightened sense of humour. For example, a five-year-old cystic girl I met, called the smell she made in the toilet her 'secret weapon'. Such humour is by no means rare among sick children. Whilst some of it appears to spring from the child itself, much would seem to be fostered by the parents' attitude to the illness, and to the child. Where they can remain positive, it is easier for the child to be positive.[79] Because of this Haller[29] has emphasised that the sick child must be 'constantly challenged by attainable goals. In this way his functional disability... will remain relative, and not become unbearably absolute'.

Clearly age is also a relevant factor in determining a child's acceptance of illness. The younger the child, the earlier the onset of symptoms, the less he is aware of alternate forms of existence, the easier it will be for him to accept the restrictions inherent in the illness state. On the other hand, the late development of illness is often 'regarded as an inequitable breach of contract and its acceptance is far more taxing'.[16]

Faith, especially the firm belief in a joyful after-life may also be of value to some children, for example one eight-year-old cystic girl who thought of God as her 'real Father' and was a regular church attender, told her mother, 'I'm tired being sick. I want to go to Heaven. I hope God will take me whilst I'm still a little girl.'

The presence of other similarly affected children may be of comfort to some ill children, especially if their mutual energies can be channelled into positive, joyful activities. Mothers of cystic children have spoken to me of the pleasure that their children gained from the company of other affected children, whether at a special school for delicate children, or at a holiday caravan, provided by the Cystic Fibrosis Research Trust.

Clearly, much work lies ahead in determining the ways in which children learn to tolerate the intolerable. Perhaps no generalisations will even be possible, but with time, and careful observation, we should be able to establish sufficient facts to enable those of us who care to care in the most effective fashion.

References

1 BATTEN, J. (1966), 'C.F. and the teenager', *Cystic Fibrosis News*, June.
2 BAUM, M. H. (1962), 'Some dynamic factors affecting family adjustment to the handicapped child', *Exceptional Children*, April, pp. 387-92.
3 BAWKIN, H. (1942), 'Loneliness in infants', *American Journal of the Diseases of Children*, vol. 63, p. 30.
4 BERGMANN, T. (in collaboration with FREUD, A.) (1965), *Children in Hospital*, International Universities Press, New York.
5 BIERMAN, H. R. (1956), 'Parent participation program in pediatric oncology', *Journal of Chronic Diseases*, vol. 3, p. 632.
6 BLOM, G. E. (1958), 'The reactions of hospitalized children to illness', *Pediatrics*, vol. 22, p. 590.
7 BOWLBY, J. (1971), *Attachment and Loss*, vol. 1, Penguin, Harmondsworth.
8 BOZEMANN, M. F., ORBACH, C. E. and SUTHERLAND, A. M. (1955), 'The adaptation of mothers to the threatened loss of their children through leukemia', *Cancer*, vol. 8, pp. 1-19.
9 BRUCH, H. and HEWLETT, I. (1947), 'Psychologic aspects of the medical management of diabetes in children', *Psychosomatic Medicine*, vol. 9, pp. 205-9.

10 BURTON, L. (1971), 'Cancer children', *New Society*, June, no. 455, pp. 1040-3.

11 BURTON, L. (1972), 'Some psychological considerations implicit in the treatment of pediatric malignancy', paper given to the Annual Conference of the Canadian Association of Radiologists in Toronto.

12 BURTON, L. (1973), 'Caring for children with cystic fibrosis', *Practitioner*, vol. 210, pp. 247-54.

13 CALEF, V. (1959), 'Report on panel: psychological consequences of physical illness in childhood', *Journal of the American Psychoanalytic Association*, vol. 7.

14 CHODOFF, P., STANDFORD, B., FRIEDMAN, B. and HAMBURG, D. A. (1964), 'Stress, defenses, and coping behaviour: observations in parents of children with malignant diseases', *American Journal of Psychiatry*, vol. 120, pp. 743-9.

15 CUMMINGS, S. T., BAYLEY, H. C. and RIE, H. E. (1966), 'Effects of the child's deficiency on the mother. A study of mothers of mentally retarded, chronically ill and neurotic children', *American Journal of Orthopsychiatry*, vol. 36, pp. 595-608.

16 DEBUSKEY, M. (ed.) (1970), *The Chronically Ill Child and his Family*, Charles Thomas, Illinois.

17 EASSON, W. M. (1968), 'Care of the young patient who is dying', *Journal of the American Medical Association*, vol. 205 (4), pp. 63-7.

18 EDWARDS, C. (1966), 'Cystic fibrosis and the medical social worker', *Cystic Fibrosis News*, November.

19 ENGEL, G. L. (1961), 'Is grief a disease? A challenge to medical research', *Psychosomatic Medicine*, vol. 23, p. 18.

20 EVANS, P. B. (1969), 'The management of fatal illness in childhood', *Proceedings of the Royal Society of Medicine*, vol. 62 (6), p. 549.

21 FREESTON, B. M. (1971), 'An enquiry into the effect of a spina bifida child upon family life', *Developmental Medicine and Child Neurology*, vol. 13, pp. 456-61.

22 FREUD, A. (1952), 'The role of bodily illness in the mental life of children', *Psychoanalytic Studies of Children*, vol. 7, p. 69.

23 FRIEDMAN, S. B. (1964), 'The child with leukemia and his parents', *Cancer*, vol. 4 (2), pp. 73-6.

24 FRIEDMAN, S. B. (1967), 'Care of the family of the child with cancer', *Pediatrics*, vol. 40 (3), p. 498.

25 FRIEDMAN, S. B., CHODOFF, P., MASON, J. W. and HAMBURG, D. A. (1963), 'Behavioural observations on parents anticipating the death of a child', *Pediatrics*, October, pp. 610-25.

26 GREEN, M. (1967), 'Care of the dying child', *Pediatrics*, vol. 40 (3), pp. 492-8.

27 GREEN, M. (1967), 'Care of the child with a long-term life-threatening illness', *Pediatrics*, vol. 39, pp. 441-5.

28 GREEN, M. and SOLNIT, A. J. (1964), 'Reactions to the threatened loss of a child. A vulnerable child syndrome', *Pediatrics*, July, pp. 58-66.

29 HALLER, J. A. (1970), 'A healthy attitude towards chronic illness', in Debuskey (ed.) (1970).

30 HENLEY, T. F. and ALBAM, B. (1955), 'A psychiatric study of muscular dystrophy. The role of the social worker', *American Journal of Physical Medicine*, vol. 34, pp. 258-64.

31 HEWITT, S. and NEWSON, J. E. (1970), *The Family and the Handicapped Child*, Allen & Unwin, London.

32 HOWELL, D. A. (1963), 'A child dies', *Journal of Pediatric Surgery*, vol. 1 (1), pp. 2-7.

33 JABALEY, M. E., HOOPES, J. E., KNORR, N. J. and MYER, E. (1970), 'The burned child', in Debuskey (ed.) (1970).

34 JENSEN, R. and COMLY, H. (1948), 'Child-parent problems in the hospital', *Nervous Child*, vol. 7, p. 200.

35 JORDAN, T. E. (1962), 'Research on the handicapped child and the family', *Merrill-Palmer Quarterly*, vol. 8, p. 244.

36 KNUDSON, A. G. JNR and NATTERSON, J. M. (1960), 'Participation of parents in the hospital care of fatally ill children', *Pediatrics*, vol. 26, p. 482.

37 KUTCZCKI, L. I. (1970), 'Adequate home care for patients with cystic fibrosis', *Clinical Proceedings of the Children's Hospital, Washington, D.C.*, vol. 26, pp. 97-103.

38 LANGSLEY, D. G. (1961), 'Psychology of a doomed family', *American Journal of Psychotherapy*, vol. 15, pp. 531-8.

39 LAWLER, R. H., NAKIELNY, W. and WRIGHT, N. (1966), 'Psychological implications of cystic fibrosis', *Canadian Medical Association Journal*, vol. 94, pp. 1043-6.

40 LAWSON, D. (1971), 'A pediatrician's comments on the development of thanatology in relation to CF', position paper to Atlantic City Symposium, April.

41 LEVY, D. M. (1945), 'Psychic trauma of operations in children and a note on combat neurosis', *American Journal of Diseases of Children*, vol. 69, pp. 7-25.

42 LEWIS, M. (1962), 'The management of parents of acutely ill children in the hospital', *American Journal of Orthopsychiatry*, vol. 32, pp. 60-6.

43 LINDEMANN, E. (1944), 'Symptomatology and management of acute grief', *American Journal of Psychiatry*, vol. 101, p. 141.

44 LOURIE, R. S. (1961), 'What to tell the parents of a child with cancer', *Clinical Proceedings of the Children's Hospital, Washington D.C.*, vol. 17, p. 91.

45 LOURIE, R. S. (1963), 'The pediatrician and the handling of terminal illness', *Pediatrics*, vol. 32 (4), pp. 477-9.

46 MACCARTHY, D. (1969), 'The repercussion of the death of a child', *Proceedings of the Royal Society of Medicine*, vol. 62, pp. 553-4.

47 MCCOLLUM, A. T. and GIBSON, L. E. (1960), 'Family adaptation to the child with cystic fibrosis', *Pediatrics*, vol. 77 (4), pp. 571-8.

48 MCCOLLUM, A. T. and GIBSON, L. E. (1971), Correspondence, *Pediatrics*, vol. 78 (3), p. 549.

49 MCCOLLUM, A. T. and SCWARTZ, A. H., *Social Work and the Mourning Parent* (forthcoming).

50 MEAD, J. (1969), *Helen's Victory*, Health Horizon, London.

51 MENNINGER, K. (1959), 'Hope', *American Journal of Psychiatry*, vol. 116, p. 481.

52 MILLER, M. L. (1951), 'The traumatic effect of surgical operations in childhood on the integrative functions of the ego', *Psychoanalytic Quarterly*, vol. 20, p. 77.

53 MORRISEY, J. (1963), 'Children's adaptation to fatal illness', *Social Work*, October, pp. 81-8.

54 MURSTEIN, B. I. (1960), 'The effect of long-term illness of children on the emotional adjustment of parents', *Child Development*, vol. 31, pp. 157-71.

55 NAGY, M. H. (1948), 'The child's theories concerning death', *Journal of Genetic Psychology*, vol. 73, pp. 3-27.

56 NAGY, M. H. (1959), 'The child's view of death', in Feifel, H. (ed.), *The Meaning of Death*, McGraw-Hill, New York.

57 NATTERSON, J. M. and KNUDSON, A. G. (1960), 'Observations concerning fear of death in fatally ill children and their mothers', *Psychosomatic Medicine*, vol. 22, p. 456.

58 O'CONNOR, G. and KNORR, N. J. (1968), 'Acute trauma from a psychological viewpoint', in Ballinger, W. (ed.), *The Management of Trauma*, Saunders, Philadelphia.

59 ORBACH, C. E., SUTHERLAND, A. M. and BOZEMANN, H. F. (1955), 'Psychological impact of cancer and its treatment', *Cancer*, vol. 8, pp. 20-33.

60 OSWIN, M. (1971), *The Empty Hours*, Allen Lane, London.

61 PEARSON, G. H. J. (1941), 'Effect of operative procedures on the emotional life of the child', *American Journal of Diseases of Children*, vol. 62, p. 716.

62 PIERONI, A. L. (1967), 'Role of the social worker in a children's cancer clinic', *Pediatrics*, vol. 40, pp. 534-6.

63 PILL, R. (1970), 'The sociological aspects of the case-study sample', in Stacey *et al.* (1970).

64 PINKERTON, R. (1969), 'Managing the psychological aspects of CF', *Arizona Medicine*, vol. 26, pp. 348-51.

65 PRUGH, D. G. *et al.* (1953), 'A study of the emotional reactions of children and families to hospitalization and illness', *American Journal of Orthopsychiatry*, vol. 23, p. 70.

66 RICHMOND, J. B. and WAISMAN, H. A. (1955), 'Psychological aspects of management of children with malignant diseases', *American Journal of Diseases of Children*, vol. 89, p. 42.

67 ROBERTSON, J. (1970), *Young Children in Hospital*, Tavistock, London.

68 ROSENSTEIN, B. J. (1970), 'Cystic fibrosis of the pancreas: impact on family functioning', in Debuskey (ed.) (1970).

69 ROTHENBERG, M. B. (1967), 'Reactions of those who treat children with cancer', *Pediatrics*, vol. 40, p. 507.

70 SAUNDERS, C. (1969), 'The management of fatal illness in childhood', *Proceedings of the Royal Society of Medicine*, vol. 62 (6), pp. 550-3.

71 SOLNIT, A. J. and GREEN, M. (1959), 'Psychologic considerations in the management of deaths on pediatric hospital services. I. The doctor and the child's family', *Pediatrics*, vol. 24, pp. 106-12.

72 SOLNIT, A. J. and GREEN, M. (1963), 'Pediatric management of the dying child. II. A study of the child's reaction to the fear of dying', in Solnit, A. J. and Provence, S. A. (eds), *Modern Perspectives in Child Development*, International Universities Press, New York.

73 SPENCE, J. C. (1947), 'The care of children in hospital', *British Medical Journal*, vol. 1, p. 125.

74 SPITZ, R. A. (1945), 'Hospitalism', *Psychoanalytic Study of the Child*, vol. 1, p. 53.

75 SPOCK, A. and STEDMAN, D. J. (1966), 'Psychologic characteristics of children with cystic fibrosis', *North Carolina Medical Journal*, September, pp. 426-8.

76 STACEY, M., DEARDEN, R., PILL, R. and ROBINSON, D. (1970), *Hospitals, Children and their Families*, Routledge & Kegan Paul, London.

77 TISZA, V. B. (1960), 'Management of the parents of the chronically ill child', *American Journal of Psychiatry*, vol. 32, pp. 53-9.

78 TONYAN, A. B. (1967), 'Role of the nurse in a children's cancer clinic', *Pediatrics*, vol. 40, p. 532.

79 TROPAUER, A., FRANZ, M. N. and DILGARD, V. (1970), 'Psychological aspects of the care of children with cystic fibrosis', *American Journal of Diseases of Children*, vol. 119, pp. 424-32.

80 TURK, J. (1964), 'Impact of cystic fibrosis on family functioning', *Pediatrics*, vol. 34, pp. 67-71.

81 VERNICK, J. and KARON, M. (1965), 'Who's afraid of death on a leukemia ward?', *American Journal of Diseases of Children*, vol. 109, pp. 393-7.

82 VISOTSKY, H. M. *et al.* (1961), 'Coping behaviour under extreme stress. Observations of patients with severe poliomyelitis', *Archives of General Psychiatry*, vol. 5, p. 423.

83 WAECHTER, E. H. (1968), 'Death anxiety in children with fatal illness', unpublished doctoral dissertation, Stanford University.

84 WAHL, C. W. (1958), 'The fear of death', *Bulletin of the Menninger Clinic*, vol. 22, pp. 214-23.

85 WALKER, J. H. *et al.* (1971), 'Spina bifida and the parents', *Developmental Medicine and Child Neurology*, vol. 13, pp. 462-76.

86 YUDKIN, S. (1967), 'Children and death', *Lancet*, vol. 7, p. 37.

3

Problems posed for staff who care for the child*

Michael B. Rothenberg

It is my impression that the reactions of those who treat or otherwise work with children who are dying of cancer or other fatal illnesses develop from a core conflict within each worker. This conflict arises because two powerful and normal, but antithetical emotional responses are elicited simultaneously when one is involved with the care of the dying—or even possibly dying—child. On the one hand, there is the response of compassion which produces the impulse to move toward the child with aid and comfort at every level. On the other hand, there is the response of repulsion by the threat of death which produces the impulse to move away from the dying child in order to begin to protect oneself from the impending shock of separation and loss. The degree of success with which this conflict is resolved determines the degree of success of the individual health care worker in providing comprehensive care for the child with cancer. Before discussing some suggested ways to approach a successful resolution of this conflict, I should like to outline some of the more common feelings and reactions of those who treat children with cancer which may interfere with such a resolution.

All those who have chosen the provision of health care services to the sick as their vocation—be they physicians, nurses, practical nurses, nurses' aides, occupational, physical or recreational therapists, or medical social workers—have in common the desire to help sick people get well. One may ask why one should find it necessary to make such a blatantly obvious statement. The answer is that when sick people fail to get well a number of not-so-obvious reactions may supervene in any or all of the aforementioned health care workers.

*First published under the title 'Reactions of those who treat children with cancer', *Pediatrics*, 1967, vol. 40.

A patient's failure to get well frustrates one of the primary goals and needs of the health care worker, and feelings of frustration lead rapidly to feeling angry. But how can one be angry at a sick— still worse, at a dying—child? And thus arises the feeling of guilt. Guilt, being an unpleasant feeling, in itself produces a reaction of anger at the one who caused the guilt feeling, and a self-sustaining emotional chain reaction has begun. This chain reaction may occur on a conscious, partly conscious, or totally unconscious level, and its intensity in a given situation will determine the degree to which it interferes with the provision of patient care.

It is safe to say that most health care workers have experienced disease and death somewhere in their own extended family constellation. Indeed, in many such workers such experiences have been important or even major motivation forces in the choice of career. It is not uncommon that the health care worker's reaction to the dying child bears a strong resemblance to or is otherwise coloured by his previous reaction to the analogous experience in his own family group. Here again we are dealing with a reaction which may be wholly, partly, or not at all conscious. Most importantly, we are dealing with a reaction which may be wholly, partly, or not at all appropriate in the current situation. Clearly, the degree to which this reaction is inappropriate will determine the degree to which it interferes with proper patient care.

The reaction of overprotectiveness is a common one in those treating children with cancer. This may represent a conscious attempt to protect the child from further damage, especially with those children whose disease has produced *sequellae*, such as partial or total blindness or unsteadiness of gait, which realistically endanger the child in his daily functioning. However, it may also represent an unconscious attempt to compensate for the kind of anger reaction which has already been described. In either case, overprotectiveness will always produce an overt or covert reaction of anger in the child, whose mobility has already been decreased by his illness and who then perceives the health care worker as intensifying this decreased mobility. Overprotectiveness is often accompanied by overindulgence, which may vary in degree from marked permissiveness to a total abolition of the boundary between freedom and licence. Rather than having the desired supportive and palliative effect, this reaction invariably imposes an added burden of guilt on the child, who has invariably responded by tyrannising the very people who are working so hard at treating him.

When the child meets overprotectiveness in one health care worker and overindulgence in another, or both reactions alternately in one and the same worker, he is forced to cope with what is probably the single most corrosive element in his adult environment—inconsistency.

When one treatment technique after another fails to arrest the progress of the child's cancer, the appearance of still another reaction among the health care workers becomes ever more likely. Individual workers in relation to each other and/or workers from one field in relation to those in another field may begin to accuse each other of failing to properly perform various services for the child. In essence, the workers displace to each other the anger and irritation they feel as a result of their frustration in dealing with the patient. Thus, for example, if the social worker had made sure that the mother instead of the aunt had accompanied the child to the clinic, it would have been easier for the child to accept the news from the physician that day that the current medication was being discontinued in favour of another which might, however, cause some nausea and vomiting. The deleterious effect of such a reaction on the provision of comprehensive care by a team of workers from a number of disciplines is obvious.

At this point, one must reiterate that we are still dealing with reactions that are well within normal limits. Indeed, in this paper I have confined myself to a discussion only of such reactions.

Illustrative case

Let us now use a more detailed case history to illustrate and elaborate some of the material we have outlined.

Jim, in his mid-teens, was the bright, hard-working, personable, older son of parents who were also bright, hard-working, and devoted to their two boys and to their upwardly striving socio-economic struggle. He had been entirely well until the sudden onset of the illness which brought him rapidly to the hospital and the diagnosis of acute leukaemia. Dr Bill, as we shall call him, was the bright, hard-working, sensitive, and dedicated young paediatrician who was taking a postgraduate fellowship in the psychosocial and developmental aspects of paediatrics with our child psychiatry-paediatrics liaison service and who was assigned by me, his supervisor, to assume the responsibility for Jim's comprehensive care. Jim's course was a stormy one—each of the usual chemotherapeutic agents was tried and found wanting, and a rapid demise was anticipated.

Jim had become profoundly withdrawn and depressed in response to his illness and hospitalisation, the haematology group and ward staff had been staggered by a half dozen leukaemic deaths in rapid

41

succession, and everyone was happy to have Dr Bill assume full responsibility for working with Jim and his parents. Indeed, everyone was so happy that they began to treat Dr Bill, Jim, and Jim's parents as if they had the plague. It was a massive withdrawal in the face of what had been a massive assault, and a withdrawal, moreover, which could be executed with little or no guilt because Dr Bill, the 'super-specialist' in liaison services, would provide for all the needs of the patient and his family. Thus, all of Dr Bill's ongoing difficulties in sorting out his own reactions to the child and the family were intensified by his awareness that, with the exception of his weekly supervision, he was very much alone in facing a formidable task.

Now the scene was fully set: the dying boy who had covered himself with a cloak of silence; the distraught parents searching fruitlessly for some way to reach their son; the hospital staff with its collective back turned in full retreat, periodically turning its head to cry out an entreaty to the embattled young physician to 'do something'; and the lonely figure of the frightened physician, struggling with mixed feelings of guilt because he could do nothing for his patient, irritation and anger at the patient for failing to respond to all attempts at medical and psychological care, irritation and anger at the hospital staff for leaving him alone, and resentment at his supervisor for placing him in this painful position. Unhappily, it is not uncommon in our work with children with cancer to find the scene set thus, all of the characters waiting to be released from the tableau by the death of the central figure.

In this instance, release was achieved by a quite unexpected and abrupt remission-release, that is, for the inpatient staff—but the tableau was rapidly restored by replacing the necessary figures from personnel in the outpatient department.

Intensive work with Dr Bill, helping him to express, face, and understand his feelings of fear, anger, guilt, and sadness in relation to Jim and Jim's parents, followed by a similar effort on Dr Bill's part with the nursing and paramedical personnel in the clinic and on the ward, eventuated in sufficient understanding, support and reassurance for all parties concerned to produce a far more pleasant milieu in ward and clinic as subsequent exacerbations and remissions supervened.

It should be noted that the single most difficult task for Dr Bill was talking to Jim about death, giving Jim the opportunity to express his fear and anger at the possibility of dying, in order that the boy's depression might be ameliorated. This is not surprising when one recognises the enormous investment of all health care personnel in the avoidance of death. It is this investment which gives rise to the reaction of avoidance of the dying patient and even of any talk of death among health care workers themselves, much less with the patient or his family.

The fatal outcome in Jim's case was never in doubt, remissions rapidly became shorter and exacerbations more severe, and another noteworthy transaction took place. Jim's parents wanted to have him at home as much a possible as he approached his terminal stage. We, tending to overprotect Jim and to avoid the accentuation of our own guilt feelings which would attend his dying at home, were unable to understand and accede to their request—until we realised that having him at home (and they had already demonstrated their ability to handle this well, including the handling of his younger brother) made them feel less guilty by enabling them to give him the comfort of being with his family.

Thus it was that Jim died in his own bed one night, as his mother spoke to Dr Bill on the phone, unknowingly describing to him what were the terminal events as they occurred. Jim had been in apparent remission, and autopsy revealed that the immediate cause of death had been perforation of esophageal ulcers caused by one of the cyto-toxic drugs used to treat the boy.

A great deal of preparation for Jim's death already had taken place. There only remained the working out of the guilt feelings surrounding the immediate cause of death, and helping Dr Bill to keep in touch with the family (and help them keep in touch with him)—instead of the usual avoidance reaction of all—so that he could help them to help themselves and Jim's younger brother regroup their emotional forces, as it were.

A postscript will end this story. Some twenty-four hours after Jim's death, while driving to my office from the hospital, I began to feel depressed. For another twenty-four hours I struggled unsuccessfully to understand why I was feeling thus, and it was not until I was telling a colleague about Jim that the obvious appeared to me. I had worked long and hard and well at helping Dr Bill, and, through him, the ward and clinic staffs as they managed Jim and prepared themselves for his death. I had neglected only one character in the drama—myself. What I had not realised was that I was using my work with the others to avoid my own feelings about Jim. Indeed, I realised in retrospect that I had tried unconsciously to place myself quite outside all of the human transactions, in the role of observer and supervisor. It followed that I had failed to work with my own guilt and anger responses, the repression of which led to my feelings of depression.

MICHAEL B. ROTHENBERG

Methods of approaching conflict

How, then, are we to resolve this core conflict which revolves about the simultaneous impulses to move towards and away from the child with cancer and his family. One might well ask, 'Can we ever really accept death, especially in children, in the deepest sense, and thus eliminate the impulse to withdraw from it?' My answer, for the overwhelming majority of health care workers, is 'No'. Therefore, we cannot resolve the conflict by eliminating one of its elements. As with the disease itself, the solution of the core conflict lends itself to no simple formula. We can only point out the right road and some ways to avoid the major potholes in it.

Our resolution must come from consciously forcing ourselves to remain moving toward the patient and his family; while simultaneously recognising, expressing, and, finally, understanding and thus coping with the many reactions which would trigger off our movement in the opposite direction. This means literally and repeatedly checking oneself out in regard to such feelings as fear, anger, guilt, sadness, overprotectiveness, and overindulgence. Is not this something that only the clinical psychologist or psychiatrist, with his special training and technique can do? My answer—an emphatic 'No'. The specialist in psychological medicine has his consultant's role to play in helping us to see unconscious and, therefore, hidden reactions. But I feel that it is the responsibility of the paediatrician, if he is to practise truly comprehensive care with children and their families, to assume the leading role in bringing himself and all other health care workers to examine, understand, and effectively use their own emotional reactions as they affect the form and content of the care that is being provided for the patient and his family.

It is not enough, for example, to understand that it is all right to be angry at a patient but not to act angry at a patient, and to understand why a health care worker may become angry at a patient in the first place. We don't have each feeling once, or even once with each patient. The feelings occur over and over again, and our seeking out and positive management of our reactions must be as relentless and untiring as our seeking out and positive management of the signs and symptoms of the disease itself. In short, our examination of our own reactions must become as automatic and exhaustive and unending as our search for tumour cells and new drugs.

We have poured an endless stream of time, money, and energy into the perfection of our instruments, procedures, and drugs in the battle against cancer. It seems to me that we owe it to ourselves and our patients and their families to do as much for the understanding and perfection of what is in many ways the most critical 'instrument' of all in the provision of comprehensive care to the child with cancer—our own emotions.

Part II

Specific problems

The child in pain

Alexander T. Mennie

What is pain?

Pain is an entirely subjective experience which has never been satisfactorily defined. It is what the patient says 'hurts' or is 'sore'. One thing is certain however, our *perception* of pain depends on the intactness of our nervous system—the free nerve endings, the peripheral nerves, the spinal cord and the various pathways to and from the brain, which transmit impulses which we interpret as painful. Our *reaction* to pain is a very complex one, influenced by genetics, culture, past experience, emotion and anxiety. Pain is a great paradox. It is protective, creative and destructive. It warns us of potential and actual damage to the body and produces a reaction—a withdrawal response, or muscular tension—which protects the injured part. It can be a powerful creative force. Great music, literature and paintings have been produced as a direct result of pain and it can also help human beings to have insight into their own nature and to have sympathy with each other. But when pain is persistent it is 'the poisoned gift which degrades man and makes him more ill'. The harmful effect of constant pain on mind and body can destroy the morale and alter the personality of the sufferer more effectively than any other single factor.

The problem of pain in young patients

The process of learning about pain starts at birth. The newborn child reacts to painful stimuli, as shown by the response to injections of drugs given under the skin shortly after birth. Newborn babies may, in fact, experience pain during birth when forceps are used, or a bone is damaged. The reaction to pain usually takes place after an interval of about half a second, and the appreciation of pain is

49

slightly longer delayed. The transmission of painful impulses depends on the stage of development of the nervous system. On the first day after birth it has been shown (Shirkey, 1972) that a fairly large electrical stimulus is required to produce a pain reaction. By the third month half this stimulus is all that is necessary for a reaction.

As with adults, the pain threshold in children—the sensitivity to a painful stimulus such as a burn or a knock—depends on the basal state. For example, a child feeding at the breast is less sensitive to pain than when it is hungry, and an anxious child is more sensitive to pain than a tranquil child.

Immediately after birth mother and child form a unit—a special life unit of complementary but different natures called a dyad. This dyad is also a pain unit and it is well illustrated by the answer of a French mother to the doctor who asked why she had called him to see her child. Her reply was, 'J'ai douleur dans la gorge de ma fille'—'I have a pain in my child's throat' (Janzen, 1970). When the child becomes aware of its own pain, the pain unit disappears. As with other processes of learning, the appreciation of pain is influenced by the mother's behaviour, so if the mother leaves the child to pick itself up after a minor fall, the child is more likely to make light of the injury than if the mother shows excessive concern.

The effect that the presence of one mother can have on a child may make the doctor's diagnosis of a pain very difficult, or even impossible, whereas another mother may make it easy. Professor Illingworth (1967) of the University of Sheffield points out how pain may be suggested by an anxious mother. He writes (pp. 84-6), 'A few minutes after I had talked to a mother about her boy's abdominal pain, telling her that I had found no disease to explain it, she was overheard saying to the boy "Of course you have pain in your tummy, darling, haven't you?". He had.'

Young children often do not know the meaning of the word 'pain', and frequently they neglect to complain of pain, or even deny its existence, despite a painful condition such as inflammation of the tonsils. They also have difficulty in describing exactly where a pain is and how bad it may be. A child may say he has a pain somewhere, but he is not aware that it is in his head. It is only when his mother, or father, tells him that it is in his head that he realises that this is true. The severity of pain may be difficult to estimate, since minor pains may be exaggerated, or severe pains minimised, but the intensity of pain in childhood is often indicated by the emotional reactions of the child. The character of the pain, whether it is a sharp, burning, throbbing, or a dull ache, which indicates to the doctor the nature of an injury, is difficult to elicit from children, since they are very suggestible and are likely to answer leading questions with a 'yes'. Acute short-lasting pain is common in young children because of frequent slight injuries at a stage of growth when control of the body is still poor. The pain pattern changes as childhood progresses and pain due to minor injuries becomes less as experience of life brings about greater awareness. In my experience, I find children tolerate pain better than most adults. They are more patient and do not feel sorry for themselves, a state of mind commonly found in adult life.

Of course, when we try to assess the importance of what we think is pain in children, we are faced with the very difficult task of estimating someone else's experience. There are, however, some guidelines. The infant usually shows he has pain by crying, although there are many reasons why a child should cry other than the presence of pain.

Paediatricians (Illingworth, 1967) often have infants referred to them on account of acute indigestion and wind, which is thought to be the reason for crying during the night. However, the crying is often due to sleep problems, as a result of anxious parents, or the formation of bad habits. Frequently severe pain produces high pitched piercing screams in a child, but some children can be very stoical and not cry at all. If the crying stops when the child is picked up, the pain is not severe. It is also unlikely to be severe if it does not stop the child from playing, or interfere with eating or sleeping. A mother's opinion of the child's pain can be of great value and it is sometimes revealing to ask if she would have known the child had pain, if the child had not told her about it.

Pains caused by stressful situations in children are nearly always located in the abdomen, whereas pains in the joints, or the head, usually have a physical basis. It is well known, though often forgotten, that it is important when studying pain in childhood to go into the history of the complaint very carefully. Frequently the beginning of the pain coincides with tension within the family, or the birth of a brother or sister. The doctor too is unfortunately often associated with the experience of pain by the child and many of us can recall unpleasant memories of early inoculations against poliomyelitis, diphtheria and typhoid fever. Dr J. L. Henderson, in a perceptive essay (Ogilvie and Thomson, 1950), points out that children of all ages should be assured of every reasonable safeguard from physical and mental pain, thus diminishing not only suffering, but also the possibility of psychological disturbances such as persistent fear.

Whether or not a child is brought to the doctor on account of pain, depends largely on the anxiety threshold of the parents. Some children are taken to the doctor when they have the most trivial and short-lasting pains. Other children may have to suffer almost intolerable pain before they receive medical aid. It is well known that anxiety by itself aggravates pain and the anxiety of parents can aggravate a child's pain by excessive attention to the child. Petting and giving warm pleasant drinks may result in more complaints, as the child uses the discomfort as an attention-seeking device. The experience of pain as an attention-seeking device is often seen in children who are suffering from a chronic illness, or who are slightly neglected. During a ward round, one child asked 'Can I have a mosquito bite too?' (Shirkey, 1972).

Children are great imitators. Sometimes they can imitate with disconcerting accuracy the painful experiences of their parents and relatives. Included in their repertoire are imitations of heart attacks, migraine headaches, and painful breathing. Children readily discover that they can use pain to protect themselves. Most of us can remember from our own experience using illness as an excuse for not going to school, or for not wishing to eat a particular food. This type of pain may be very difficult to distinguish from pain due to a disease process. As mentioned previously, pains in the area of the stomach often have a psychological element and occasionally they suggest to the doctor that the one who should be treated is the parent and not the child. In assessing the child's pain, it is important to assess the family pattern of behaviour and to find out if other members of the family have similar pains. If the father complains of stomach pains, or the mother is seen to have attacks of migraine, it would not be surprising if the child also has pain which is not directly due to any pathological process. Pains in the head or the abdomen are frequently experienced by the child because of anxieties about school. He may be having difficulty with a particular subject, or he may be a sensitive child and may be worried because other children are teasing him about his clothes or his appearance in general. The pain he experiences is real enough, although it is entirely psychological in origin.

An unusual response to pain has recently come to light with the battered baby syndrome. Here the child may suffer considerable injury from the parents. These unfortunate children react quite differently to children who are brought up in a different environment. The pains they suffer tend to be damped down almost as a protective measure, since any reaction to physical violence produces more pain. These children therefore, react by not making the normal response to a painful stimulus. When the battered child finally goes to hospital, fractures of the arms and legs are discovered which the child may have forgotten about. It is remarkable that when the parents who have caused so much damage visit the child in hospital, the child receives them with trust. Such children are often homesick when in hospital and the injuries they have experienced tend to be overshadowed by the loneliness and lack of affection which they have also sustained. The battered child usually comes from a large family and the other children of such families often have normal care and attention.

The battered child is the scapegoat and literally the 'whipping boy' (Janzen, 1970). These poor children often long to be permitted to return to the family circle. They will even remain quiet and uncomplaining in spite of harsh treatment, if only they are allowed back with their brothers and sisters.

Very rarely a condition is seen in infancy or early childhood where there is a failure to react normally to painful stimuli. This abnormality is usually first recognised when the child is apparently undisturbed by an injury which should be painful. The cause of the disorder is unknown and remarkably there is no apparent damage to the nervous system. Here is an illustrative case (Ogden *et al.*, 1959).

The patient was a fourteen-year-old girl who developed normally during her first year of life. When she was about one year old, her parents noticed that she was inclined to chew her tongue causing large ulcers, which appeared to be painless. When she was two-and-a-half years old handfuls of her hair were pulled out by her playmate; at the age of three she smashed her fingers in a door; at four she severely lacerated her forehead. With each of these injuries there was no evidence of pain and on several occasions the damage was unsuspected until noticed by her parents. At the age of six her right hip became swollen over the period of two weeks and eventually she complained of being unable to move the leg. Three weeks later she was admitted to the hospital where a fracture of the right femur was diagnosed. At no time during this period, even while walking, did she complain of pain. At the age of ten she fell while playing and noticed while getting up that her wrist bent the wrong way. She had sustained a painless compound fracture of the left wrist, which was set without an anaesthetic and without causing her any discomfort. She cannot recall having a headache, earache, stomach ache, colic, or having experienced pain of any kind. She realises when she has a foreign body in her eyes, but is not disturbed by it.

This of course is a rare condition and at the time of writing there is no explanation for it. Apparently there is no obvious damage to the nervous system.

An illustrative case history of another kind shows how mental abnormaly can affect the appreciation of pain (Goodhart and Savitsky, 1933). A young girl of sixteen was admitted to hospital because of a mild infection of both eyes. A few hours after admission the nurse was called to the patient's room. The patient said to her 'My eye just popped out' and showed the nurse her enucleated right eye held in her right hand. Attached to the eye was the optic nerve in its entirety. The patient showed no excitement or physical discomfort and was evidently not in pain. Within two hours of this experience, with a bandage applied to the head covering the empty cavity of the removed eye, the patient again made some commotion calling the attention of another nurse. When the nurse went to see her, the girl, again apparently in no distress, explained that her other eye had popped out. Subsequent statements by the patient made it clear that she had suffered no pain in the act and completion of her mutilating effects. The act of mutilation was, of course, evidence of an abnormal mind.

A strange condition known as 'asymbolia for pain' occurs in children who have brain damage which is usually confined to the parietal lobe of the brain. This brain damage does not prevent them from recognising painful stimuli, but it does interfere with their response to pain. They are not able to respond in the normal way. For example, if they burn their fingers in front of a fire, they are unable to take appropriate action by withdrawing the hand from the source of heat. This 'asymbolia for pain' is also present in patients who have had frontal leucotomy, in schizophrenics and in certain depressive states.

Cultural attitudes to pain

The response to painful stimuli is greatly influenced by upbringing, and the environment, and in some societies the fortitude with which pain is borne is a measure of manhood. This is seen in the painful initiation rituals carried out by various tribes in Africa.

The Scots, the Irish, the Scandinavians and 'old Americans' (Sternbach, 1968, p. 74) do not have approval from their cultures for the public expression of pain. When they are in pain, they tend to withdraw from society, and cry or moan only when they are alone. The Italians and the Jews are less inhibited. Their culture does not disapprove of the public expression of pain, and public suffering for them is designed to bring forth family and professional support and sympathy. There is also a strong belief amongst Jewish people of the undoubted therapeutic value of crying out when pain is present.

With the recent great interest in acupuncture, it is also clear that the Chinese have a different attitude to pain from our own in the West.

During a recent visit to China, a general practitioner, who was interested in acupuncture, had an opportunity of observing closely the use of this procedure in adults as a pain reliever for dental extractions and surgical operations, including removal of the thyroid gland and hysterectomy. The acupuncture technique appeared to be successful in adults but had little or no effect in children. The explanation given for this was that it was easier to convince an adult that this particular method was going to succeed, but that it was much more difficult to convince children. Whatever the explanation, the Chinese doctors approached children in a different way as the following report shows (Brown, 1972):

> While visiting a children's hospital, we saw a queue of smiling five year olds standing outside a room where tonsillectomies were being carried out in rapid succession. The leading child was given a quick anaesthetic spray of the throat by a nurse a few minutes before walking into the theatre unaccompanied.
> Each youngster in turn climbed on the table, lay back smiling at the surgeon, opened his mouth wide, and had his tonsils dissected out in the extraordinary time of less than a minute. The only instruments used were dissecting scissors and forceps. The child left the table and walked into the recovery room, spitting blood into a gauze swab. A bucket of water at the surgeon's feet containing 34 tonsils of all sizes was proof of the morning's work. This tonsillectomy technique is significant in as much as it indicates that, without recourse to acupuncture, the Chinese patient is conditioned from early childhood to accept surgical interference of his body with the full knowledge that it is going to be successful and he will experience little or no discomfort.

The attitudes of the medical and nursing profession to pain

It is quite remarkable that for a long time it was believed by the medical profession that infants did not experience pain to the same extent as adults, and even in my lifetime I remember operations, such as the removal of tonsils and circumcision, being done on children without the use of anaesthetic. From the results of a study I did in the last year on the treatment of leukaemic children in hospital, it was obvious that this mistaken idea was still with us. Changing of dressings, taking of bone marrow samples and the

55

insertion of needles into the spine are procedures which often cause a great deal of pain to children and yet they are still done without adequate analgesia. In a modern hospital there is no excuse for any child to suffer pain from such diagnostic or therapeutic measures.

It has been noted earlier that persistent pain is both harmful to the body and the mind and although there are a number of published studies highlighting these facts (Gold *et al.*, 1943; Wolf, 1943), it is astonishing that even doctors and nurses appear to ignore the facts. Many people think that pain is something that you have to put up with, and that to take too much time over the treatment of pain results in making the patient soft. Men in particular are expected to bear pain, especially in general medical wards and it is found that whereas women patients tend to be given analgesics whether they require them or not, men are frequently denied them. A revealing letter appeared in a medical journal recently from a general practitioner (Senex I, 1970), who himself was in hospital for a prostate operation. Owing to some infection, he had surprisingly bad pains before his operation, and he felt strongly that they could have been alleviated in some measure if the approach to pain had been different. He writes:

During some nights, pain was such that I could not stay in bed (I was in a single room at the time), but got up, one or two nights as often as 20 times, to go and sit in a bathroom or lavatory solely for the purpose of weaving back and forth there to help bear it, groaning and with considerable total strain— in itself, I thought, as dangerous as any pain-killer would be, for a person of 79. On my way I often passed the ward sister, at or near her desk; I was breaking rules, but there was no protest—she knew my reason. I would beg sometimes for something to reduce the pain, if only a couple of aspirins. But sister never acceded; she could not, I suppose, increase the quantum of sedation. She would look up at the clock and say, 'Not for another hour' (or more or less)—words I found desperate in my deep need then and there. In short, I might as well have walked into the middle of the Sahara, for any prospect of aid, as out into the ward. Every member of the staff I saw was completely conditioned against paying any attention; they had their jobs to do; all were used to patients in pain and used to their asking for relief, a request apparently beyond their power to grant. Even the ward doctor seemed to lack authority to give off his own bat, increased doses of sedatives. (Why should a patient not be allowed to take his own risks?)

56

In my dreary predicament, unassuaged by hope of alleviation, (I may have missed some words of concern or sympathy, being hard-of-hearing), I formed the concept of a kind of ombudsman for excessive pain, or, as others have put it, 'a nurse for a pain round'. Probably numbers of patients suffer pain which could be reduced. I found it a mental as well as physical strain to agonise through the night.

Two weeks later in the same journal another GP wrote in almost identical terms (Senex II, 1970):

It was a remarkable experience to read the letter by Senex, because, word for word, it was an almost exact picture of what I was suffering contemporaneously with him. After a prostate operation in a famous teaching hospital I was allowed to suffer hours of what seemed to me the greatest pain I'd known in 81 years of life. My respiration gasped under it, the sweat streamed, I wondered if—indeed I hoped—I would faint under it. And yet the instant the glorious total relief was perfectly possible—as was later proved three times—by recatheterisation. But the business of the ward just went speedily and rather merrily on.

Treatment of painful states

It is clear to me from the patients that I see in hospital that the best way of dealing with pain is to try and prevent it from occurring. When it is present it must be eliminated as quickly as possible, since, if it is allowed to persist, the pain escalates and becomes more difficult to treat. It seems self-evident that before you treat a pain you have to find out what is causing it, but frequently the busy doctor takes the line of least resistance and prescribes an analgesic drug. This is not very helpful if the basic condition that the patient is suffering from is fear or anxiety, and this is particularly relevant in the treatment of children, who may be terribly frightened at their first hospital visit. It is important to spend sufficient time with them to gain their confidence before any operative procedure is carried out. It is equally important not to deceive them intentionally. If the introduction of a needle is going to hurt them, you must say it is going to hurt, since there is nothing that wrecks the confidence of a child more readily than telling lies. It is surprising what fortitude a child shows when you ask for his co-operation in performing some difficult procedure, which may have to be done without a general anaesthetic. Many children are stoical when their parents are present, but the percentage of stoics is in inverse proportion to the number of parents who remain with their children during medical, or surgical treatment. Usually medical treatment proceeds more smoothly when parents are not there.

'Distress from diagnostic procedures', one mother told me, 'can be overcome, if parents keep out of the way. My daughter made more fuss when we were about. She should have the doctor she trusts who keeps her talking throughout the procedure.'

Occasionally a calm reassuring parent can be of undoubted benefit once a proper relationship between the doctor, the child and the nursing staff has been established.

However, with the drugs and techniques at our disposal there is no reason at all why a child should suffer anything but the slightest discomfort from diagnostic and therapeutic measures. Unnecessary pain can be prevented by careful handling of the sick child to minimise the production of painful stimuli. According to one authority (Ogilvie and Thomson, 1950), in minor surgical procedures, such as lumbar puncture and sternal puncture, preliminary local anaesthesia should always be given, even in babies.

It is remarkable that in young children a local anaesthetic is often omitted on the assumption that it is almost as painful to prick the skin and introduce an anaesthetic solution into the tissue as to insert a needle without an anaesthetic. There is no evidence for this and the practice is certainly unjustified. It is unreasonable to deprive a child of the benefit of analgesia which is regarded as indispensable for adults in similar circumstances.

There is a wide range of analgesic drugs, from simple aspirin to compounds of opium, which, administered skilfully, can remove pain speedily, and, combined with drugs that remove anxiety and depression, they can make the life of a child with an incurable disease relatively pain free and comfortable. If the drugs are in-effective for the treatment of intractable pain, surgical procedures, such as cutting the nerve fibres which carry the painful impulses, can produce relief. If cancer cells are causing the pain, radiotherapy may give relief. Some authorities believe that hypnosis may have a place in the relief of pain in children and certainly, in this country, self-hypnosis has been successfully tried in children who showed stress from asthma.

I believe that the study of pain and its relief should occupy a larger part of the medical curriculum. After all it is usually the first thing that brings the patient to the doctor, and its relief affords both doctor and patient the greatest satisfaction.

References

BROWN, P. D. (1972), 'Use of acupuncture in major surgery', *Lancet*, vol. 1, p. 1328.

GOLD, H., KIVIT, N. T. and MODELL, W. (1943), 'The effect of extra cardiac pain on the heart', *Proceedings of the Association for Research in Nervous and Mental Diseases*, vol. 23, p. 258.

GOODHART, S. P. and SAVITSKY, N. (1933), 'Self mutilation in chronic encephalitis', *American Journal of Medical Science*, vol. 185, p. 674.

ILLINGWORTH, R. S. (1967), *Common Symptoms of Disease in Children*, Blackwell, Oxford.

JANZEN, R. (ed.) (1970), *Pain Analysis*, John Wright, Bristol.

OGDEN, T. E., ROBERT, F. and CARMICHAEL, E. A. (1959), 'Some sensory syndromes in children', *Journal of Neurology, Neurosurgery and Psychiatry*, vol. 22, p. 261.

OGILVIE, H. and THOMSON, W. A. R. (eds.) (1950), *Pain and its Problems*, Eyre & Spottiswoode, London.

SENEX I (1970), Letter, *Lancet*, vol. 2, p. 1040.

SENEX II (1970), Letter, *Lancet*, vol. 2, p. 1132.

SHIRKEY, H. C. (1972), *Paediatric Therapy*, 4th edition, Mosby, St Louis.

STERNBACH, R. A. (1968), *Pain*, Academic Press, New York.

WOLF, G. (1943), 'The effect of pain on renal function', *Proceedings of the Association for Research in Nervous and Mental Diseases*, vol. 23, p. 358.

5

The 'doomed family'— observations on the lives of parents and children facing repeated child mortality*

Margaret Atkin

> With unerring doom
> He sees what is, and was, and is to come.
> *Dryden*

Twentieth-century Western society ill-prepares its members for the loss of children. Life is for living—death is remote and taboo. Yet some families must face death in not only one, but several, or all of their children. In a very real sense this 'doomed family' has to try to make dying a part of living. The integration of the two may be an agonising part of their total experience. Each family has to use to the full the inner strengths and resources of every member to face the recapitulation of death. It throws into sharp relief the whole purpose and meaning of life.

The emotive word 'doomed' is used therefore to describe a family who feel that they have little future together and whose hopes for further happiness and fulfilment have gone. Occasionally it means literally a family for whom the present generation is the last. There are a number of fortunately rare diseases in which a child is either born with severe handicaps or develops them and deteriorates. The manifestations of these diseases include: mental retardation, dementia, epilepsy, weakness, unsteadiness, and failure of vision and hearing. The term 'dementia' implies not only mental retardation but progressive loss of intellectual function.

The stresses on all members of such families are well known theoretically, if not always fully appreciated in practice. Why then should we separate a group of families and consider them as 'doomed'? A number of these diseases are genetically determined and the chances of a further child being affected may be as high as one

*I am greatly indebted to Dr B. G. R. Neville for his encouragement and medical guidance and to Dr J. Wilson for reading the manuscript.

in four. Many such conditions are progressive and there may be a period of months or years of normal development before the disease begins and then runs its relentless course. Most parents who are given as high a risk of recurrence as this decide not to have further children (Carter, C. O. *et al.*, 1971). Hence, if the first child is affected, this usually means the parents will lose the only child they will ever have. Others may already have younger children before it is clear that an older child has such a disease. The parents then have to wait to see whether or not their younger apparently normal children are going to escape. This problem reaches the ultimate in the case of Huntington's chorea in which parents will usually have had children before they themselves develop the abnormal movements and dementia of that disease. Their children have a one in two chance of developing it and there is no way of knowing in the apparently normal twenty- to thirty-year-olds if they are going to do so and therefore if they will transmit it to any children they may have.

The major medical advances in the management of families with genetically determined diseases have been detection of the abnormality in the first three months of pregnancy. As yet this only applies to some diseases, but can be offered to these families who have had one affected child. The parents may then make a decision—uniquely their own—to have a termination of pregnancy performed if the foetus is affected. For some parents this may enhance attitudes towards themselves and hence raise them above a sense of hopelessness and despair.

The observations here described are based on recent experience in helping families whose children have been referred for diagnostic studies to the neurological unit of a children's hospital. In no sense the result of systematic study, they offer but fragmentary glimpses into the lives of parents and children facing repeated loss. The pain and heartache so caused are frequently well camouflaged by a family struggling to function normally. It is easier and more acceptable for society that way.

The parents of such children are confronted with specific painful emotional adjustments in their family life. They also face many practical concerns. The two are interrelated, for the greater parental emotional adjustment, the more effective is their capacity to handle day-to-day problems of management. The family's ability to meet the many stresses made upon it depends on the personality of the parents and the kind of marriage they have, together with the quality of support and guidance they receive from those who help them in the hospital and community services.

The hospital-based social worker's intervention should be early and preferably at the first visit or while investigations are being undertaken as an inpatient. Hospitals are not without their stresses and the setting poses many problems for parents already harassed and bewildered. The social worker's approach is based on the view that just as the family is the unit of living, so it is also the unit of illness, and sometimes of dying. For it is within this framework that all family members experience most deeply those events in life which involve beginnings and endings, unions and separations and the many emotions engendered by such events. The task initially is to try to understand the very real concerns and fears parents may have about their child. This includes learning what referral to hospital has meant, what has been told and what is understood about the child now. Parental comments as to how they have coped with preceding weeks of anxiety may be supplemented by information forwarded by caring figures in the community. Since an approach to the sick child involves every family member, awareness of their pre-illness adjustment, and the patterns of communication and respective roles within the family unit need to be understood. The unique qualities inherent in each family—their strengths and weaknesses—are gradually appreciated.

Referral of children to such a specialised centre may bring added parental stress. It frequently heightens expectation of what may be achieved for the sick child. Waiting for the results of tests is a crisis phase, described by one parent as 'living in a state of limbo. The hours seem like years. I feel exhausted doing nothing but just being here. I don't feel this tired when I do the spring cleaning.' At such times some parents are unable to share concerns with each other. It is almost as though each has to exist in isolation of the other. Perhaps they think the expression of fears makes them too real. Baby Julie's mother explained this feeling:

'I have dark moments. Black fears that lurk at the back of my mind. I shut them out. But sometimes I think Julie will never grow—just stay as she is. I can't tell my husband. He adores her and he's so optimistic now we're here and things are being done. We don't talk about Julie—it's better that way.'

Whatever deeper meaning may lie behind such comments, the social worker should enable parents to begin sharing a maze of confused and jumbled thoughts whilst awaiting a medical verdict.

The diagnosis in such circumstances must always be a shock, but perhaps parents who have had appropriate support of this kind are a little better able to tolerate bad news however painful this may be.

The giving of the diagnosis is part of the overall therapeutic management and needs careful preparation. It is a point of maximum stress for parents. Sadly it is also a situation which may be repeated as other siblings become ill. Efforts are made to ensure that both parents are seen together, in relative comfort and with no rigid time limit. The task is usually undertaken by the consultant whose sensitivity tempers the frequently fatal news he has to give. For those parents who have not realised what is happening to their child, I believe the dying process starts with the giving of such a diagnosis. How crucial then that this interview should be handled with considerable medical competence—and compassion. As Dr Edelstyn has stressed (chapter 13, p. 158), for many reasons, the qualitative pace and level at which each parent hears what is said varies considerably. Hence whilst one parent may have grasped the implications of the doctor's words before the end of the first sentence, the other may continue a long dialogue asking one question after another, overtly oblivious of the partner's distress. Allowance for this must be made and opportunity given for more discussions and questions when the parents are less shocked and can together participate in further talks. All members of the medical and nursing team are concerned to support parents with the avalanche of different feelings that may engulf them at this time. For many the diagnosis is the culmination of restless and anxious months—wondering and waiting. In spite of anguish there is relief. Their child's condition is recognised—even if untreatable and incurable. Reflecting back on this experience a mother wrote:

> It's shattering to get such news and to know it's so final. You are the last court of appeal—we have nowhere else to go. But we now know what's wrong and that's a relief. You can't understand how we really feel but I certainly think you try very hard to. To be treated as responsible parents is very helpful at such a time.

However frightening the implications of brain diseases may seem, once the diagnosis is given, parents very painfully start to mobilise their earlier feelings of helplessness.

As they begin to peer through the mist to grapple with the content of the doctor's words, parents wonder how to convey their sad news to other members of the family. Whilst some inform relatives at once, others prefer to defer this task until they themselves have begun to sort out their own feelings. Just because stalwart friends usually are not so involved, they may be the people to whom parents first turn. The comfort of relatives may be sought a little later.

Talking with the sick child's siblings is usually a continuing dialogue and one with which help is frequently sought. Parents who have achieved a relatively satisfying marital adjustment can share sadness and sorrow about what some of them call having 'bad genes'. Together they begin to look at profound questions affecting their philosophy of living to which they will constantly return. Although intra-uterine detection is possible in an increasing number of conditions, many couples still cannot safely seek solace in having another baby of their own without high genetic risk. Lucy's brain disease was diagnosed when her mother was in the early stages of a second pregnancy. The mother wanted her pregnancy to continue; her husband preferred a termination, feeling they could not again face the suffering they were still experiencing with Lucy. They received considerable professional help in talking through their differences. They decided the pregnancy should continue and Peter was a delightful baby. Lucy died shortly after her brother's birth. Peter died of the same disease later that year. The inner resources of these parents were such that they were able to share the pain and desolation of losing two children within a year even though they had differing views about the second pregnancy. In time they were able to adopt children and remake their family life.

Whatever fantasies and fears parents may have about the 'why' of their child's illness, guilt feelings are very common and genetic factors may exacerbate them. A mother sitting beside her dying ten-month-old first baby John commented:

'Friends at my office said I'd never cope with a baby. They used to tease me about being up in the small hours for a night feed. I always said I'd fix a tube from my room to the baby's tummy. He's got a tube—I feel I'm being punished for what I said. Now I might never have another baby because of genetics.'

For other parents the genetic aspect reduces their sense of guilt since they see it as beyond their control.

The admission of a second or subsequent child for investigation may reactivate in parents dormant feelings about an older child whose death occurred years earlier. Tina was admitted for investigation of loss of skills. At three years of age her seemingly normal development had ceased. She was no longer speaking and had become withdrawn. Tina was a few weeks old when her parents' first child died as a result of a mysterious neurological disease of uncertain cause. It was a great shock to them to learn that Tina probably had the same illness. Tina's mother voiced the feelings of many parents: 'The first time, every day I was hoping for a miracle. Each day was new. I didn't know what to expect and kept on hoping. Now Tina is already so like her brother in her biting and everything... how much is a mother expected to bear?' The answer to the mother's question is unique to each situation. Tina's mother, with other family difficulties, had much unresolved grief over the loss of her son. She was overwhelmed at the prospect of a full-time caring programme all over again. She did not have to face it, but shared Tina's care by regular visits to the local paediatric unit.

Perhaps some of the most distressing cases are those in which the family circle had been completed and the potentially dying children are at different ages and phases of life experience. The eldest of three children, Ann, was eight when she became ill. Her early behaviour problems disguised the underlying nature of the condition for about a year, by which time it was obvious that she had ceased to learn and had lost some abilities. She was then referred to the hospital, and found to have a degenerative brain disease. Parental distress was heightened—'We punished Ann for being naughty and all the time she couldn't help it'. Two younger brothers had exploratory tests carried out. Their mother oscillated from wanting, to not wanting, to know whether they had the same condition. 'I don't need any doctor to tell me the signs—I'll know before he does' was her frequent comment. Coexisting was the wish: 'They're not going to keep anything from me. I have a right to know the truth.' Ann's physical state necessitated nursing care and she was hospitalised for a long time. Her speech ceased, her eyes failed to focus and she became increasingly less aware of her surroundings. A flickering smile was one of the last definite communications noted by her mother. The parents understood Ann's life expectancy was to be short—yet she lived on for many months. Her illness was no part of their experience. Although physically recognisable, all communication, awareness and emotional responsiveness had gone. As her mother explained: 'She's there but she's not'. Or in Dryden's words: ...'And doom'd to death though fated not to die'. The parents would comment that 'everyone is too good to Ann' almost as though she was not being allowed to die.

The brothers Roy and Adam visited their sister. Bewildered by her lack of response to their chatter, they would scamper off to play with others in the ward whom they found more receptive. At home these children would touch none of their sister's possessions. They asked permission to play with her toys. Articles especially favoured by Ann her brothers would not play with—'That's Ann's special'. Their parents tried to prepare them for Ann's non-return home but whilst she lived, and for some months after, the boys handled their sister's belongings with great reverence. They did not want her bed removed. They understood their sister had gone to live with Jesus, and was helping Him to look after children. A Sunday School teacher very sensitively helped Roy with his feelings of disappointment that God had not answered his prayers that Ann should be made better to be his 'special mate'.

The family were still grieving Ann's death when Roy began to exhibit symptoms of the same disease. His mother first noted the early signs, as she said she would. The doctors confirmed her worst fears. Having lost one child the parents faced the situation once more. Because of his learning difficulties, Roy was transferred to a special school which he found stressful. Later he went to a training school. As the dementia slowly increased he had to remain at home. Roy could not settle, walking aimlessly from room to room, hand-clapping, grimacing, gradually losing remaining skills. He made only odd noises, hardly knew his parents and could find only fleeting contentment listening to records. He became incontinent and had to be fed. Eventually he was hospitalised for a short time before he died.

Adam has a similar form of the same illness. The parents detected the early symptoms some months before Roy died. 'We know it all now—we shall be left with nothing—no children—nothing.' The family moved after Ann's death, but their hopes of making a new start were never allowed to materialise. Farther afield from extended family members and amenities, they became socially isolated. Though contact with the hospital was maintained, social work support from the community was rejected. The family accepted intermittent help from clergy and faith healers. The father said little—his face portrayed his inner thoughts: 'It's terrible to see healthy children go subnormal and have fits'. He took on evening work, thus tending to opt out of his caring role in the home. The mother was filled with feelings of anger, shame and guilt at what was happening to her children. She expressed fears of 'going mad locked up all day' with a dementing child. After Roy's death this mother obtained a job and was surprised how much this helped her. Of her youngest child, she remarked: 'I've not got the same patience as I had with the other two. I get so cross with him. It's not his fault, but it's no good; it's difficult to be bothered any more. I know where it will all end.'

Overwhelming and poignant tragedy. Each member of the family has only so much energy and many mechanisms come into play as to how it is used. Faced with similar problems another couple pulled together in spite of earlier marital stress. However this mother complained: 'My husband is very good. He's in every night but he won't feed the sick one for me. He says—"no, you do it". I have no break. Still I s'pose it's something he'll play with the well one; I haven't time to.' In yet another family three out of four children were in varying stages of dementia. Both parents became heavily involved with the first two who developed the disease. When these children were hospitalised they had little emotional energy left for the third child still at home in the early stages of the same illness. Their physically well boy of three was being driven into an early independence because his careworn parents did not feel he needed them. The child was confused and frightened by the comings and goings at home. One day he said to his parents: 'I don't like it here. I'm going to auntie's'. This he did.

Over a period of time the parents received considerable emotional and practical help from community sources. They came to believe their three-year-old was physically fit. They learnt anew how to enjoy their son who had been so emotionally traumatised by family events. In spite of all the sadness, there was some restoration of confidence in themselves as parents. Realignment of parental roles in such situations calls for great resourcefulness on their part.

The continual sense of loss gnaws away at the very fabric of family life. It is as though the 'doomed' family are in a chronic state of mourning. Facing the loss of his third child a father described his feelings:

'It's always the same. You've no peace. You're always getting over a loss. It's a sort of stalemate. It's bad enough to watch a child lose what he's learnt and gradually die. But it's not the end and you know you've to go through it all over again. There's nothing you can do to stop it.'

He spoke sensitively of the different stages of deterioration, as though each regression was in itself a little death—repeated many times in each afflicted child. Repeated too for the parents: 'My wife and I feel we lose bits of ourselves'.

The sometimes sudden cessation of the affected child's speech leaves the family bewildered: 'How many times have I told her to shut up—but I never meant it'. The silence seems intolerable. The bizarre behaviour unfathomable. What is going on in his brain? Perhaps he'll talk tomorrow. Does he still recognise us? Does he know what we say to him? It is difficult for medical advisers to have the answers. Individual parents will deal with these successive 'losses' in their own way. 'As far as I'm concerned my daughter died six months ago' was the comment of a father on being informed of the child's death. Emotionally he had begun to withdraw from her when she first became unresponsive though he continued to help in care. The child's mother said: 'I went on hoping she'd be able to respond to me in just some little way, but it was not to be'. Her preoccupation with her sick child was almost total.

The 'hanging-on and letting-go' process varies from one parent to the next. A wish that their children should have been taken early has been voiced by several facing repetitive loss. 'It'd be easier if they were taken as babies if they're not to grow up.' Others have spoken of the 'sheer waste' of the potential in their children and what they might have achieved had they lived to adult life. Where the marital adjustment has been precarious the family faced additional inner turmoil. The loss of self-image seems to be particularly marked if one or both parents see themselves as father/mother first and husband/wife second. In some cases reality pressures have tended to seal over the marital cracks whilst there are still children to be loved. In other instances the stresses act as a bridge between the couple who are drawn closer together. But sometimes there is a tendency for a child's plight to reinforce the negative aspects of personality already present in one or other parent. Faced with repetitive loss, such persons may well need skilled help if they are to survive emotionally.

One of the most stressful periods for the afflicted child must be in the initial stages of certain degenerative brain diseases. Adam was able to talk about 'being teased at school like Roy was'. When confronted with something familiar he had done before he would say: 'I did know once'. Another child faced with a change of school would say: 'Why am I at another school? I'm not mental am I mummy?' Perhaps the next bit of peculiar behaviour would bewilder his mother and confirm her fears that he 'wasn't normal'. It is very hard to know the capacity for insight and awareness that such a child may have, coexisting with much that seems to deny its existence. How do we know what such children suffer during this period of early dementia? It would seem that there is some blunting of their affective faculties but this can be a distressing phase for the child. Once further deterioration takes place, insight fades. Mercifully there is no physical pain. The suffering is in the family. It is as though its members exist in a chasm of sadness, glancing back to a happier past, fearful of the future and with a present that is almost unbearable.

Healthy children are deeply concerned over their sick siblings, whose gradual loss of intellectual capacity is at once bewildering and threatening. Many are well supported not only by their parents, but by members of the extended family, school teachers and friends. Yet inevitably they become 'Mummy's eyes' from time to time, watching the sick one's antics and seeing there's no danger. An adolescent, visiting a younger sick sibling on the ward blurted out to the doctor: 'You've no idea the demands she makes on my parents. They wait on her day and night.' After the sister's death, this same young person acknowledged: 'She wasn't really demanding, she never had been. It was her condition and she couldn't help that'. Another teenager, observing a brother's weird noises, commented: 'It's strange. He grins when there's nothing funny and he makes awful crying noises for nothing. It's kind of eerie. He can't help it I s'pose. You just get used to it.' A younger child of yet another family experienced minor psychosomatic symptoms. He had lost one sibling and was facing the experience a second time. His sister, in the latter stages of her illness, seemed unaware and unresponsive. Yet her little brother seemed to evoke some faint recognition. She appeared to smile with her eyes— a last window into the darkness. He said: 'I don't mind if you don't talk to me. It's lonely without you. I can talk to you.' He prattled on about his rabbit, his cars and his wish to have a party on his birthday. It is indeed sometimes difficult for parents to keep up with such events normally treasured in family life.

Another group of neurological diseases in which dementia is not a major manifestation is that of neuro-muscular disorders such as muscular dystrophy. If the problems for parents are as stressful and onerous, perhaps the situation is a little more clear cut for the siblings. The most obvious difference is that such afflicted children can still converse, communicate and be supported. They still retain an active role in the family however disruptive this may sometimes appear to be. The disability and the wheelchair may be used as mechanisms for bargaining but they serve to remind brothers and sisters that the physically handicapped member still has outlets of expression. Parents bear the pain of having to face awkward questions about the future as the disease progresses. 'Mummy what would you do if you found me unable to move in bed one morning?' A question suddenly put by a seven-year-old to an unsuspecting mother over breakfast. The mother was speechless. Later she said tearfully: 'My daughter is leaps ahead of me—I'm not ready for it'. She began to understand that because of her knowledge about the disease, her own anxiety for the future was perhaps greater than that of her daughter. Although questions should be answered truthfully, it is important not to assume the child is always asking fundamental questions. Some-times parents are so fearful of this that they take each query to be

69

'the one'. Other members of the family or helping persons may share the task of talking with such children but there can be no escaping it. There is a sense in which such children can and do support their parents and siblings. Their enforced physical inactivity allows for more thinking, and many young people are innovative in the adaptation of their remaining skills. The child's physical dependence on his parents and others is to some extent offset by a continuing intellectual contribution to life at home and in school. Sadly this cannot be so for children with dementia.

During the latter stages of a child's disease, parents may wish to talk with hospital staff about the question of resuscitation. Recognising that the quality of life is ebbing away, some parents explicitly state they do not wish their child to be resuscitated. Most share the medical viewpoint that vigorous treatment of intercurrent ills is fully justified whilst a child is still capable of giving and receiving love. It may be considered meddlesome if used to prolong the life of a child whose brain has virtually ceased to function.

After a child has died the doctors may ask for permission to undertake a post-mortem examination. Some parents themselves raise the issue because it is evident to them the doctors cannot answer all their questions. Certainly management of the family and genetic issues are the normal medical reasons for such a request. In addition there is an obvious need for further research into such diseases, for it is recognised the brain yields limited knowledge during life. It is only after death that further work can be continued which, hopefully, will help other children in the future. So many factors, however, may colour the response to what appears a bleak and distasteful request. Whether or not they feel able to agree to it, most parents understand the reasons behind such a request.

How do families bear the recapitulation of death in their children? Whilst experience of these conditions is fortunately limited, certain trends seem to emerge in a situation where meaningful relationships are broken one after another. Common to all families with older children who have brain disease is a sense of guilt and sometimes bitterness that their offspring were seen as 'behaviour problems' in the early stages of their condition. Understandably parents feel it questions their capacity, causing tensions within the home and at school. Perhaps it is only later they can accept that children displaying such problems would normally require special help—and it is rare indeed for such difficulties to be due to brain disease. Retrospectively, most parents are appreciative of the help received earlier. Parental investment in individual children is very high in our society. Whilst all of them are much loved it does seem that parents may grieve the loss of each differently. Hence in one family, where three children have died, the loss of the first remained the greatest sadness for the father. He had seen a developing intellect and envisaged the child's very special success in later life. To the mother, the loss of her second child was the greatest heartache. In life this child had epitomised laughter and high spirits. The mother commented sadly: 'With all our troubles we had laughter; now there's none. Nobody makes up for that.' Is it perhaps that, for varying reasons, one parent is closer to one child than another? Or is it that the parents in some hardly conscious way share the work of grieving, as they shared the caring during the children's lifetime? There is too a sense in which family members are unable to fully work through the grieving process for each child. Whilst mourning the loss of the first child they become involved with the death of a second. It is a coping with the practicalities of death all over again, and then adding new hurts to old. Hence grief work is incomplete for each child, with resulting unresolved feelings for parents and surviving siblings. It is difficult for parents to recall what thought belongs to which child as memories blur and merge into one long period of mourning. Described by a father thus: 'It's like going through a cycle each time, only you don't finish it'. The dependency of such sick children on adult care leaves a large void. Hence for one mother: 'For five years I've been the brain first for one and then the other. Now they're both gone and I'm lost.'

Within the families there appears to be a thinning out of inter-personal relationships. There has been a reluctance for surviving siblings to take on any part of the dead child's role. This may even have meant disposing of much-loved pets. For the adolescent sibling sorrow has been kept away from all but the most intimate friends. 'Taking the mickey' and 'roughing you up if you cry' are under-standable reasons for keeping silent about what has gone on at home. The teenager too has many questions about the 'why' of the illness and seeks reassurance that his own body is working well. Yet another adolescent expressed disappointment that his brother never grew up to share his interests. The only survivor of three children, he commented: 'I suppose you think I'm the lucky one. I suppose I am in a way but I feel unlucky …. It's a strange feeling and partly frightening.' The younger siblings too need considerable help in being able to play out their feelings and anxieties within the home situation. Their brash way of doing so may sometimes cause anguish to their already distressed parents. Words like 'silly', 'stupid', 'mad', 'mental' and 'crazy' ripple off their tongues as grim reminders of earlier teasing when their siblings were ill. Is it also that perhaps

71

they fear for their own sanity? Understandably they tend to become more clinging to their parents and decline activities that take them out of home. Some siblings may require specialist help in coping with the long-term effects of repeated loss.

Parental ambitions are considerably reduced as a result of so much trauma. As each child dies the expectations for the surviving children are diminished further. 'So long as she remains well I don't mind about her reading and writing just so long as she can get by.' In one or two instances there has been a lessening of ambition in the parents. To quote a father: 'My priorities are different now — getting on at work doesn't matter any more'.

Whilst families experiencing multiple grief situations are mercifully few, they may well wish to draw on a network of services to assist them. First, they require ready access to doctors who understand the overall management of their sick children and can anticipate potential crisis points in the deteriorating course of the disease. They also need to feel that medical advisers have themselves come to terms with their own sense of failure to cure these children. As with any sick person, there must be open channels of communication between hospital, family doctor and the local health authority.

Second, such families appreciate consistent and continuing support. Whereas some may seek this through their church and/or family members, others may have regular contact with a social worker. There are separations aplenty for them within the family and it is most important to them not to have to keep on making new relationships with caring people. A few may wish to be linked with groups such as that for Muscular Dystrophy or the Society for Compassionate Friends. Additionally, psychiatric, casework and groupwork skills are all potentially valuable in helping such families.

Third, in addition, families may need access to local resources of every kind. These may include: home nursing; rehousing; rest-breaks; pre-school play groups; home helps; baby sitters; night attendants; special adaptations in the home; installation of telephones and financial grants. One mother commented: 'Somebody from the welfare services said I could have what I liked — but I don't know what there is and I don't know what to ask for!' Social workers have always been diffident in putting over their role to other colleagues and those needing their help. The 'welfare lady' was apparently seen by this mother as a source of practical help. She had not understood that additionally this person or one of her colleagues could also give of herself in a caring casework relationship. 'Just being' through so much heartache can be of great value to many parents.

Fourth, families recognise their own plight is overwhelming but express concern that they in turn overwhelm everyone else, so that society feels impotent to help them. A mother voiced the comments of others: 'People don't know how to handle you. They can't believe you survive. They don't know what to say. They stare—like I'm a sort of leper.' Words that aptly put into focus the evasive, clumsy and fumbling way in which society reacts to death. Amongst the families themselves there seems a greater sympathy for others and a willingness to reach out to those who are also in trouble. Asked how she felt she coped with so much sadness a mother thoughtfully replied: 'Because I know I'm not the only one whose been through this with their children. It helps to know there are others who have sat by their beds trying to understand their wants.' Did she perhaps feel a part of corporate suffering? A father, who had lost two children remarked: 'I manage now because of what I've already been through and because I know we've done our best for the children .... But sometimes I wish people would understand a bit better—it makes the slog that much harder.' It is as though through bereavement their status in society changes and they feel socially isolated.

It is indeed true for some parents that through great suffering their lives have attained a larger perspective. They have lost children who represented the continuity of life and the fulfilment of their hopes. They have experienced the sense of utter hopelessness and the unbearable separation from loved children. Yet in a very real way they and their families are gathering up the fragments that remain, and, even as this is written, are moving forward, falteringly ....

Reference

CARTER, C. O., FRASER ROBERTS, J. A., EVANS, I. A. and BUCH, A. R. (1971), 'Genetic clinic—a follow up study', *Lancet*, pp. 281-5.

6

The family coping with a heavy treatment régime

Lindy Burton

> Diagnosis is the hopeful search for a way out: but the setting
> forth on the way which one discovers and the unflinching
> persistence in making the effort—that is the treatment, that is
> the self directed, self administered charge.
>
> *Menninger* [21]

For many parents the possibility of giving treatment for their child's
illness comes as the first shaft of hope in the gloom of despair following diagnosis. Treatment is seen as a means of potentiating the
child's existence and undertaken as a challenge. As such it brings
immediate strength and encouragement to continue, diminishes
feelings of guilt and lowered self-esteem[1,9]—fostered by the
diagnosis—and makes it easier for parents to accept the help and
advice of medical personnel. Many clinicians[8,12,15,17,23] have noted
the way in which active participation, even in the hospital treatment
and care of their children, helps mothers to adapt to the illness.
Feelings of shame and isolation are reduced, the mother is brought
into contact with other mothers and given something essential to do.
Because of this, her sense of protecting and nurturing her child is
accentuated rather than diminished. She does not feel she has
abandoned him to another's ministrations, and she involves herself
in treatment with obvious satisfaction.

Involvement in treatment, necessitating, as it does, activity on the
parents' part, can also be of use in helping parents to forget some of
their otherwise overwhelming anxiety. Obviously, as with any other
excessive activity, it may tax their overall strength, producing a loss
of personal energy[29] and enthusiasm, and a consequent diminution
in leisure time activities. However, as Henley and Albam[15] have
noted when describing mothers of children with muscular dystrophy,
the gratification afforded by the opportunity to directly care for the
sick child may more than compensate for the strain imposed.

Most usually it is the mother who shoulders the burden of treatment. In some instances this may occasion feelings of guilt on the father's part,[15] or even feelings of rejection.[18] Either emotion, if it is excessive, may prejudice the mother's own ability to cope, and several clinicians[4,22] have noted the negative implications of marital disharmony for treatment. Essentially the mother should feel that just as she cares for and gives strength to the child, so her husband cares for her. When such security exists—no matter how inequably treatment procedures are divided—the couple may experience a growing closeness, and subsequently state that the marriage was actually strengthened by the experience of nursing the child. Recently, I found that over half the families in Northern Ireland coping with cystic fibrosis expressed the feeling that their marriage had been strengthened and was better because of their shared task of caring for the sick child. As one mother of a three-year-old boy explained: 'It's bound to draw you together. My husband never says a lot, but you can tell. When out little boy is poorly, my husband goes quiet, and we talk about it, and it helps. I feel I understand now how he feels, and we feel the same.'

Perhaps nothing reflects family stability and integration so much as the way in which the challenge of treatment is met. Bruch and Hewlitt,[5] working with diabetic children, found that poor regulation was frequently associated with emotional disturbance in the family. Erratic or persistently poor management was associated with a maternal attitude of self-pity, or a dislike or rejection of the child. Diabetes was then viewed as one of the child's 'undesirable and annoying traits'. Equally damaging was an attitude of repressive, perfectionistic overcontrol in which the family was able to follow a restricted regime to the letter. The most desirable attitude, and one found in half of the twenty-one families they studied, was one of tolerant, relaxed acceptance of the task.

It is certainly true that in some cases, despite full intellectual understanding of the necessity for treatment, and verbal acceptance of the task, parents quite knowingly do not comply with the advised regimen, and the guilt that arises may produce a general resentment towards the clinicians involved and even greater difficulty in following through on treatment. As one young professional father, who found it 'impossible' to give morning physiotherapy to his cystic child, said,

'We feel very guilty that we don't get up earlier and give it to her, but I believe that we do what we can. We're not neglecting her. What we're told to do is the ideal—absolute perfection—and we fall short of it and we feel guilty.'

In some instances this failure to comply with treatment requirements reaches pathological proportions, the parents shying away
from the challenge of the task. Perhaps it is the seemingly unpleasant nature of many treatment procedures which produces this
aversive reaction. Insecure parents may be unwilling to accept
responsibility for apparently accentuating the child's pain, either
because they cannot bear to see the child suffer, or because they
cannot tolerate any expression of hostility[19] which such suffering
might produce against themselves. In such instances parents argue
that as the condition is presently incurable and the treatment purely
palliative, they are not morally justified in subjecting the child to so
much discomfort for such minimal gain. (Some paediatricians are
themselves anxious about this point:[27] see also chapter 1, p. 13). In a
few instances parents may refuse even hospital treatment.[20] More
usually, where treatment is begun, they will absent themselves from
the hospital ward, not visiting for weeks on end, or they will fail to
bring the child to the clinic for necessary procedures. Their attitude
to medical personnel may be hostile, and their remarks, aimed to
give the child the feeling that they side with him against his
'tormentors', may arouse negativism in the child.

Problems occasioned by treatment may arise for parents in other
ways, perhaps the most crucial being that, where the parents feel
themselves to be wholly responsible for the child's treatment, any
slight exacerbations in the disease may produce a 'disproportionate
amount of guilt and frustration'[24] on their part. By contrast to
parents of children who are receiving treatment from medical
personnel, and who may be able to displace frustration occasioned
by the child's ill health on to staff, parents who are themselves
administering treatment have no one else to blame for flareups.
They are therefore doubly frustrated—by the exacerbation in the
child's condition, and by their own inability to control it. One such
mother, of a six-year-old cystic girl, told me: 'If she's unwell and has a
cold, I feel it's my fault, and sit down and think—where was she? It's
my fault. What did I let her do?'

Where parents feel over-responsible for their child's physical well-
being, attention may tend to rivet on treatment to the detriment of
the child's wider social and emotional needs, a factor noted by
Schoelly and Fraser[25] when studying families coping with muscular
dystrophy. In such instances parents fail to appreciate that quantity
of life is insufficient without quality, and that treatment—albeit
meticulously given—is only a means to an end and not the end itself.
Whilst physical care is essential for any child, most especially the
child with the potentially fatal disease, emotional warmth, com-

panionship, intellectual stimulation, and joyful experiences are equally crucial. Not only may overemphasis on treatment obscure the need for such a full existence, but also it may diminish opportunities for this by fostering overprotectiveness on the part of the parent. Thus, instead of encouraging the child to experiment and participate in all manner of activities, parents may fearfully restrain him, lest somehow he mysteriously injure himself. Over-protection may lead inexorably to overindulgence,[14] producing erratic disciplinary limits. As a result, the confused child may become disobedient, irritable and argumentative.

Some parents experience difficulties in explaining the need for treatment to their child. Either they are reticent about explaining too much, for fear of frightening the child, or their own basic knowledge of physiology and anatomy is so limited that they have to fall back on weak generalisations, for example, 'It's to make your tummy better', or 'It will make you feel a lot less tired'. Whilst explanations of this kind may be sufficient for some children, others find them lacking, especially when faced with continuing symptoms. Equally, they may mislead some children into believing that at some point, when they have received sufficient therapy, they will be completely cured. Invariably, failure to thrive then produces bitter disappointment and recriminations against parents who 'promised' he would get better.

Questions raised by family friends or even strangers can be a further source of embarrassment to parents. Coming unexpectedly, they can catch the parents off-guard and make them feel ashamed and guilty. For example, some mothers of cystic children comment on their shame in public places when the child begins to cough and they have to slap his back, or when at meal times they have to sprinkle replacement enzymes on his food. One mother of a two-year-old girl said:

'It's when she coughs—when she wants a thing and goes into a fit and cries and coughs, and people come and say, "that's a bad cough", or say, "she's not bothering with that child". I can't have that. People say "You'll have to watch it"—they make me feel uncomfortable.'

Where parents feel shame this sentiment will quickly convey itself to the child and to his siblings.[1] In the end the family may prefer to isolate themselves, and normal social outings may be halted.

Perhaps the most tragic problem concerning treatment is the problem of finally withholding it. Because, for many, it becomes a symbol of hope, its withdrawal, at the last, can be resisted vehemently. One mother of an eight-year-old girl dying of a brain tumour could not accept the gradual withdrawal of treatment and the inevitable slipping away of her daughter's will to live. Despite the protests of her own mother, and the feeble entreaties of the child, who only wanted to be left alone, she insisted on getting a psychiatrist to see the child and treat her for depression. 'She's lost the will to live, to help herself', she told me, 'and they don't want to bother. They say it's part of her present disease—but her will to live is her only hope and I won't let her give it up.'

In certain instances, paediatricians find themselves pressurised by parents to continue treatment even though they themselves feel the child has reached a point where he should be allowed to die in peace.[30] There can be few hospital wards which have not, at some time, had a drip, or a heart machine going solely for the sake of the parents.

What of the children, how does treatment affect them? As yet we do not fully know, and further research is clearly indicated. Clinical assessments[5,7,15,24] would suggest that overdependence on the mother, and babyishness are increased, either of which may represent a threat to the child and also a temptation. If the child yields to this temptation to regress, no longer struggling for independence, but allowing himself to develop a 'putty like submissiveness'[5] he may become guilty and discouraged. Treatment may then be viewed as a symbol of this dependence, and during those periods when he is temporarily stronger, or more anxious, he may resist it. Bruch and Hewlitt[5] talk of the 'passing sabotage behaviour' of diabetic children, who use refusal of treatment to curb disliked parental behaviour.

Alternatively the child may equate illness with treatment, and if he is driven to deny the reality of his condition, he may refuse treatment, arguing to himself that, as he is well, he no longer needs it. Chodoff[7] cites instances in which children with muscular dystrophy repudiate their wheelchairs, and Lawler and his colleagues[18] noted the rejection of treatment by cystic children who were denying the severity of their condition. One particularly disturbed nine-year-old cystic girl I met had refused all medicaments and physiotherapy for two years, would shake her head vigorously or rush from the room whenever illness was mentioned, refused to undress before the paediatrician, and exhibited symptoms of acute anxiety such as nightmares, sleeplessness and preoccupation with fear of failure at school work. But denial of illness state does not always encompass refusal of treatment. Sometimes the child expresses denial directly through an accentuation of normal energetic competitiveness.[7] Such children become compulsively involved in competing with their more fortunate non-handicapped siblings.

Perhaps the most desirable response, from the child's standpoint, is one which occasionally allows him to regress and become dependent, regaining strength and comfort, and then, when he is renewed, permits him to actively attack the environmental and personal problems which beset him. Too extreme a reliance on either regression or compulsive competition is disadvantageous.

From the child's viewpoint, treatment procedures frequently have a punitive colouring,[3] for example, those requiring bedrest or immobilisation, the swallowing of unpleasant substances or the limitation of food intake. It is not surprising therefore that some children develop consequent 'fantasies of being unloved, different, singled out'.[11] The depth and degree of such fantasies bears no objective relationship to the severity of the treatment regime, some children being inherently more reactive to even minimal stress.[6] Such fantasies are accentuated by the lack of privacy[10] and loss of independence occasioned by the illness. Understandably real feelings of hostility may develop as a result, both directed towards the treatment, and at those who are administering it. In children whose movements are restricted, the problem may be further compounded by their inability to release and rid themselves of these hostile feelings through normal movement. Several clinicians[25,26] have noted a 'need to be violent' in dystrophic children, with negativism and verbal aggression replacing direct physical attacks.

Such aggression may be unacceptable to the adults who care for the child, and it may also frighten the child, for, as Chodoff[7] has emphasised 'to be angry at those who are taking care of us is to deprive ourselves of support which may be vital for the very necessities of life'. The angry child is placed in a dilemma. If he attempts to redress supposed wrongs he may deprive himself of vital support, but if he chokes back his anger and submits, he loses his self-esteem. Some children attempt to solve this problem by developing a marked concern for their own bodies. They love themselves in lieu of others, and are thus less dependent on external goodwill. Where such hypochondriasis is temporary,[3] it may be useful, enabling the child to accept the regime without excessive upset. But where it is long-lasting—as in the dystrophic children studied by Sherwin and McCully,[26] or the cardiac children observed by Bergmann[2]—it may be disadvantageous to the child, limiting his ability to adaptively struggle towards maximum physical, intellectual, and social functioning. Such children become self-absorbed, anxiously scrutinising their own diets, rigorously guarding themselves against draughts and damp. Any normal, youthful exuberance is lost in the process.

Hypochondriasis would seem to be most prevalent in those children whose disease processes have no marked external symptoms or outward trappings, only a 'mysterious internal ailment difficult to verify'.[2] External symptoms such as cough, mucous, or tummy pains give the child some objective yardstick by which to assess his progress. Where there is nothing but a mysterious debilitating, and possibly deteriorating, condition the child's self-absorption may be increased. In such instances treatment may be of actual value to the child in giving him some outward trapping to which he can attach his fears. In essence therefore the child substitutes fear of treatment for fear of disease process. Thus regular treatment, accompanied by regular protest, gives him some controlled way of expressing his apprehensions. In addition, because he appears to be protesting against something tangible, with which the adults can empathise, it is more likely that he will receive reassurance and support. By contrast, were he able and willing to verbalise his more pervasive illness fears, he might meet with evasion or speedy withdrawal.

In some children the constant need for treatment produces feelings of unworthiness, the child feeling lessened or subtly diminished by the illness and its therapeutic trappings. In order to compensate for this supposed inadequacy and also because of his sustained contact with adults, the sick child may develop a repertoire of behaviours designed to please well—especially adult—people.[7] (Oswin comments on the usefulness of such behaviour in chapter 8, p. 112). He may become excessively polite. He may try to dress more neatly, or he may become more highly verbal.[28] In certain instances the child may try to change his entire personality in order to become more socially acceptable. For example, one lively seven-year-old cystic girl told me that if she could be someone else she would be 'an understandable person, who could be nice to people so that they wouldn't say to her "You cheeky brat". A person who could talk to them, without them saying, "I don't really like you".' She confessed subsequently to great feelings of loneliness and observed that no other children really wanted her. In this she was not unusual. Many sick children express such feelings of isolation, though they are apparently well integrated into home and school communities. Not surprisingly such feelings are accentuated when the child has to sustain treatment procedures demanding physical isolation. Jabaley and his colleagues[16] noted strange bodily feelings, perceptual disturbances and an acute loss of identity in children who were physically isolated for the treament of burns, and I have observed similar distortions in bodily image in children who were given barrier nursing for leukaemia (see chapter 2, p. 29).

It is often thought by casual observers that children who are maintained on a heavy treatment regime for a long time must somehow adapt to it, so that, in the end, it becomes a matter of course. This may be true for children whose treatment is commenced in infancy. They have known no alternative, and the frustrations produced by the situation relate solely to the impositions of the procedures themselves. For older children such happy adaptation is much less likely. They have known days of freedom, days without diets, medicines, exercises or restrictions, and they resent not only the frustrations of their illness, but also the loss of this freedom. Sometimes they bear their lot without protest, to please medical staff or parents, sometimes they bear it because they are too cowed to rebel, but rarely do they accept it willingly. When any additional stress is placed upon them, especially if this is not connected with the medical régime, they react with severe temper tantrums and despair.[2] Changes in school, family moves, discord between parents, illness or death of relatives or friends, are all reacted to with what superficially appears to be excessive emotion.[13] A visit to the dentist may assume ghastly proportions, and even changes in simple domestic and school routines may be resented. For example, the mother of a seven-year-old cystic boy told me;

> 'This past week (the end of term) the teacher hasn't been doing much work and he got quite annoyed and said he didn't like school. He's not really one for running about. He gets annoyed too if the teacher hasn't time to do his reading. I notice you have to keep your promise with him—everything has to be exact.'

The small boy in question seemed to have an exaggerated fear of new clothes. He had insisted on wearing the same jersey since he was two, and consequently it was up around his armpits. He had worn two sets of trousers alternatively for the previous four years, insisting that his mother darn and redarn the knees, and refusing to wear anything else—to her great embarrassment when they went out socially! In addition, Bergmann[2] has noted how in some instances fear of hospital may accentuate, rather than diminish, with experience, for on each readmission 'fears and anxieties belonging to former occasions are revived'.

Freedom to cry and express dislike of procedures—and the acceptance that such feelings are justifiable—would seem essential for good emotional adjustment to therapy. So also is the younger child's tendency to play out the therapeutic saga, taking the active role as nurse, doctor, or mother, and administering treatment to some passive self-substitute, such as teddy, the dog, or Daddy. Many pre-school children adopt this method of coping, becoming enthusiastic torturers or aggressive martinets in their turn.

Even very young children benefit from simple straightforward explanations concerning symptoms, and the way in which treatment ameliorates them. For example, young cystic children, who found difficulty in accepting postural drainage and physiotherapy, derived satisfaction from seeing upturned jars of honey and water, demonstrating the difference between the sticky mucous found in their lungs and the more runny variety found in the lungs of other children. This simple demonstration helped them to understand why their parents had to clap and tilt them to get the mucous up.

It is equally important for the child to be certain that whoever is giving the treatment has his best interests at heart. Whilst it is wrong to foster unrealistic, excessive hopes of cure, it is essential for the child to know that the adult is giving treatment to potentiate his health and ease his suffering. One mother of a seven-year-old cystic girl who had been persistently questioning the reason for, and protesting against, treatment, put this point to the child. Observing that her daughter was devoted to her dolls, and had expressed every intention of becoming a mother when she herself grew up, she finally said to her:

'If you have a little girl when you grow up, and that little girl isn't well and the doctor says she must have exercises and medicine or she'll get very sick, will you say to yourself, "Poor wee thing, I won't bother. I'll just leave her peacefully" or will you say, "Oh, goodness me. I must do my best to keep her well, so she can grow up to be a Mummy herself"?'

The little girl sat and thought, eventually replying:

'I'll give her the medicines and help her grow up.'

'Well, that's what I'm doing for you', said the mother, and marvellously the protests vanished.

Hospital personnel should be equally prepared to explain the reasons for their procedures, and be available to reassure the child that such procedures are in his best interest. In many respects this task should be easier for them, because professional objectivity should diminish the tension and overconcern frequently experienced by parents, themselves undertaking therapy.

Where the child is properly informed and supported in this way, his illness and treatment may afford him an opportunity to grow emotionally, through learning to master his anxiety and environmental threats.[3] In addition, the intimacy of his contacts with those who are administering the treatment may afford him a chance to develop richer and more meaningful relationships than might otherwise be possible. More than ever, he may be certain that he is loved for what he is, be it weak, tired, or protesting against the 'unfairness of it all'. As a consequence feelings of closeness[16] may develop between the sick child and his parents, so that not only is the child enriched, but the parents also obtain comfort from the relationship. I have found, despite all the difficulties imposed, that it is not unusual for a family to prefer their sick child to his well siblings, and to feel that they personally have learnt much about life through their experiences with him.

References

1 BAUM, M. H. (1962), 'Some dynamic factors affecting family adjustment to the handicapped child', *Exceptional Children*, April, pp. 387-92.
2 BERGMANN, T. (in collaboration with FREUD, A.) (1965), *Children in Hospital*, International Universities Press, New York.
3 BLOM, G. E. (1958), 'The reactions of hospitalized children to illness', *Pediatrics*, vol. 22, p. 590.
4 BOZEMANN, M. F., ORBACH, C. E. and SUTHERLAND, A. M. (1955), 'The adaptation of mothers to the threatened loss of their children through leukemia', *Cancer*, vol. 8, pp. 1-19.
5 BRUCH, H. and HEWLITT, I. (1947), 'Psychologic aspects of the medical management of diabetes in children', *Psychosomatic Medicine*, vol. 9, pp. 205-9.
6 BURTON, L. (1968), *Vulnerable Children*, Routledge & Kegan Paul, London.
7 CHODOFF, P. (1959), 'Adjustment to disability. Some observations on patients with M.S.', *Journal of Chronic Diseases*, June, p. 653.
8 CHODOFF, P., STANFORD, B., FRIEDMAN, B. and HAMBURG, D. A. (1964), 'Stress, defences, and coping behaviour: observations in parents of children with malignant diseases', *American Journal of Psychiatry*, vol. 120, pp. 743-9.
9 CUMMINGS, S. T., BAYLEY, H. C. and RIE, H. E. (1966), 'Effects of the child's deficiency on the mother. A study of mothers of mentally retarded, chronically ill and neurotic children', *American Journal of Orthopsychiatry*, vol. 36, pp. 595-608.
10 DEBUSKEY, M. (1970), 'Orchestration of care', in Debuskey, M. (ed.), *The Chronically Ill Child and his Family*, Charles Thomas, Illinois.
11 FREUD, A. (1952), 'The role of bodily illness in the mental life of children', *Psychoanalytic Studies of Children*, vol. 7, p. 69.
12 FRIEDMAN, S. B., CHODOFF, P., MASON, J. W. and HAMBURG, D. A. (1963), 'Behavioural observations on parents anticipating the death of a child', *Pediatrics*, October, pp. 610-25.

13 GREEN, M. (1967), 'Care of the child with a long-term life-threatening illness', *Pediatrics*, vol. 39, pp. 441-5.

14 GREEN, M. and SOLNIT, A. J. (1964), 'Reactions to the threatened loss of a child: a vulnerable child syndrome', *Pediatrics*, July, pp. 58-66.

15 HENLEY, T. F. and ALBAM, B. (1955), 'A psychiatric study of muscular dystrophy. The role of the social worker', *American Journal of Physical Medicine*, vol. 34, pp. 258-64.

16 JABALEY, M. E., HOOPES, J. E., KNORR, N. J. and MYER, E. (1970), 'The burned child' in Debuskey, M. (ed.) *The Chronically Ill Child and his Family*, Charles Thomas, Illinois.

17 KNUDSON, A. G., JNR and NATTERSON, J. M. (1960), 'Participation of parents in the hospital care of fatally ill children', *Pediatrics*, vol. 26, p. 482.

18 LAWLER, R. H., NAKIELNY, W. and WRIGHT, N. (1966), 'Psychological implications of cystic fibrosis', *Canadian Medical Association Journal*, vol. 94, pp. 1043-6.

19 LEWIS, M. (1962), 'The management of parents of acutely ill children in the hospital', *American Journal of Orthopsychiatry*, vol. 32, pp. 60-6.

20 LOURIE, R. S. (1961), 'What to tell the parents of a child with cancer', *Clinical Proceedings of the Children's Hospital, Washington D.C.*, vol. 17, p. 91.

21 MENNINGER, K. (1959), 'Hope', *American Journal of Psychiatry*, vol. 116, p. 481.

22 MURSTEIN, B. I. (1960), 'The effect of long-term illness of children on the emotional adjustment of parents', *Child Development*, vol. 31, pp. 157-71.

23 RICHMOND, J. B. and WAISMAN, H. A. (1955), 'Psychological aspects of management of children with malignant diseases', *American Journal of Diseases of Children*, vol. 89, p. 42.

24 ROSENSTEIN, B. J. (1970), 'Cystic fibrosis of the pancreas: impact on family functioning', in Debuskey, M. (ed.), *The Chronically Ill Child and his Family*, Charles Thomas, Illinois.

25 SCHOELLY, M. L. and FRASER, A. (1955), 'Emotional reactions in muscular dystrophy', *American Journal of Physical Medicine*, vol. 34, pp. 119-23.

26 SHERWIN, A. C. and MCCULLY, R. S. (1961), 'Reactions observed in boys of various ages to a crippling, progressive and fatal illness (muscular dystrophy)', *Journal of Chronic Diseases*, January, pp. 59-68.

27 SIGLER, A. Y. (1970), 'The leukemic child and his family: an emotional challenge', in Debuskey, M. (ed.), *The Chronically Ill Child and his Family*, Charles Thomas, Illinois.

28 SPOCK, A. and STEDMAN, D. J. (1966), 'Psychologic characteristics of children with cystic fibrosis', *North Carolina Medical Journal*, September, pp. 426-8.

29 TURK, J. (1964), 'Impact of cystic fibrosis on family functioning', *Pediatrics*, vol. 34, pp. 67-71.

30 YUDKIN, S. (1967), 'Children and death', *Lancet*, vol. 7, p. 37.

Part III   Helping the child

7

'The care of our dying child'— a
          parent offers some personal
        observations based on recollection

Yvonne Craig

> The child who can live through the process of dying in the care
> and understanding of a dedicated and mature team and a
> loving family will come to appreciate the fullest meaning of
> life itself.
>
> *Easson*

Background

On Christmas Eve, 1964, our youngest daughter, Claire, aged two-
and-a-half, collapsed, and we were told that she had acute leukaemia
and faced death. We rushed her to the nearest hospital, a grim
Victorian workhouse, whose vast children's ward had crumbling
ceilings, no cubicles or curtaining, its few screens sheltering large
families with sick children from the neighbouring slum. Yet this alien
anchorage protected Claire from distress, calmed our fears and
sheltered our experiences in caring for her.

In sharing these remembrances we hope to help others to understand some of the problems of terminal care. We do not presume
that our experiences apply to other hospital systems or family
relationships, for each sick child is a uniquely developing person
having acutely varied needs and unpredictable responses to changing
regimens.

Claire, affirmative, and fun-loving, enjoyed the warm security of a
long, happy marriage, plus well-integrated hospital and home care.
Unfortunately, many children suffer incomparably in struggling
against isolation, occasioned by family incapacities, excessive pain
or overwhelming hospitalisation. For example, five-year-old Trudie
had an illiterate mother who blamed her husband for the disease,
because it developed in their damp flat. His guilt and anxiety made
him desert, eventually fathering another woman's baby. Whilst this

87

reassured his threatened mortality, it deeply shocked Trudie. He never visited and she constantly cried for him. Nine-year-old Adrian, weakened by many painful procedures carried out in private European clinics, died cruelly from drug overdosing, away from home, though visited by wealthy parents. Eleven-year-old Jane became grief-stricken when two friends died in a terminal ward. She died prematurely through respiratory paroxysms, her terror reinforced by anxious parents travelling many miles, doctors attempting resuscitation, nurses constantly observing.

All dying children are stretched on racks of physical and emotional endurance, yet they can surpass their potential, fulfilling shortened, brave lives, whose significance transforms experience and ennobles memory for parents who loved them, as we loved Claire. Her life and death became meaningful and regenerative through the loving care of family, friends and local communities, plus the devoted treatment of hospital staff, whose insights and skills kept her happy and free from fear. We specially remember with gratitude a junior doctor, who, watching a visiting haematologist fail to establish transfusion during a terminal crisis, gently kissed Claire's collapsing vein, successfully connecting the relaxing arm.

Enriched by our debt to sensitive paediatricians and abundant samaritans, we gratefully, though inadequately, offer these recollections.

The crisis

A child closes as a sea
anenome
In mysterious seas of
suffering . . .

No hopes no fears
Can touch these sleeping
eyes and ears . . .

From poems by bereaved parents

Claire, normally noisy and naughty, never before hospitalised, lay silent in her cot. Carolling began, nurses gathering around with white-winged caps and lighted candles. 'Are they angels?' Claire whispered. We said that they were nurses who would love and care for her. Years later, I read an article by Dr Cecily Saunders called 'Watch with me' (1965) exactly describing this service of vigil. We sang through our bitter grief, 'Unto us a child is born', plunged into an unknown abyss of anguish.

Doctors arrived, un-uniformed, grouping behind the Christmas tree, the only private and pleasant space. One gave its fairy to Claire, who smiled. Another gently took us aside, speaking simply and slowly, scanning our anxious faces for barriers of shock and fear, denial or antagonism (Kubler-Ross, 1970). Perhaps my professional training—as a social worker—invited honesty, making it easier for me to accept the diagnosis, but my eyes were tear-blinded and senses numbed like those of other parents confronted with catastrophe. Despite their carefully measured answers to our immediate, and subsequently increasing questions, it was difficult to be objective as reassurances primed us 'to bear the unbearable'.[1]

The chaplain entered, calmly practical: could he contact relatives, help in any way, bless Claire? He stroked the fairy's hair, then lightly touched Claire's head. 'Jesus is looking after you', he assured her, winking secretly: 'See you later!' Those three confident words turned flooding fears into surging hopes, as Claire relaxed the cold little hand clutching mine. Her Daddy's goodnight kiss immediately prompted 'Mummy will stay with me', a confidence unshared by children facing sickness and death, separated from their mothers (Bowlby *et al.*, 1956).

A young male nurse asked Claire if she'd like me to sleep in the next large bed, kept for very fat children! Contented, she lost consciousness.

Watching, waiting, I clung to my husband, seeking his strength, he my comfort. Mercifully, my good mother lived with us, and would keep up traditional festivities with our other children, despite their sorrow.

The consultant appeared unobtrusively, greeting staff, and welcoming us with friendly, Jewish gestures of sympathy. His handshake symbolised our feeling that he shared our parental concern for Claire, and that we would share in his medical care of her. He promised every attention, inspiring the trust which all parents of critically ill children need, though he offered only care, not cure (Jones, 1971). He inspected Claire's transfusion closely, consulting with staff.

We experienced those memorable moments in the shadow of death which can petrify parents, or generate 'the internal energy which strengthens and extends' (Erikson, 1965). Unfortunately, not all parents experience such energy. For example, ten-year-old Paul had respiratory disease, and was suddenly deteriorating. He was attached to a heart machine, and was terrified. His inarticulate mother, forced outside, became immobilised, subsequently suicidal. Her popular school-captain son died alone. By contrast, eleven-year-old Elizabeth had tumours distorting her sight and face. Her crisis lasted twenty-four hours, and her father, an academic writer, was constantly by her. He described the waiting as a gradual transfiguration by which the child passed from her disfigured childhood into radiant maturity. His words comforted many parents.

Transfixed by our own comatose child, I remembered Biblical stories of parents pleading for their children's lives, seeing them restored. I prayed and pleaded too, like any mother, whether begging miracles from paediatricians invested with magic (Thomas, 1971), sacrificing herself to expiate the punishing power of disease (Mackenzie, 1969), or bargaining with specialists for latest cures.

Our tragedy magnified awareness of other children's sufferings. We watched as a nearby Cypriot wearily scanned her sicklecell anaemia scars, and haunting thoughts of the innocents of Vietnam, whose preventable deaths were unsolaced and untended, increased our sense of guilt, impotence and inadequacy. Yet anxiety released energies, and mobilised our resources to protect our threatened child (Wolff, 1969). The situation was as metamorphic for us as for Claire, who seemed cherubic.

Suddenly the consultant smiled: Claire was transfusing well and should recover, her natural vitality sustaining treatment. Christmas would be made happy for her, the staff giving us freedom to use the ward as home. This explained curry smells from the nurses' kitchen, where a Hindu mother cooked for her child. Dazed with delight, I hugged my husband, relief only exploding in laughter next day when a big, black, nephrotic boy informed Claire that she would look like him, having had the same pills!

Sensing our close family relationships, the consultant offered to share all developments with us, whether favourable or critical, so we were able to help Claire 'cope as best she could with each stage' (Glaser and Strauss, 1965). Later, I gratefully recalled the imaginative sensitivity of his communications, not expressions of information but of relationship, as Buber (1961) says. For example, Claire's first examination was preceded by doll-cuddling; later, he always kissed her; his final prolonged hug warned me her borrowed time was ending.

However, her remarkable initial reprieve indicated healthy resistance. The length and quality of her life depended on controllable factors, one he encouragingly attributed to our ability to give Claire a happily purposeful existence; another was his family-orientated ward. Although it unfortunately had no facilities for advanced chemotherapy, or appropriate accommodation, willing parents were offered partnership in the ward team.

The staff believed that 'Mother is the chief instrument of child care'[2] providing she is not 'captive' (Meadows, 1964), spreading anxiety, nor depriving home, husband, and other children. (Later we discussed difficulties parents face in freeing themselves from stresses (Bennett, 1972) so they can care for their child without panic, over-protection, spoiling or withdrawal.) The nurses valued mothers' assistance and personal knowledge (Stacey, *et al.*, 1970), and those who tolerated ward diet, early bed hours, lack of privacy, and helped other children, were pronounced heaven-sent by the Jamaican ward sister.

It was that crowded, ugly ward which seemed like heaven as Claire's Christmas crisis ended. Nurses pinned mistletoe onto caps. Doctors wore funny hats—why don't they clown more often? The chaplain came with messages from churches praying for Claire, saying her recovery was a miracle, blessed by God, typical of his hospital's marvellous care.

Silently, I thanked God, the hospital, our family, friends, all those caring for Claire.

She woke: 'I want some Christmas pudding!' she chirped, her appetite, her life, regained.

In hospital

This ward is my little home   Solitude is a torment
      West Indian girl, 11   Isolation is a fear
                                         Donne

Claire enjoyed her ward Christmas, surrounded by family friends. Her brother and sister toured labs, had reassuringly positive blood-tests, and immediately regarded the hospital as a friendly place of healing. Thereafter, they visited Claire freely with her friends, so she retained home identities, unpreoccupied with her illness or other patients.

This open ward community minimised formalities inhibiting children, removed barriers with the outside world, encouraged familiar relationships, and stimulated fruitful contacts with teachers, play-ladies, therapists and general entertainers, though not as surrogate-parents. Popular junior cadets jousted gently with con-valescents; a camera enthusiast gave photos of favourite nurses for taking home; an old lady told goodnight stories to lonely children; troupes gave plays and ballets. Parents planned parties, and Claire was enraptured by an indoor fireworks display, when we made a guy from doctors' clothes. The dietician saved us scraps to feed squirrels in the park, where I took ward children to collect caterpillars for nature trays.

The children's days were filled with creative experiences, keeping them contentedly busy, releasing both constructive and destructive energies without brooding, promoting natural tiredness and sleep (Montessori, 1936). Claire never needed sedatives. When ill, she still insisted on daily programmes of favourite activities and ritualistic doll-care (Noble, 1967):whilst dying she lovingly re-wrapped 'poor cold Rosebud', unconscious of her own frozen fingers. As Maureen Oswin observes (chapter 8, p. 101) most children prefer lively wards, though too ill to participate.

Yet some children face empty hours (Oswin, 1971). For example, three-year-old Barbara, tormented by nightmares in hospital was too afraid to tell the staff. They refused her teacher-mother's request for unrestricted visiting, saying Barbara was their quietest, easiest patient. Sally, aged six, pined, so was removed by her parents from a teaching hospital, where the elderly sister allowed no play activity, home toys, or frequent visiting.

Loneliness enlarges threatening phantasies, particularly in disturbed children, who need special care to absorb them in external interests (Winnicott, 1969). The care of pets is therapeutically valuable for hospitalised children who feel caged and vulnerable themselves. So also are birdwatching, floristry and gardening, involving contact with nature, from which hospital has removed them. Claire loved looking restfully through lenses, and my beautiful prismatic pendant. A Swiss paediatrician caring for dying children advocates cathartic dressing-up and acting.[3] Playlists from an American hospital (Plank, 1964) include suitcase packing and unpacking for newly arrived and long-stay children, punchball games for the aggressive, and museum-making for intellectuals! A British paediatric unit is constructing artificial beaches, with rocks, sand and water!

Our consultant considered play prophylactic, and encouraged all joyful activity for its developmental and recreational normality. Parents were encouraged to become active supporters, not passive present givers. They thereby received insights into their child's imagination, obsessions and fears, and so recognised opportunities for encouraging independence, or signals for help. Giving children such diverse satisfactions minimised behavioural problems (Burton, 1968). Pressurised parents sometimes exploded with normal irritability, discouraging childish manipulations, and restoring homely realities (Robertson, 1970)!

The nurses protected us from depressive preoccupations, teaching us essential nursing procedures so we returned home more confident and competent. Having washed, fed, shopped for, and played with our children, we were too tired for overconcern with treatment, or other maladaptive attitudes, which would have antagonised the staff. Sister never minded mothers smoking discreetly, but she disliked children being propped up before unsuitable TV. Our consultant deplored seriously-ill children watching death agonies, believing that fears increased thereby. In this he differed from others, though there is still insufficient research to warrant conclusions.[4]

During Claire's rest-hours, I learned much by listening to staff and parents, discussion initially raising anxiety, though dispersing it later, so my husband never suffered disruptive visits. Spontaneous comparisons of experience developed compassion for others, understanding of their adjustments, and opportunities for anticipatory grief. We progressed through personal conflicts, without reinforcing them, nor becoming pathogenic as some organised groups, because individuals withdrew if sensitivities were overexposed (Friedman, 1967). Interested staff were available on an informal basis, and sought to learn, with parents, the child's situation. Parents greatly respected the openness of the staff. Shared responsibilities minimised over-involvement and stress, and the happy relaxed sister was the centre of a circle, not the apex of a pyramid, her nurses sharing family confidences and case conferences. As Dr Rothenberg has observed (chapter 5, p. 39) many staff bear unrelieved suffering, however. For example, one consultant was so distressed at the failure of his new treatment to save three children that his hair turned white. A surgeon's operation failed, so he stopped visiting his patient who felt rejected, and sister was over-stressed by demanding parents and loyalty conflicts. A chaplain resigned because the children's terminal ward made him cry. Another, himself bereaved, dedicated his life to this work.

Our paediatricians orchestrated the care of their critically ill children with deep sensitivity, demonstrating to us how emotions can be controlled and used to balance processes of life and death (Debuskey, 1970). Mutual misunderstandings were reconciled forgivingly, and we relied on staff as lifelines of support, in and out of hospital.

At home

Never again leave me to be the peaceful child I was before	There is a land of pure delight Infinite day excludes the night And pleasures banish pain
Whitman	*Watts*

During remissions, Claire's home life was the normal, gay round of cooking for her dolls, mucking up the garden with her friends, going

93

to shops, parties, outings. Fattened by steroids, she flopped happily in ballet and swimming, on holiday puffing determinedly up castle towers, and on to donkeys' backs.

Failing to prevent friends spoiling her with presents, we teased her meanness in clinging to them, and increasingly to us, as disease spread. We praised her dry-eyed endurance of unanaesthetised lumbar punctures and daily blood-tests, ignoring the tantrums caused by cortisone and pent-up frustration. We encouraged her to be proud of her achievements, laugh at difficulties, and feel that doctors and nurses loved her for being helpful and brave. This sense of being secure and valued in hospital was reinforced by her daily prayers containing long lists of staff to be blest (Dean, 1971). Self-confidence and sociability prevented loneliness, dissociation and regression, absorbing her in pleasurable activity, which, with increasing rest-routine, balanced any newly threatening developments. When a small haemorrhage started, the consultant visited, and suggested possible readmission on Sunday. However, Claire, having rested sufficiently to recover, dressed herself and her dolly, for the preferable regular pram-push to church!

Claire's gaiety and commonsense came from her eighty-year-old Granny who did a Russian dance on hospital days to make her laugh. My mother's devoted help endorsed Bozemann's insight (1955) concerning maternal support, and made our ménage viable, even protecting us from the pejorative vocabulary of an interested psychiatric social worker, who became fascinated by what she termed 'Claire's sporadic non-specific reciprocal inhibitions'!

My husband amused Claire tenderly with rude rhymes and funny pictures, treating her with patient firmness. He used his own anxiety-energy to gain a First Class Honours degree, and we spent exhausted evenings listening to music, deepening our marital relationship. He upheld me constantly.

Our older children, happily active outside, consciously and unselfishly expected us to concentrate on Claire. Their understanding, compassion and sorrow developed naturally as she faded, and they faced the storm, involved, not excluded.

Our friends were marvellous, supplementing hospital transport arranged by social workers, planning family treats, always sympathetic. Their churches and synagogues sent parcels, praying regularly, as did Muslim friends.

My own feelings had become almost psychedelically sensitive to the heights and depths of life, though I never took sedatives or stimulants. I wept and laughed, whispered and sang, hoped and feared: a hothouse of emotions in which Claire seemed a precious plant entrusted to my care for the final unfolding of a perfect and unique flower, whose seeds of trust, courage and long-suffering had yet to ripen for harvest. Whether skies were brilliant with sunshine or cloud, each day was a celebration in which every joyful moment was wrung out drop by drop. The circus, the pantomime, her first mouthful of dewberries, and hilarious afternoons dancing under the hosepipe, gave reality the lustre of enchantment.

Remissions were periods of 'peak experience'[5] when our whole community surrounded Claire with love and kindness which sustained her through later crises. One such incarcerated her for six weeks in a tiny ante-ward, with me her only masked nurse-companion. Yet she regularly slept ten hours, clambering into my bed for early morning cuddles, contentedly colouring pictures like those later published as a children's prayerbook. When she became resentfully angry, she rocked desperately on a playhorse until peace came. Needing similar relief, my own ridiculous rides delighted Claire, and the terminal room became identified for its laughter, not its silence; transformed into a little 'home'.

Unfortunately, some children in the terminal stage suddenly find home-life distorted. For example, four-year-old Betty was subjected to unorthodox medicaments by her vigorously compensating physiotherapist mother who denied her imminent death. She prepared dietary regimens, whilst Betty cried for favourite titbits and cuddling. A nine-year-old Cypriot boy, Nicholas, slept in the same bed as his separated mother, who dressed completely in black, becoming his constant shadow. She spoke no English and Nicholas abused his self-administered drugs. During relapses she wailed traditional elegies whilst he became hysterical.

Claire's background of activity and peacefulness kept her healthy despite damage by disease and drugs. She seemed to contain and localise the cancer, becoming physically and emotionally immunised from its malignant power by personal biochemistry (Gillis, 1967), or protective antigens, which our doctor called psychosomatic, and my mother attributed to maxidose rose hip syrup! Although Claire nearly died on three occasions, she rose from each coma to demand sausages, her dolly, or the potty!

It was her first bed-wet, plus increasing restlessness, which symptomised total disease invasion, associated with severe CNS depressions, which Hinton (1964) says characterise many cancer patients. She became pathologically tyrannical, urgently demanding my continual presence, our symbiotic bonding becoming parasitic, pitiful. Acute pain started, provoking fear in her, and nervous conflict in me, increased by a hospital locum who only suggested readmission or paracetamol, not that our GP should take over.

Claire had previously suffered pain uncomplainingly. Soon her tumbling tears and clinging weight, as I carried her everywhere, made me collapse emotionally and physically, my ability to cope exhausted. I felt suddenly finished, just as she was. My husband whitened, kissing our ashen faces, knowing it would be selfish to prolong her life (Yudkin, 1967). We had to help her die.

Death

He who respects the infant's
   faith
Triumphs over hell and
   death.
Blake

The night be dark
The world seem dim
But the anchor held
I got hold of the strong hand
   of the Saviour.
Words of a dying child

Claire's death was simple; it was our thoughts and feelings which were complicated and distraught, reconciled only by realising we must respond to Claire herself, undeterred by cultural fears.

Many such fears torture present-day parents and children, who seem lost amidst changing traditions. Protective guardian angels come strangely disguised: for example, twelve-year-old Kathy formed death images from Dracula films, and feared dark churches (Anthony, 1971). She drew strength from Batman and her crucifix. Peter, eight, cheerfully connected Heaven with space travel. His mother, opposed to religious morbidity, comforted him and his mourning brother, with visions of interplanetary visiting.

Children's questions demonstrate their longing to find meaning in existence (Madge, 1965), expressing their need to maintain hope in life (Illingworth, 1971) and find beliefs which catalyse and comfort diminishing senses. Sensitive listeners, remembering age (Piaget, 1969) and background differences (Beadle, 1971), may help children find anchors.

Easson recommends Psalm 23. Sigler (1970) stresses the spiritual unacceptability of children's deaths, and many parents feed imaginations on rebirth of bulbs and seasons, hibernation and metamorphoses of butterflies, the resurrection of the egg—sophisticatedly used by Kubrick in '2001'. Autton's (1969) parable of the dog sensing his Master's presence reassured one child. Older children are fascinated by perpetuation through transplant and even as changing electrons—'bits of one buzzing around everywhere!' Younger children may think of a sleeping journey in their parents' arms, waking in a holiday place, where the family will also come. Many who write to me trust Jesus to care for them, feeling He will make them well and happy when they are with Him. Those who are unconscious of approaching death may be mercifully spared unexpressed fears and final loneliness.

Young children choose their comfort with faith and wonder that adults lose, providing they are sure parental love will never forsake them, and that they have their own spiritual security. They can rest in peace, returning to primal dependence on their mother's nourishing love and their father's steadfast strength. Just as a mother brings her baby to the breast, so can she cradle him into the cocoon of his final sleep. The last precious moments, like other family rituals of birthdays and festivals, can be filled with flowers from friends, messages from loved ones, warming candlelight, all creating an atmosphere of calm and communion which children may sense as nearness to heaven. Release from pain, and reassuring touches of love, may help the child feel, like Hazlitt, 'it was not like death, but more like life'.

Claire was too little for questioning. Trusting the world as she trusted us, she accepted the changeover from her sister's bedroom to our lounge, filled with flowers. I took her to church for the last time, thanking God for having kept her whole and unhurt throughout her trials, begging Him to prepare a peaceful return. Friends called with cooked meals, prayer groups gathered again, and I felt uplifted, an old-fashioned word many parents use to describe similar experiences.

She haemorrhaged, vomiting blood, passing it, breathing it down pinched nostrils, covering me with stains as I sponged her with rose-water. Bidding her lie still to lessen pain, I asked if the doctor could help, but she said Jesus would look after her. During a respite, she wanted Daddy to take her to Granny's room for 'Top of the Pops'. She made us sing her favourite Beatles' song, 'All I need is love'. Then she wanted her bed again, she wanted her cuddly blanket, Rosebud, drinks, kisses, her potty . . . we gave her everything she wanted, surrounding her with her family of dolls, tucking her up gently. Turning the lights off, I lit some candles, saying it was time for sleep. We lay down together, saying her favourite prayer, picturing Jesus enfolding us. Claire nestled in my arms, Rosebud in hers. Her eyes closed, her translucent face suffusing with peace. She had gone—without having known the fear of separation, which suddenly stabbed me like a sword. Gasping, I rushed to my husband, bent over his books, though it was his birthday. He caught me in his arms and we clung together until we found the strength to go and give our last kisses and final services.

I covered Claire's bed with her beautiful baptismal shawl. Having washed her with Holy Water, and placed Rosebud in her arms, I forced myself to make the symbolic Cross of Committal on her brow. She lay there, transfiguring death and enshrining love in the little life which had lifted us all into new dimensions, making paradise out of purgatory, now finding that the cherished kingdom of childhood was eternal. Through our tears, throughout the lonely, silent, aching months of missing and mourning, we knew that she who had left us was not lost, and that we all should one day be wherever she is.

Renewals

> A son or daughter dead
> Can bend the back
> Or whiten the head
> Break and remould the heart
> *Edwin Muir*

Some parents, renewing family life, bury grief in the grave; others mourn pitifully; many sublimate sorrow in active parent-doctor associations, offering similar families domestic and financial assistance, help with transport, holidays, childminding, plus advisory, consultative and educational services. Sharing in this work affords me privileged confidences and insight into major parental concerns which stress that:

(1) Research must increase, its benefits being applied more accessibly.

(2) Unrestricted visiting and necessary living in accommodation for parents should be available.

(3) Hospital and home treament should be co-ordinated by regular, specialised, supportive visiting, for example by the GP, M.S.W., H. V., or District Nurse.

(4) Community provisions should be stimulated.

(5) Reports such as Ministry of Health, 1958, 1966; National Association for the Welfare of Children in Hospital, 1969, 1972; Department of Health and Social Security and the Welsh Office, 1971 and Department of Health and Social Security, 1972, regarding the needs of hospitalised children should be urgently implemented. Treating personnel should be paediatrically trained, ward recreational facilities developed and parental participation encouraged and valued.

Then the sufferings of our children, and our own unique experiences in caring for them, might be redeemed, as in the words of the poet:

Love is not changed by death
and nothing is lost
and all in the end is Harvest.
Edith Sitwell

Notes

1 Inscription on Tomb of Mumtaz Mahal, Taj Mahal.
2 Attributable to Sir James Spence.
3 Information verbally given by Professor Strang of University College Hospital.
4 Personal correspondence with Professor H. Himmelweit of the London School of Economics, 1971.
5 Attributable to Professor Abraham Maslow.

References

ANTHONY, S. (1971), *The Child's Discovery of Death*, Allen Lane, London.
AUTTON, N. (1969), *The Pastoral Care of the Dying*, SPCK, London.
BEADLE, M. (1971), *A Child's Mind*, MacGibbon & Kee, London.
BENNETT, D. N. (1972), *Parents should be Heard*, Hutchinson, London.
BOWLBY, J. *et al.* (1956), 'The effects of mother-child separation: a follow-up study', *British Journal of Medical Psychology*, vols. 3 and 4, pp. 211-47.
BOZEMANN, M. F., ORBACH, C. E. and SUTHERLAND, A. M. (1955), 'The adaptation of mothers to the threatened loss of their children through leukemia', *Cancer*, vol. 8, pp. 1-19.
BUBER, M. (1961), *Between Man and Man*, Collins, London.
BURTON, L. (1968), *Vulnerable Children*, Routledge & Kegan Paul, London.
DEAN, J. Q. (1971), *Religious Education for Children*, Ward Lock, London.
DEBUSKEY, M. (ed). (1970), *The Chronically Ill Child and his Family*, Charles Thomas, Illinois.
DEPARTMENT OF HEALTH AND SOCIAL SECURITY (1972), *Meeting the Training Needs of H.M.*, HMSO, London.
DEPARTMENT OF HEALTH AND SOCIAL SECURITY AND THE WELSH OFFICE (1971), *Hospital Facilities for Children*, HMSO, London.
ERIKSON, E. (1965), *Childhood and Society*, Penguin, Harmondsworth.
FRIEDMAN, S. B. (1967), 'Care of the family of the child with cancer', *Pediatrics*, vol. 40 (3), p. 498.
GILLIS, L. (1967), *Human Behaviour in Illness*, Faber & Faber, London.
GLASER, B. and STRAUSS, A. (1965), *Awareness of Dying*, Aldine, New York.
HINTON, J. (1964), 'Problems in the care of the dying', *Journal of Chronic Diseases*, vol. 17, p. 201.

ILLINGWORTH, R. S. (1971), *The Treatment of the Child at Home*, Blackwell, Oxford.

JONES, R. S. (ed.) (1971), *The Care of the Critically Ill Child*, Arnold, London.

KUBLER-ROSS, E. (1970), *On Death and Dying*, Tavistock, London.

MACKENZIE, N. (1969), *Psychology for Nurses*, Cassell, London.

MADGE, V. (1965), *Children in Search of Meaning*, SCM, London.

MEADOWS, S. R. (1964), 'No thanks, I'd rather stay at home', *British Medical Journal*, vol. III, p. 813.

MINISTRY OF HEALTH (1958), *The Welfare of Children in Hospital* (Platt Report), HMSO, London.

MINISTRY OF HEALTH (1966), *The Visiting of Children in Hospital*, HMSO, London.

MONTESSORI, M. (1936), *Secrets of Childhood*, Longmans, London.

NATIONAL ASSOCIATION FOR THE WELFARE OF CHILDREN IN HOSPITAL (1969), *Survey on Visiting Children in Hospital*, NAWCH, London.

NATIONAL ASSOCIATION FOR THE WELFARE OF CHILDREN IN HOSPITAL (1972), *Survey on Visiting Children in Hospital*, NAWCH, London.

NOBLE, E. (1967), *Play and the Sick Child*, Faber & Faber, London.

OSWIN, M. (1971), *The Empty Hours*, Allen Lane, London.

PIAGET, J. (1969), *The Language and Thought of the Child*, Routledge & Kegan Paul, London.

PLANK, E. (1964), *Working with Children in Hospital*, Tavistock, London.

ROBERTSON, J. (1970), *Young Children in Hospital*, Tavistock, London.

SAUNDERS, C. (1965), 'Watch with me', *Nursing Times*, 26 November.

SIGLER, A. Y. (1970), 'The leukemic child and his family: an emotional challenge', in Debuskey (ed.).

STACEY, M., DEARDEN, R., PILL, R. and ROBINSON, D. (1970), *Hospitals, Children and their Families*, Routledge & Kegan Paul, London.

THOMAS, K. (1971), *Religion and the Decline of Magic*, Weidenfeld & Nicolson, London.

WINNICOTT, C. (1969), 'Communicating with children', in Tod, R. J. N. (ed.), *Disturbed Children*, Longmans, London.

WOLFF, S. (1969), *Children Under Stress*, Allen Lane, London.

YUDKIN, S. (1967), 'Children and death', *Lancet*, vol. 7, p. 37.

8   The role of education in helping the child with a potentially fatal disease

Maureen Oswin

I have spread my dreams under your feet;
Tread softly because you tread on my dreams.
W. B. Yeats

All children in Britain today are entitled to education, no matter how handicapped or ill they may be. This education may take place in ordinary schools, if the staff and physical amenities of the school make this possible; or, it takes place in day special schools, residential special schools, hospital schools, in the wards of hospitals, or at the child's own home with a home teacher. There are local education authority teachers working in all children's hospitals, sometimes they teach in purpose-built school blocks in the hospital grounds, sometimes they work at the child's bedside in the ward. All mentally disabled children are entitled to education, and even when a child has a deteriorating brain disease he still receives some form of education in his ward. Various illnesses and handicaps call for various education arrangements, e.g. children with leukaemia may be educated at ordinary schools or in day special schools between treatments and whilst they are well enough; during hospitalisation, if their treatment requires sterile isolation, a teacher speaks to the child by telephone through the partitioning. Bedside tuition in hospital wards, or at home, is available to children even during the final stages of terminal disease, and adolescents may study for O and A levels although their illnesses are advanced.

Traditionally, a child's education is considered to be a preparation for adulthood, but this philosophy cannot be adhered to by teachers who work with sick and disabled children. The question arises: 'Why educate children with life-shortening diseases or incurable handicaps if they have no chance of employment or higher education, or marriage or parenthood? Why not just let them stay at home and do what they like?'

But, to concentrate entirely on the fact that these children may not possess futures is a very negative approach to their problems. Small children, whether healthy, sick or chronically disabled, do not regard school as a preparation for adulthood. They live very much for the pleasures of the present, and enjoy books, play, companionship, conversation, music and creative activities for their own sake, without considering future values. Education is a way of life for the small child, and its value cannot be measured in questions of how long his life will be. The older child, however, especially the intelligent adolescent with a potentially fatal disease, may himself question why he needs education and here the teacher needs to be sensitive to the child's possible depression and sense of futility in his growing awareness of the seriousness of his complaint. The sick adolescent needs school sessions to be as inventive and interesting as possible, with the teacher making use of creative work and current affairs and providing as much out-of-the-classroom activity as she can. Far better, if the child is physically capable of doing so, for him to go to theatres, concerts, or sports meetings than to sit in the hospital school classroom listening to a teacher talk at him about subjects which can, in truth, have little present or future value for him.

My first contact with children who were handicapped or suffering from life-shortening illnesses was when, as a student, I visited a residential school for blind children. Innocently imagining that I would see straight-limbed, healthy, blind children learning Braille, etc., in preparation for a busy adult life, I was shocked and upset to discover that many of the blind children also had complicated life-shortening diseases of which blindness was only one result; some were so physically handicapped that they were confined to wheelchairs, and others had deformities which would prevent them from ever living a normal adult life. Ignorantly, I questioned the purpose of education for these children. Wisely, the headmistress made no attempt to explain her ideals, but took me round the school and let the children themselves show me that education was essential for them, providing challenging occupations, companionship and interest. The incredible feeling of hope in that little school left a lasting impression on me. Children came up and felt my coat, my buttons, my hair, they asked me about my own home and what my name was, what I looked like and if I would come again. They explained, with giggles and arguments and waving hands, how the snowfall on the previous day had enabled them to toboggan all over the garden slopes and how their hands had frozen as they made snowballs and a snowman. A fast shrinking snowman stood on the lawn in the sunshine and they pulled me to the windows and asked me if I could see him, was he much melted now, did I know that he measured four feet tall.

The headmistress took me to see Ellen, a very sick girl of thirteen, grotesquely paralysed as well as blind. She had a lovely smile and voice and told me about her favourite books, and how she did not like maths, and that she was hoping to learn French very soon. She was deteriorating rapidly and had to have school by her bedside, but, with a determined laugh she told me that she would be up for her fourteenth birthday party.

We saw George, aged seven, who was not expected to live for very long and whose fingers were swollen into such banana-like shapes that he would never be able to learn Braille. His main enjoyment was singing in the school choir. He had been able to see a little when he had first come to the school two years previously, but had recently lost the rest of his vision. When his mother had fetched him from hospital after his latest treatment he had caught hold of her coat and asked 'Will I always be in the dark now, Mummy?' Mother had dreaded that question, having hoped against all medical evidence that he would not become totally blind. But it would have been wrong to have lied to such a sensitive child so she gently explained that 'yes, he would be in the dark now'. For a short while George was very silent, then he said 'But I can go back to school, can't I? I shall be like all the others there now, all the other children are blind.' That child, newly discharged from hospital and faced with permanent blindness wanted most of all to get back to the other children and his school. He wanted his school activities to continue, it was a way of life that he understood, needed and enjoyed, without any question of what future use education would be to him.

The profusion of beautiful pictures hanging on the walls of that school for blind and short-lived children seemed to symbolise the fine philosophy of the teachers who worked there: beauty was not excluded from the environment just because the children could not see it, nor was education excluded from their brief lives just because they were not going to have a long future in which to use it.

The children's educational needs

The educational needs of children who are handicapped or ill do not, broadly, differ from the needs of well children. *All* children need stimulating interests, all want to satisfy their natural curiosity. No matter what their disability might be they have a normal desire to make a mess and a noise, dress up, act, handle and look after pets, hear music, collect treasures, make jokes, play with others, learn to

103

read and appreciate books and creative activities. First, then, their education has to satisfy a basic need for *experiencing the normalities of childhood*. These normal experiences will be especially important for the disabled child with brothers and sisters: having a teacher and a school and interests like the other children in his family and the neighbourhood makes him feel the same as everyone else and is a boost to his social esteem.

Next, there is a need for the school activities to be *practical*. Children who are permanently in wheelchairs, or who are likely to be confined to hospital for long periods, are in danger of missing many of the practical experiences of childhood, so an 'active education' is very important for them. This means getting away from the traditional idea of classroom teaching, by giving the disabled child as many practical experiences as possible. A trip on the river is better than listening to the teacher talking about rivers. *Posting* letters is better than looking at pictures of letter-boxes. One school for multiply handicapped children lets even the deaf-blind children post their own letters; not escorted by any teacher, they walk slowly along the school drive, holding onto each other, down to the village post-office, where they hand over their money, buy stamps, lick them, put them on the envelopes and finally feel for the letter-box and post the letters. Full of triumph they fumble their way back up the school drive, relief at successfully completing the challenge making them gleefully careless so that they mischievously bump each other into trees. Being able to actually feel the letter-box, handle the money and taste the glue of the stamps is an infinitely more satisfying and memorable experience than staying in a classroom to merely hear about it from the teacher.

A programme of *practical education* for such children should start at an early age, because their illnesses may result in them getting very heavy and immobile in adolescence. For example, children with spinal diseases and muscular dystrophy often have a very empty and restricted adolescence due to the practical difficulties of manoeuvring them and their wheelchairs into interesting places, but if they have been taken out as much as possible when they were small enough to carry around, then it can help a little towards giving them some rich memories and topics of conversation. Marie, aged six, and confined to a small wheelchair due to a rapidly advancing spinal disease was taken on holiday to the sea, and went on to the pier which at that time had only two or three fishermen on it as the time was out of season for holidays. She was able to spend a long time, undisturbed, peering through the slats of the pier floor, watching the dimpling of the water far beneath her. Then she watched the fishermen, hanging their rods over the side into water which was so calm that she could clearly see the dark shapes of fishes. It was joy for Marie to see the swift movements of the fish and the varying colours of the sunlight and shadows on the water, and to be up so high with no walls around her. Normally she lived in the enclosed world of a hospital ward, where the only sun she knew came through ward windows and the only fish she knew came encased in thick batter from the hospital kitchen. She had never been physically well enough to experience the normal childhood perils of tree-climbing or sitting on high, forbidden walls. As she watched the dark bodies of the fish she remarked: 'How quiet the fish are, they make *me* feel all still, too'. When a fish was caught she was fascinated to see the silver body and the men's excitement at their capture. Shutting her eyes against the destruction she agreed that it was cruel, but added, 'I want to tell the others all about it though'. So she went back to the other children, with lots of conversation, and impressed them with her simple adventures on the pier.

The children need sensory and emotional experiences, such as feeling different materials, tasting exotic foods, smelling unpleasant and pleasant smells, watching sunsets, enjoying storms, cooking, getting fond of animals. Visiting a Safari Park with a group of sick and disabled children I found that they were most impressed by the chance they had to go inside the children's zoo to see and handle the many small animals housed there: hamsters, rabbits, goats, pigs, calves, lambs and chicks. Taking turns to stroke the baby animals, they argued about which were their favourites, some liked the feel of the lamb's coat, others the firm heads of the fierce little kids, or the chicks which swiftly pecked their teeth if held up to their laughing faces. Others favoured the silky rabbits which they were allowed to cuddle, and the guinea-pigs which amused them by making one or two puddles in laps. The pungent animal smell in the barn was very vivid to them, accustomed as they were to the clean smell of hospitals.

The children can gain sensory experiences from the most ordinary childish interests. One day, we found a baby pigeon who had fallen from his nest and he provided the children with many happy moments as he was fed and gradually gained his strength and learnt to fly. When he had flown away we forgetfully left his food dish of bread and milk lying in the shed, and several days later the children were suprised when we showed them a huge pale hairy mould covering the dish. This provided a great deal of interest and they took turns to have the dish on their tables, gently blowing the hair of the mould and stroking it with strips of paper. Making smelly mixtures is another sensory experience that the children enjoy; this

105

can be done quite simply by mixing up any vegetable mixtures and leaving in a jamjar for a few days, the resulting odour causing considerable interest and amusement.

Children who are confined to hospital wards should not be deprived of the pleasures of cooking, for it gives interest and aesthetic satisfaction. Even if the children are too weak or disabled to do the mixing and weighing on their own, the teacher can take the ingredients into the ward so they can watch her mix it, then she can make use of the ward kitchen for cooking it. Some hospital teachers get the children to mix the ingredients in the ward, and then they take the mixture home with them at lunch time, cook it and bring it back to the hospital in the afternoon for the children to put on icing or fill with jam. But, ideally, all children's wards should contain a small cooker for the children's use, so that they can see at first hand exactly what cooking really means and smells like. They like to prick sausages, melt jellies, break open eggs, cook richly smelling vegetables such as onions, and help to make each other's birthday cakes and lick out the basin afterwards. It is very important for the teacher to look for experiences that disabled and sick children might be missing, experiences that are not only important for learning and intellectual development, but which are also essentially part of the joy of a normal childhood, for example cleaning out the cake mix basin with a busy spoon and tongue after mother has made a cake is one of the simplest of pleasures for a small child at home with his mum, but it is likely to be one of the many childish experiences missed out when a child is unwell and confined to hospital for long periods.

The teachers in one hospital once took their children round the back of the single-storey ward on to some waste ground, where they collected sticks, built a little fire and cooked sausages, eggs and fried bread. After a good feed the children lay on blankets round the fire, watching its embers, whilst the teachers put long sticks across it which burnt in half and dropped into the ashes, making a myriad sparks. Finally, before returning to the ward, they found an old tyre and decided to make a disgusting smell by putting that at the edge of the fire! Several of the children in that little group had no hope at all of ever reaching their teens, others would not attain adult life, others were so totally physically handicapped that adulthood promised only a meagre existence in a hospital or home. But, despite all the physical frailties, and despite the fact that it was the teachers and not the children who had done all the running round finding sticks and stoking and cooking, the afternoon had been most successful. The children were full of good smoky food, they had been in the fresh air, they had been a bit scared in an exciting way when the wind had blown the fire fiercely towards them, they were decidedly dirty; in fact, their afternoon had been packed with normal happy childhood experiences. Even when the children cannot physically participate in experiences themselves they can get vicarious pleasure from watching others do it.

It is also important to develop the children's imagination. Even when they cannot speak, nor see, or are too weak to move around freely, they can still appreciate language and the excitement of stories and drama, and can identify inwardly with colourful characters. Imagination can be developed by letting the children have plenty of books around them, by telling them stories, helping them to listen, and by backing up the stories by practical experiences if possible. One teacher tells her group of hospital children a never-ending tale of some country children named Molly and Simon; the adventures are very simple and childish, but to watch the children's faces as they listen is a revelation of how vividly they are able to identify with story characters. One day the teacher brought to the hospital a small tent and sleeping bag to illustrate how Molly and Simon had camped out; the children's excitement was intense as she gently lifted them into the sleeping bag to feel how squashy it was inside. A well-developed imagination can give the children a rich fund of things to think and talk about, which can momentarily release them from dull surroundings, illness, physical discomfort, pain, and homesickness.

Sometimes, children with potentially fatal diseases may be over-protected by their teachers. This is understandable, but unless there are medical reasons for taking extra care then it would be wrong to overprotect the children to the extent of depriving them of experiences that will give them pleasure and teach them about the world. Physically well children will play all day in the fields or on farms, perhaps getting hungry, wet, cold and dirty, but some children with handicaps or life-shortening illnesses never even go out in the rain. I remember visiting a farm with a group of disabled hospital children, and it poured with rain most of the day. We covered the children with dusty farm-sacks and sat just inside a barn, eating sandwiches and fruit and watching the rain. The sound and smell of the rain, and the formation of dark, discoloured, puddles in the uneven farm-yard remained vividly in the memory of one child, now a grossly deformed twenty-year-old living in a Cheshire Home. She recently recalled, 'do you remember that lovely day at the farm when it rained, it was the first time I'd ever been wet and out in the rain, and my hair went all curly'.

Another day at that farm we all went for a ride in a farm-cart, when some of the children's bottoms got pricked by the bales of straw we sat on and we were all in some danger of falling out. The adventure caused plenty of merriment from the tougher children, and a need to reassure the more timid ones. Opportunities for small adventures like this are a very normal part of childhood, but unwell children may not get them unless teachers, parents and medical staff make deliberate arrangements for them to visit farms, the seaside, rivers etc.

Teachers and parents

The teacher's relationship with the child's family has two main aspects. First, the family and the teacher will be united in their aims to *help the child*. Ideally, this takes the form of great co-operation between teachers and parents in making the child's education as interesting as possible. It is very important for parents and teachers to know each other. This knowing is fairly easy in a day special school, as parents attend open-days, and may bring the child into school each morning themselves, and there is often frequent correspondence between teachers and parents, e.g. one very handicapped child who was unable to speak or use her hands and was brought into day special school every morning in a coach, used to carry little notes in her satchel every day, telling her class teacher little bits of family news and what she had done the evening before or during the weekend. So that the child was able to take part in 'newstime' with the other children in her class and could 'talk' through her mother's notes all about what went on at her home, and did not get left out in spite of her terrible handicaps.

But, in a residential special school, or a hospital school, the teachers may find it very difficult to keep in close contact with parents, especially if the hospital is some distance from the child's home. Under these circumstances it is helpful if the teachers try to maintain family links by writing to parents and letting them know what their child does in school, so they can share in his education and talk about it to him when he is able to have periods at home. This was the situation for Bebe, who had deteriorating epilepsy; her teacher and mother rarely met but they maintained a friendship by corresponding regularly about Bebe. The teacher told the mother what Bebe did during school-time in the hospital ward, and sent her small bits of work, such as cutting out and paintings. And, when Bebe went home for brief holidays, the parents sent back messages for the teacher and a list of things that the family had done together in the holidays. Bebe worsened quite rapidly one summer and did not survive long after her eighth birthday, but a few weeks before her death there was a hospital school pageant which included a procession around the hospital grounds. Children on spinal carriages were dressed as Humpty-Dumpties or Bo-Peeps and Miss Muffetts and there were plenty of 'Pollies' to put the kettle on as it was so easy to make old fashioned poke-bonnets and give wheelchair children a little kettle to hold. Some children were dressed as Queens of Hearts and proudly held trays of little plasticine jam-tarts. Bebe's mother, knowing about the school pageant, sent a special long dress to drape over her wheelchair, with a tray of plastic flowers to tie on the front of the chair, so Bebe was able to go as Mary, Mary, Quite Contrary. Although Bebe was then considerably brain-injured and unable to speak, it was obvious that she appreciated what was going on and the effort that her mother had made to provide her with a pretty costume, for she grinned and wriggled with joy during the whole procession.

The second relationship that is important between parents and teachers is the one of *mutual help in personal emotional stress*. It *is* emotionally distressing to work with children who may not get better and who are perhaps terribly handicapped, and both teachers and parents need to support each other—the teacher helps the parents by giving them confidence that their child is receiving as interesting an education as possible despite the particular illness, whilst the teacher is reassured by knowing that the parents understand her efforts to help their sick child. When Bebe died, the teacher's letter to mother described 'how much Bebe enjoyed school, she joined in everything as much as she could for as long as she could and I was glad to have her in my school group'. Bebe's actual contribution to the school group was very meagre, consisting in the final months of perhaps only a slight hand movement in percussion band time, or a smile in story time; an unperceptive person may have deemed it a waste of teaching time to have included Bebe in school at all, but it was very important to mother and father and to Bebe herself that she had been included for as long as possible right up to the end.

When a child has an illness which progressively impairs her mental abilities, as in Bebe's case, school can be a help to parents in so much as it retains some semblance of the normal social pattern of childhood happenings for as long as possible. One does not wish to give parents unrealistic ideas about their child's recovery (most parents are only too well aware of the hopelessness of their child's illness and his deteriorating mental ability, so this is a small risk) but education is the *right of every child*, no matter how bad he is, and all

109

the time he has life in him he is entitled to receive attention from educationalists. Just as nobody yet has the right to decide when life-saving medical apparatus should be 'switched-off', so no one has the right to decide when a child's education should cease. The attention of a teacher for as long as possible throughout a deteriorating illness makes all the difference between maintaining that child's dignity as a thinking, feeling child, and giving him up as a hopeless medical 'case'. This applies in particular to children who have been irreparably brain-injured in road accidents and have small chance of full recovery. The child may lie unresponsive and silent, but should not be excluded from school. Some teachers who work in wards which include road accident brain-injured children always include those children in the school group, by putting toys on their beds or by moving their beds round so that the child is included in the singing or story circle. No matter how brain-injured the child may be, it is still important for him and a comfort to his parents, to know that he is included in the education that is taking place in the ward. His reponses may be meagre and his personal contribution may be nil, but he is still a living child and entitled to a teacher's attention.

The teacher's relationship with the children

Unlike the teacher of well children the teacher of sick and handicapped children inevitably develops a deep relationship with her children; and if the child has long periods away from home, in hospital or residential school, then the teacher may be regarded as a substitute parent by the younger children. Because of this deep relationship, the teacher may have to cope with innumerable difficult questions, some of which may be very distressing, e.g. 'Why can't I walk?', 'Will I get better?', 'Why can't I go home?', 'Can you be my mother as my mum doesn't come to see me any more?', 'Why do people hurt me?' Many of these questions can never be answered satisfactorily, and, unfortunately, no one can give advice on what to say, for the answers depend on the teacher's understanding of the individual child, and her sense of what will be most helpful for him.

Children who live a sheltered existence in residential special schools and long-stay hospitals may get a very distorted idea of childhood and adulthood. Because they are surrounded by unwell children and handicapped children and very healthy adults, they sometimes come to believe that *all* children are handicapped and grow into physically well adults. One child of six, confined to a wheelchair and with a life-shortening disease, said 'Of course, I'll be able to walk about when I'm as old as you, won't I?' That child had never mixed with children who could run about, as she had been confined to hospital for as long as she could remember, and she did not have a family, so it was understandable that she had developed the unrealistic belief that handicap and illness was a normal part of childhood.

If handicapped children are taken out into the community and given a chance to see other groups of people of mixed ages and abilities, e.g. old people, babies in prams, businessmen, trades-people, etc., then it could help a little towards correcting their distorted ideas of childhood. I once took a group of severely crippled children into a restaurant, some of them had spina bifida and some had muscular dystrophy; there we saw a legless man in a wheelchair. 'But he's grown up and *still* in his wheelchair', one of the children cried out in amazement.

Seeing that man made them ask some very penetrating questions when we got back to the hospital, about whether *they* would still be in wheelchairs when they grew up, about what happened if you did not 'get better' and suppose the doctors did not make them better and they died.

The children's demands on their teachers can be emotionally exhausting as they seek these explanations about their illnesses and handicaps. Sometimes they seem to ask their teachers difficult questions more readily than they ask their parents, perhaps unconsciously wishing to spare their parents from distress. (A point discussed also in Dr Burton's chapter, p. 25). Some questions actually relate to adult distress, for example 'I saw Debbie's mummy crying the other day, why do mummies cry sometimes?' Children can be uneasy and fearful when they see adult tears and they want to have the subject openly discussed, so a question like this may be just another way of asking for reassurrance about whether their *own* mummy ever cries and *why* she does; fear at seeing parents' tears expresses fear about themselves, too, as if they are sharing with their parents the grief of premature loss of each other.

Children who are handicapped or ill are not always easy to work with, for they can get as angry, bad-tempered and rebellious as any group of well children, but, because they are unwell and may have short lives or be incurably disabled, there is sometimes the tendency to feel uncomfortable if one grumbles at them. But unpleasant behaviour should not go unchecked. Children need the security of being controlled, and it is a sentimental mistake to condone a child's anti-social behaviour because he is sick or disabled. Jerry, aged seven, handicapped by muscular dystrophy, was a particularly

111

disgruntled child who possessed a gift of making cynical remarks aimed at spoiling other children's enjoyment of school activities. His teacher felt guilty because one day she justifiably got very angry with him. She said, 'I completely forgot that Jerry might not be here in a few years' time and I feel upset now to think that I got so angry with him'. But, Jerry's illness should not permit him to spoil everybody else's pleasures as well as his own; a cure for muscular dystrophy could give Jerry and other boys like him a normal span of life, and they would not be socially helped if their patterns of behaviour were shaped by adult reluctance to correct unpleasant attitudes.

It was understandable for the teacher to feel guilt at treating Jerry as a normal disgruntled little boy, but it was surely the best thing she could do for him. Handicapped and sick people depend so much on other people and if in later life Jerry was alive and in a Cheshire Home or hospital ward, he would be very unpopular with staff and other patients if he had been allowed to grow up in the habit of behaving selfishly and unkindly. It is a hard truth that disabled people really need to develop *extra nice* personalities because they are very dependent on other people and at a social disadvantage to begin with. If the teacher can show the children what sort of behaviour is tolerable in a social group, and how to be pleasant to other people, and if she reacts to unkindness by becoming normally cross then she is in fact educating the children in how to live happily with other people.

Some relevant problems

Some difficulties of teaching children who have life-shortening illnesses relate to physical and environmental pressures. For example, children with muscular dystrophy often become very large and the sheer physical problem of getting them and their wheelchairs out may result in them staying indoors for months on end, leading very empty lives, and becoming dull and morose. It is always useful to try and get over this problem by calling on volunteer 'pushers' when taking groups of wheelchair children out. Having enough 'pushers' makes all the difference when on trips to shops, the seaside, farms, zoos, etc. If each child has his own helper he feels independent, and is saved from awful interminable waits for *his* turn to be shown the lion or pier or particular shop window.

One of the most difficult jobs is teaching children with leukaemia who are in isolation units. Although the teacher and child may communicate visually through the partition and can use an intercommunication telephone system, nobody can ever pretend that the situation is good, for children rely so much on activity and personal touch when they are learning. One can only concede to the serious-ness of the child's illness and the importance of that particular medical treatment in combating the disease, and hope to be able to make up his education in plenty of practical ways and affectionate relationships during the periods he is able to be away from the isolation unit.

Home teaching is another aspect of teaching which has its own special problems. Home teachers are most often employed for the older multiply handicapped child, especially those who may be studying for O or A levels, or doing commercial courses. Perhaps the child's physical condition is rapidly deteriorating and the parents prefer him to be at home rather than in a hospital unit, and he is keen to get on with his O or A level exams; in such cases the teacher may call into his home on several mornings a week. The teacher may find that home tuition is a lonely job because she is away from contact with other children and colleagues, and it will be distressing as the youngster is so frequently at a terminal stage in his illness, but there is no doubt that she is very welcome to the young person and his family.

Another problem in educating the sick or handicapped child is the reaction of some parents to the knowledge that their child needs to attend a special school instead of an ordinary school. But, uneasiness about special schools may lessen after the child has started there, and the parents discover that the teachers frequently have additional qualifications beyond the normal, and that the buildings are purpose-built and permit easy movement from room to room if the child is confined to a wheelchair. Many of the children in special schools will *appear* physically able, because schools for physically handicapped and 'delicate' children have a high proportion of children in them who have haemophilia, heart diseases, cystic fibrosis, asthma, leukaemia, and rheumatic diseases, in addition to cerebral palsied children and those with muscular dystrophy and various crippling orthopaedic conditions. Parents are often bitterly disappointed at their child having to attend a special school but eventually they may become reconciled to the fact that it is better for their child to be 'king' in a special school than odd-man-out in an ordinary school, where the pace and physical demands would rapidly single him out as unwell or 'different'.

It is most helpful if the special school has a lively Parent-Teacher Association and the parents feel that they can take an active part in helping their child's education. Parents of sick or handicapped children should never be excluded from being involved in their child's education, however unorthodox that help might seem when judged by ordinary school standards. For example, some parents of special school children invite small groups of children back to their houses for a look round their garden or a picnic. One teacher in a day special school takes her group of infant age children out to tea in a friend's garden each summer, aided by parents. The fact that the house has a large tree-filled garden, is near a pond and has a grassy bank to slide down, makes the afternoon a happy time. Another reason for having a good Parent-Teacher Association is that it enables parents to meet *each other*, and can be an invaluable source of friendship for parents who are going through periods of deep stress.

Of all the professions who work with children who have life-shortening diseases, it is true to say that the teacher really has the *easiest* task. Unlike the nurses, she does not have to give painful treatments: she does not have to make the decisions about treatment or surgery as a doctor does: she does not have to make the physical demands on the child as a physiotherapist might have to: and, professionally, she is not called on to cope with parents' grief in the role of social worker. The teacher's work is essentially hopeful, for, in spite of often grave medical prognosis, she is only asked to deal with matters that interest the child *as a child,* and, no matter how crippled or unwell a child is, in some miraculous way he so often retains his young hope and young curiosity—a hope and curiosity which seem to generate a vitality that hides the fact that his life may only be very short. I have even seen young children within a few hours of coming round from difficult operations stretching out their hands to feel for toys and asking questions about something that interests them.

Edward was a child who made us all 'forget' how very frail he was. His muscle control was deteriorated to such an extent that the only thing he could do was to speak. But, his spirit was so fierce and alive and his personality so strong that staff and children forgot that a mere knock would have left him as helpless as a beetle on its back. He was the acknowledged leader in his school group, controlling the other children with his beautifully expressed ideas and bright conversation. His favourite hymn was 'Glad That I Live Am I'. Cynics might have thought the words incongruous to the meagre quality of life that Edward led. But those of us who knew him well understood that it was his normal reaction to life, he *was* genuinely glad that he was alive, and, singing this hymn, simply and sincerely expressed his joy in life. We learnt to accept Edward's strange ability to be happy.

In the same way as we accepted Edward's happiness without questioning, so we must accept the children's dreams which express

114

ambitions which we know may never be fulfilled. Liz was aged seven and already hopelessly crippled by a disease that made death inevitable by the age of eight or nine; one day she returned from the ballet, breathless with excitement, saying she would be a ballet dancer when she grew up. 'I *can* be a ballet dancer, can't I?' she asked her teacher. Her teacher's prompt reply of 'yes, you will be a lovely dancer' was not dishonest. Childhood dreams are as much part of a sick child's life as they are of a well child's life, and nobody has any right to destroy those precious dreams in the name of honesty. And, anyway, who is to say that their dreams will not be fulfilled? Medical science advances quickly, so dreams about being dancers, doctors, singers, teachers, pilots, and explorers, might well become reality for them. Education, providing interest, hope, friends, and imaginative adventures, is an essential part of their dreams, and can never be considered a waste of time, no matter how short the child's life may be.

Social work help for children whose life may be shortened

Pamela Gibbons

We have come a long way in recent years in acknowledging and meeting the emotional, social and physical needs of the adult patient whose life is threatened. Despite this most of us still experience difficulties in responding naturally to children placed in similar circumstances. Perhaps it is that we find it harder to be objective because death is not normally expected in the young. But sick children, from earliest days, do have very real physical and emotional needs which must be understood and responded to appropriately if the child is to be fully helped in the situation.

Sources of help—the family

All with whom the child is in contact can help him in varying ways, whether they be medical, para-medical, educational or social workers. The ones who can best help however are the child's own family, particularly the mother, who is in a position through her physical proximity and 'emotional closeness' to communicate an essential feeling of security and belonging to the sick child. Some parents however may find it particularly difficult to impart such feelings, and therefore a social worker endeavouring to help their child, must first help them.

In some families the problems arise from the mixed feelings parents have towards their handicapped child. These have already been discussed earlier (see chapter 2), and I will not reiterate them. Suffice to say that such feelings create a barrier in the natural parent-child relationship, the parents reacting primarily to the handicap rather than to the baby or child as a person. Whilst such parents remain anxious to do their best for their child, they may be unsure of their capability to help him. Unless parents can be helped to recognise, understand and 'work through' such feelings, they may find it extremely difficult to face the future with their child. Only when they have come to relate to him normally as parents can they hope to help in relation to his illness.

This was clearly illustrated recently when one of our caseworkers was asked by the medical social worker at the maternity hospital to visit a mother who had just gone home after the birth of her fourth child, who was a mongol. She was warmly received by the mother who felt she had no knowledge of how to handle her child. Throughout the interview she left the baby in his cot and asked for 'instructions' as to how she should handle him. With skill and patience the worker was able to get her to talk about how she had handled and cared for her other three children very competently. In turn she was able to relate this to the needs of the new baby. By the end of the visit the mother was able to verbalise how initially she had only been able to focus on the handicap, but now the worker had helped her to see that the baby had the same needs as all her other babies. Instead of focusing entirely on the handicap, she was now able to see the baby primarily as a person, with the handicap in perspective.

In some extreme cases the parents' self-confidence may be so shaken when they produce a handicapped child whose life expectancy is short that they feel unable to take the baby home from hospital. This child's acceptance into his family then depends on how the parents are told, and the expertise with which the situation is handled. Only too frequently do we see children whose parents rejected them at birth left in long-term hospitals or left to live out their short lives in the care of the local authority.

Even when the handicapped child has been satisfactorily accepted at home, frequent hospital admissions may be necessary. At such times the child has very real and pressing needs (summarised earlier p. 25). Again much help in meeting these needs can be given to him through his family. Often parents and siblings find it difficult to accept that the child needs special hospital treatment which they are unable to give. They need help to understand that this is in no way a reflection on their own care of the child. The importance of keeping the link with home needs to be stressed, and encouragement and sometimes practical help given to enable visiting to be maintained. Particularly when the child is very young, it may be difficult to explain why he needs to go into hospital and he may see it as a rejection. It does not make it easy to maintain the contact if, when the parents visit, he turns away from them because he does not understand why he has been, as he sees it, 'sent away from home'. Skill and patience on the part of the social worker is needed to help parents to understand why their child reacts in such a way and to encourage them to continue visiting until he gradually accepts that they still love him.

Other children in the family are undoubtedly affected by the situation. Younger siblings may be fearful that they in turn may be 'sent away to hospital' and it is necessary, although not always easy, for the parents to help allay these fears both by being honest about the situation and also by not focusing all their attention on the sick child to the exclusion of the other children. Older siblings are sometimes expected to take on responsibility beyond their years either in relation to, or because of, the handicapped child, and it is vital that this situation is not allowed to develop.

The important part played by non-verbal communication, particularly with a younger child, cannot be over-emphasised with parents. Included here is the importance of familiar links with home when he goes to hospital, e.g. special favourite toys, clothes or even a piece of cloth to which he is especially attached. If the child is a little older regular picture postcards from his family can help maintain the link between visits. By working in close co-operation with the hospital staff the caseworkers are able to help parents to understand the need for treatment and encourage them to maintain it. It is often easier for the family to discuss and explore any difficulties with the worker in their own home where they can be encouraged to accept and participate in treatment and care.

As well as help at the emotional level, parents often need practical help. Frequently, for varying reasons, parents do not fully utilise available facilities. With her knowledge of the handling and treatment of illness or handicaps and all the voluntary and statutory sources of help available, the social worker enables the family to accept and use relevant help.

Direct help for the child—from babyhood through to adolescence

However, even from an early age the child can be helped directly from outside the family. The earliest help comes through medical and nursing skills and knowledge and their contribution has been considered elsewhere (chapters 10 and 13). Although this is not within my province, our work must be closely related if the child's best interests are to be served.

It is not surprising that in many cases children with a poor prognosis tend to be overprotected. Whilst appreciating the parents' feelings we encourage them to allow the child to lead as normal a life as possible for his own sake. As he develops the child himself often finds it frustrating if he cannot join in the play of his peers. In the case of an only child, or one where the siblings are considerably older and he is virtually an only child, it can be extremely important for him to have the opportunity of playing with other children. If the child is severely handicapped he may not be able to participate in a playgroup for ordinary children and will only become more isolated. In this case a playgroup for handicapped children can help. Here he has the opportunity to participate at his own pace and at the same time learn to mix and play with other children. In a well run group, where the leader and staff are trained, he is stimulated at the appropriate level by the play material and toys provided. The child has the opportunity to express himself through a variety of media, e.g. paint, modelling clay, etc., and has the scope and facilities for using play materials which may not be possible in his own home, e.g. paint, water, trampaulins. Although this is basically a play experience it is also a learning situation and is the basis for a gradual preparation for school. Some groups termed 'opportunity classes' are being run in conjunction with the schools, and in certain hospitals the importance of play is recognised by playgroups within the hospital setting.

As well as being a preparatory learning situation for school, the playgroup affords the climate in which both mother and child are able gradually to lessen their dependency ties on each other. We are well aware of the tendency for any handicapped child to become overprotected and live too sheltered a life and it is not surprising that this is often accentuated in the case of a child whose life expectancy is known to be severely reduced. It is, indeed, hard for a parent to allow such a child to explore and develop like an ordinary child, but with skilled help she can often accept what is best for the child. Sometimes it is the fear of the unknown that prevents a parent from allowing the child to join the playgroup. If she is allowed to accompany him initially and the only gradually increase the time during which she leaves him there on his own, this allays her own fears and gives the child the opportunity to develop his independence step by step. The child himself needs to feel secure before he can undertake new things; this can only be accepted if his mother is able to help him towards this end. It is important to remember that a mother with a handicapped child herself needs a break from the twenty-four hour care. It is because of this that it can be helpful if she is not expected to participate in the running of the playgroup, but be free to follow her own devices.

A mothers' group run by the social worker at the same time as the playgroup is in progress can well prove to be most helpful. In this situation mothers feel able to talk about their very real fears in relation to their children. The fact that they have something in common, i.e. a child with a handicap, enables them to talk freely about how they feel. It is important that the social worker is skilled in guiding the group to think along constructive lines, but the mothers themselves all make their individual contributions and gain tremendous mutual help from one another.

We have found from our own experiences that both children and mothers benefit from the pre-school playgroup with a mothers' discussion group attached. The children take a later transition into school much more easily and the parents themselves are more able to accept this big step.

There is sometimes a tendency not to think of the baby growing beyond childhood, but with the vast developments in medical science many illnesses which in the past took their toll in early years, do not do so until later. Bearing this in mind we need to look carefully at how best to help the child in order that he may live his life as fully as possible for as long as possible.

Out of our particular concern with the handicapped adolescent has arisen new knowledge of his very special needs for help at this time, in addition to those common to any maturing young person. It is vital that these needs are catered for if he is to be prevented from simply withdrawing into his family. As he approaches adolescence he can often use, and benefit from, social work in his own right. Sometimes this is best given in the one to one casework relationship with another social worker working with the parent, but increasingly we are finding that the adolescent is often best helped in the group setting which provides the right opportunity for him to discuss objectively his own fears about the future and what it holds for him. He is able to express and work through his anxiety in this neutral situation outside the home. Here he can feel free to air his, sometimes very strong, feelings, without impinging on his own parents who are too closely involved.

Whilst appreciating the adolescent's needs and difficulties we must not forget that the parents may also need considerable help during this difficult transition from dependence to near independence. Although the teenager with a handicap needs special help we do not lose sight of the fact that he (or she) is going to have to hold his own in society alongside those without a handicap. Because of this we must try, right from a very early age, to help him integrate into society. This can start in a playgroup situation where even if it caters specially for handicapped children, able-bodied brothers and sisters can be included. Later, if it is possible, he may be taught in an ordinary school alongside ordinary children. As an adolescent he can mix with others on a social basis at a PHAB Club, that is, one for both physically handicapped and able-bodied.

Facing reality

Whilst stressing the importance of integration into the community as far as possible, we must not lose sight of the reality situation. There will be things that a child with a life-shortening illness is unable to attempt or achieve, and we have to help him to face this and to channel his interests and capabilities more appropriately. Remembering that every child is an individual and that every individual has his rights and needs we must endeavour to help him on an individual basis.

The advances in medical science make it a constantly changing scene and we have to be adaptable. Honesty and sincerity to the patient, whatever his age, is of the utmost importance. It is only if this honest relationship is established, and he can trust what is said and done to him, that he has the opportunity of facing the situation realistically. At every stage all who are in contact with him must remember not to underestimate his degree of comprehension and, with this in mind, respond to both his physical and emotional needs as fully as possible.

10   The role of nursing staff in helping the hospitalised child[1]

Janet Duberley

What are the fears that face a child when he is admitted to hospital? Even if his mother and father have prepared him for his admission he may still be very frightened when that awful day arrives.

The building itself is unfamiliar with its long corridors, mysterious doors, furniture, instruments and odd smells. He is wary of the number of nurses wearing different uniforms, people in their white coats who could be doctors or porters: the hustle of hospital life and in general the noise that issues forth from any children's ward. Coming from home, where he is used to mother and father and perhaps one or two siblings, to a large room, where children of different ages are shrieking and running about, may in itself frighten the child, and may make him feel insecure so that he clings to his mother or father. Having to remove one's clothes to be weighed and measured may also be unnerving especially if there are other children and parents in the bathroom. Meal times might seem a nightmare, sitting at a table with children of varying age groups; the fear of being given something one does not like and having to eat it. The distraction of toddlers feeding themselves and each other may to some children be amusing, but to more sensitive children very upsetting. As the day wears on he wonders when mother and father will be going, how it will be when they have gone and when they will return. Has he really got to sleep with all those other children and babies? Will the babies cry during the night and wake him up? Please can he go home tonight and come back in the morning to see the doctor? He would much rather sleep in his own small bedroom where there is no noise to disturb him and where he can turn to mother and father if he is frightened.

The child's fears are influenced by any fantasies he may have. He may have watched television programmes about hospital life, or have been threatened with hospital if he misbehaves himself, so that he

122

thinks of it as a place of punishment. Relatives young or old may have been admitted to hospital and not returned: where do they go? People go to hospital to have operations, injections and to die.

How can one overcome these very real fears of the child and thereby make the ward a happy and secure place for him while he is ill and in need of hospital treatment? Not all children have these fears. Those who are ill and suffering great pain may not be as frightened by the environment as by their illness. A child in status asthmaticus, or severe congestive cardiac failure, may feel so ill that he is beyond caring what is done to alleviate his symptoms. However, on recovering, fears may well come alive, especially if certain morbid expectations, such as the receiving of painful injections, have been confirmed.

It is important for the nursing staff to be aware of these fears and to recognise them. In some ways, children who are acutely ill present the least psychological problem: however, as will be discussed later, this does not apply to their parents. It is the children who are least unwell that are probably most vulnerable to psychological trauma, particularly if they are admitted for elective procedures. The danger is that they may come to look on a hospital as the place that makes you ill. Contrary to apparent needs, it is essentially with children in this group that the nurse must establish a personal relationship, thereby gaining their confidence.

This may be done by greeting the child by name when he arrives on the ward, and by talking with, and not at, him. I usually get the child to tell me why he has come into hospital, what he thinks about hospitals and if he, or any of his brothers and sisters, have been in hospital before. Through such a conversation I can assess his level of comprehension, and the way in which he uses speech and language. This makes it easier for me to find words that he will understand. With such words I then try to tell him as exactly as possible what is likely to happen to him while he is in the ward. I tell him when his mother, father, brothers and sisters can come and visit him, and in the course of such a conversation the child is able to ask questions about the things that worry him. He may volunteer his likes and dislikes particularly of food; he may not be English and therefore unused to a typical ward diet, in which case arrangements can be made for mother to bring in food from home. By constantly addressing the child by name both mother and child become aware that I am truly interested in him. Mother may prompt him helpfully, but it is unusual for her to butt in and take over the conversation unless there is an underlying psychiatric disturbance. This conversation is very important as it is the beginning of a rapport between child and ward sister. He feels that he is important, and that the ward sister trusts him. They are beginning to find out about each other.

At this point attention may be turned to mother. She is shown where her child's bed is and is able to put away his belongings in his bedside locker so that she takes possession of his corner on his behalf. It is not necessary to introduce a new child patient to other children in the ward, as by this time they are all too eager to find out for themselves who the new boy or girl is. This moment must be watched as it may be rather overwhelming, and it may be necessary to single out one or two of his own age group who are more likely to befriend him.

The first indication that the child will really stay in hospital comes when he is asked to undress. This is therefore a very delicate moment. It could be a very traumatic experience for him suddenly to be undressed, bathed, dressed in strange clothes and put into bed. Whenever possible it is better for the child to keep his own day and night clothes whilst he is in hospital, the psychological gain being well worth the extra trouble. Mother should be encouraged to do as much as possible for her child. She may weigh him, preferably at bedtime, if there is no urgency, as this allows him to settle in his new environment, before having to remove his clothes. Many children over the age of five years have been weighed and measured at school, and are quite pleased to show mother and nurse how to set about the procedure.

If mother is unable to stay with her child all day, she is asked if she will return in the evening, so as to prepare her child for bed, and to remain with him until he is asleep. It is of course preferable that mother should be with her child all day, but this is not always possible; not all hospitals have sufficient facilities for resident mothers, and not all mothers are able to remain with their children even if the facilities are available.

It is very important in the organisation of a general paediatric ward to ensure that the individual personal relationships built up through the admission procedures between the child and his nurse are not allowed to lapse. It is tempting to pay more attention to the very ill or very young patients at the expense of the older ones who may seem to be more independent. The nurses may feel very guilty about simply sitting and talking to a child. They are inclined to feel that they are only achieving something for their patients if they are actively doing something for them. One may have to campaign from time to time that nurses do not merely cope with the physical needs of a miserable homesick two- to four-year-old but that they must take time to hug and comfort him, and, if necessary, rock him to sleep.

The ward in relation to the hospital

There are several problems that arise when a children's ward is part of a General Hospital. Nurses in training are obliged to spend part of their time, a minimum of eight weeks, nursing sick children, and, although most enjoy their experience, there may be some who feel that this is a difficult, even frightening, time. They may have unresolved anxieties from their own childhood or, at a quite simple level, they may be unable to converse with and nurse young children. The nurses require constant support and encouragement from a full complement of trained staff. Senior administrative nursing personnel in the hospital must be aware that there may be special needs in a children's ward because of this, and extra nursing requirements. This may cause misunderstandings unless there is proper liaison.

The ward

Duty rosters must be carefully arranged in order to ensure that the children are allocated to the care of the minimum possible number of nurses. In this way the children will learn when to expect 'their' nurses during the twenty-four hour day.

Convalescent children running about the ward, perhaps disturbing the more sick children may create quite a nuisance. Physical grouping can make a lot of difference; one or two lethargic children placed between two 'fire brands' may in such a situation prove sufficiently enlivening for their neighbours without disturbing the ward.

There are certain pitfalls in the everyday care of children on a ward whatever their illness. Contact with the family must be maintained. Some parents withdraw from reality, and sit back whilst the nursing staff care for the physical needs of their child. Parents should be encouraged to become involved in the nursing of their children, to wash and feed the child instead of standing by and watching the nurse. Some sense of continuity and reality must pervade the ward and its activities, as otherwise the whole experience could become frightening and unreal, and the child withdraw from reality.

It is most important that the child does not become bored for it is then that his security is threatened. Children may become lethargic and sullen if they are bored or they may become noisy and uncontrollable. As nursing staff are largely concerned with the actual day to day care of the sick children, other staff also work with them on many children's wards, for example, the play therapist. As well as assisting with painting and model making, she may help those children who wish to re-enact their experiences in hospital. Just as small children at home play 'Mothers and Fathers', children in hospital play 'Nurses and Doctors' and it is surprising how accurate they are in their interpretation of the roles. In my experience the most popular situations are the administration of general anaesthetics and intravenous injections. It is important that such 'play' is encouraged, as children are able to express and overcome their fears in this way. To make play more realistic in our hospital a sister's uniform, several nurses' uniforms, and doctors' white coats are available in miniature sizes for dressing up. Play comforts the child in other ways, by making the hospital environment more normal. Perhaps this should be the essential function of nursing staff in helping the hospitalised child — to make an otherwise strange and challenging environment into one as comfortable and consoling as possible.

Note

1 I would like to acknowledge the encouragement given to me in writing this chapter by Dr Eva Frommer, Consultant Child Psychiatrist, St. Thomas's Hospital, London.

The psychiatric care of children with life-threatening illnesses

Roy Howarth

This chapter is concerned with what very sick children think and feel about their illness, how they behave, and how they can be helped if they are distressed. A specialist in psychological problems may act as part of a team of doctors, nurses and social workers discussing whole-family problems, or ward and out-patient policies. The children's psychiatrist, in particular, has knowledge of children's ways of thinking and their emotional reactions, and has developed experience in relating to children. With these skills he is sometimes asked to advise because a child is showing some uncharacteristic behaviour, or emotional reaction, while ill, or in hospital. Often staff are already wondering how much the child knows about his illness; whether he knows the illness is serious or even fatal, and if this is the cause of any psychological upset he may be showing. But obviously children vary in their understanding of death and dying depending on their age and experience. Also there are many other more common reasons for sick children to show emotional upsets, for example, as a reaction to their parents' own behaviour, or the events surrounding the onset and development of the disorder, or to the child's misconceptions about his symptoms.

Social workers and doctors in various parts of the world have documented their experiences of looking after the physical and emotional welfare of children with life-threatening diseases. As Dr Burton has already stressed (chapter 2) some advocate telling the children the name of their illness and their outlook for the future; others maintain that this information should be kept from the child so that he will not become upset or depressed. The different approaches tend to be used in different settings, and what works out well under one set of circumstances for some people is clearly not appropriate for other workers in a different situation. Whatever the conditions, the child's parents obviously must take part in deciding these issues and give their approval to a particular approach, even if they need a great deal of support in order to take an active part in the child's care. When you get down to it, each fatally-ill child and his family have to be known extremely well by their medical team, so that each can be given the most appropriate help in their particular circumstances.

However, in addition to knowing the individual child and his family, there are general guidelines about psychological management which can be drawn out from the slowly growing knowledge about children's concepts of, and attitudes towards, illness and death. There is a gradual appreciation of the meaning of death during childhood, until by the age of nine or ten years the universality, physical finality and permanence of death is comprehended by all children. By about this same age of pre-adolescence the implications of chronicity of disease and disorder seem to be realised also. Younger children, when ill, tend to be most concerned about separation from parents and home when in hospital, or about whether their symptoms or treatment will hurt, or whether their body will not be the same after the illness—worrying that it might be damaged, scarred or in some way look or function differently. In addition to these worries, after about the age of ten years, children are more likely to be concerned that they might always have their illness or that their life might be threatened by it.

Most children who are ill are upset for short periods in reaction to their symptoms or treatments; some seriously ill children show disturbances of behaviour for longer periods, not just as an immediate response to their unpleasant experiences. Sometimes these children's longer periods of disturbance can be attributed to repeated episodes of physical distress, so that there is perhaps a build up of anxiety and upset, without the chance to recover fully before the next unpleasant experience. Under these circumstances children have been observed to become increasingly anxious and agitated, and finally lapse into a depressed withdrawn state.

The other frequent cause of prolonged emotional upset is the disturbance in family behaviour which sometimes accompanies serious sickness in one of the children. The stress on family members shows itself in the physical and emotional symptoms of the parents and the other children at these times, and in the changes in relationship between the parents—some quarrelling more and others quietly withdrawing from one another. The results of these stress responses are changes in the psychological atmosphere of the family, and, in particular, changes in the ways in which the parents and others behave towards the sick child. Some children are especially sensitive to these changes.

There is a great deal of concern about how much these children know about their illness, what they think is happening to them and what they believe will happen in the future. At the same time some workers believe that a large proportion of the children become aware of the seriousness of their state without always letting this be known overtly, while other workers in the field suggest that this is not the case. The apparent discrepancy in opinions probably occurs because of the use of the concept of awareness; it being assumed that there are degrees of awareness of one's state. However, a child is either aware that he has a life-threatening disease or he is not; and if he does know his illness is fatal, it is more important whether he believes it, or whether he uses some psychological mechanism to put the knowledge 'out of his mind'. A more useful approach is to consider what various symptoms and treatments mean to each child, how he sees himself with his illness in relation to other people, and what predictions he makes about the future course of the disease.

Young children may categorise their illness by the type of symptom and treatment experience they have; that is—by what happens to them in the form of changes of appearance, functioning, and other people's behaviour towards them. The meaning of these experiences for each individual child varies with his age and stage of maturation, and also with the type and extent of previous similar experience. On the basis of what illness experiences he has had in the past, he will make sense of his present experiences, and try to anticipate what will happen to him at least in the near future. Of course one of the ways for a child to speed up the process of making sense of his present experience is to ask parents and others in authority what is happening to him, or for him to be given information by them spontaneously. He can then test out the information given against the evidence of his senses, and knowledge of what has occurred previously. On this test will depend whether the information-giver can be trusted or not for future discussion about his illness. As Dr Mennie has observed in the context of preparing the child for a painful procedure (chapter 4, p. 49) it is always necessary to be honest, factual and consistent about the information you do give, even when you are deliberately withholding some of your knowledge about the child's state, and the likely future course of the disease.

A child learns about his illness then by what he is told and what he otherwise gleans from the behaviour and attitudes of those around him; and he makes sense of this information by relating it to what has happened to him in the past in this and previous illnesses. In practice there is a variation in the amount children are told about their illness by doctors, nurses and parents. This depends partly on the policy adopted by the people in charge, but also partly on the type of illness. For example, I have found that children with cystic fibrosis often learn a great deal about the disease, as explanations of the pathology often accompany the discussion of medication, dietary care and physiotherapy given by the physician to the parents. On the other hand, children with leukaemia are told very little about their disorder, and so are more reliant on other ways of understanding what is happening to them. Considered in this way there is some evidence that the majority of children with cystic fibrosis predict their illness going on in much the same way as it has already, with a few of these children becoming depressed and pessimistic as they get older. Children with a more acute life-threatening disease like leukaemia, however, show greater variation in their predictions, perhaps as a result of having to rely more on their own assessment of their progress in the light of their relapses and remissions. A small number of children with fatal disorders predict that their illness is getting worse. This does not mean that they believe they are going to die, but the possibility of their illness being fatal is more likely to be considered by those over the age of nine or ten years who are predicting deterioration in their state.

It is obviously important to know whether there are any be-havioural signs in these children which accompany their underlying knowledge or anxieties. Change of usual behaviour pattern seems to be the most useful indicator of this sort of stress. There may be questions about other children's treatment or symptoms; they may show concern about other children (hiding their own self-concern); occasionally they may talk of death—usually of others or in general, rather than in relation to themselves. One twelve-year-old boy who had realised he was very ill, changed gradually from being a quiet, fairly studious boy, to showing difficult aggressive behaviour at home and at school, with periods of withdrawal, as well as outbursts of temper. Another twelve-year-old boy had a friend with the same serious disease. His friend died but he was not told of this, he just did not see him any more, and no one mentioned him for fear of causing distress. He became very clinging to his mother, made no further friendships, and was more demanding, and behaved generally more like a much younger child. A younger boy, aged seven years, with severe chest disease had been difficult to deal with at home and in hospital, partly because he had always been given his own way. Getting him to co-operate in his treatment was particularly difficult; but in the terminal phase of his illness he became very compliant, accepting and swallowing tablets eagerly, clutching the oxygen tube to his face mask and accepting the physiotherapy he used to rail against.

A nine-year-old girl who learned that she had leukaemia was very talkative and excitable, began to talk of others dying and pets dying, and when the disease relapsed later she became very quiet and subdued, becoming agitatedly anxious when she had to go into hospital.

A ten-year-old girl, full of life, bounce and intense curiosity about everything, realised after a series of hospital admissions that her illness was getting worse, and became apathetic, no longer interested in anything and just did not want to talk to people or discuss herself and her situation.

What can be done to help these children?

Parents and family atmosphere

Parents' mental anguish clearly has an effect on the children, not always directly but usually by the changes in relationship between themselves and in their behaviour towards the child. There is an associated danger that other members of a family with a very seriously ill child will become isolated, not only from friends or relations outside the family, but also from one another within their own family. The result is sometimes a further increase in tension between family members, or a gradual withdrawal from one another. As Audrey McCollum so ably points out (chapter 15, p. 177), a skilled social worker will often be able to mitigate these effects with consequent improvement in the sick child's emotional state. The parents need to know that both you and they can do some things to help their child, to keep him comfortable, and support him through difficult times.

Repeated physical distress

There are two ways of helping children who suffer repeated unpleasant physical experiences. One is to render the experiences as little distressing as possible by adequate sedation and general care during the periods of unpleasant symptoms or upsetting treatment procedures. The other main way of reducing the child's emotional stress is by giving him some explanation of his experiences, so that he is better able to make sense of what goes on; in addition these explanations can be coupled with some hope of alleviation and improvement in the future, so that he dares to anticipate the future to some extent and can do so without despair. But before being able to give explanations and reassurance to the sick child, the doctor

131

must have established some approach to him and formed a relationship with him. Often signs of emotional upset have already become
apparent and the paediatrician asked for a child psychiatrist's
advice. In this case it is wise to see the child on his own familiar
ground—either at home, or in a hospital ward to which he is
accustomed, or in the children's outpatient clinic he usually
attends. In this way the association of the psychiatrist or social
worker with the rest of the paediatric team is confirmed, and there
can be a natural approach to the child's feelings about his state,
through discussion of his physical symptoms and treatment in the
first place. It often seems helpful to explain to the child that the
people working in the hospital are interested to find out what
children of different ages and with different symptoms think and
feel about their illness and coming into hospital.

An introduction on something like the following lines is often
appropriate:

'I am one of the doctors here, working with Dr .... I see many
of the children who come to the hospital with all sorts of
illnesses, and they tell me what it feels like being ill and being in
hospital. Some children when they are ill are sad, or worried
or upset, and some are not. We know a lot about how to make
people better and how to keep them comfortable, and we
would also like to make sure that children do not get too sad or
upset by coming to hospital and having treatment.

We need to know what children think about being ill and
having to come to hospital; what they like and don't like, what
upsets them and what doesn't.

Can I ask you what you think about it all?'

Here are a few of the sorts of questions, or areas of enquiry. Each
is mainly useful as a stimulus for the child to talk around; and his
attitudes, ideas and feelings about the things that seem to be
important to him, should be brought out particularly.

How long have you been coming here?
Why do you have to come here?
When did it all start?
How did it start?
How can you tell you have an illness?
Has the doctor told you anything about it? or the nurse—or
your mother or father? .... or, did you get any idea what was
wrong with you when the doctor spoke to your mother or father?
What did they say?

What do *you* think caused your illness?

What happens inside you to make these ....(symptoms)?

What sort of things do you have to have done here? (blood tests, medicine, etc.)

What other things do people have to have done to make them better sometimes?

Have you been ill before?

When? What sort of illness?

Have other people in your family been ill much?

Mother? .... Father? .... Brothers? .... Sisters? ....

What about friends, or children you know at school?

Who is your best friend?

Who else do you play with?

What do you like doing together when you are not at school?

—and from here a general enquiry about his emotional life and relationships can be made in the usual way.

Most young children seem to think of their illness in terms of the bits of experience which go to make up the whole picture which we as doctors recognise as a particular disease and its treatment. So when trying to find out what the child feels about his present state it is necessary to enquire about the sorts of illness experiences he has had recently, his understanding of them, and his emotional responses to them. With this information as a baseline it is possible to make comparisons with what has happened to him in his illness prior to this recent period, and perhaps more importantly to gain some idea of his predictions about the future, at least as far as the next few months are concerned. These enquiries can either be made very informally for the clinical investigation of an individual child, or can be systematically recorded using a standard form of enquiry for research purposes.

The questions children ask

Although they tend to divide their illness into its component experiences—older children often like to have a name for the disorder—something they can call it when talking to others. If the disease is inevitably fatal in a short time, then it is doubtful whether the real name should be used, unless the parents, on careful reflection of all the issues, wish to be totally open about the disease and its implications. If the name is used, almost inevitably the older child will find out all about the illness from books or other people—so you might just as well give the information yourself and maintain the child's

133

trust in you. The alternative is to use a descriptive label which covers at least some of the pathology, so that the child can identify himself with his illness, e.g. various forms of anaemia, instead of leukaemia.

Is it serious?
Am I going to die?

The information you give should depend on what you know of the child and his family—how much he and they can take, and also depends on what you know you can give honestly and consistently and are able to follow through with social and psychological support and guidance to the child and his family. For most paediatricians and social workers, working with limited resources of time and personnel, this means avoiding giving the whole truth about the disease to the child (although the parents must be told immediately after the diagnosis is made).

A good deal of knowledge must be given to the child too, in order to help him to maintain trust in his doctor and others. This can be done by promoting the idea of chronicity of his illness. The idea is gradually conveyed that this is not a disorder which can be treated and then is all over, but is one that can be controlled—has an up and down course, needing hospital and medicine sometimes, and for as long into the future as you can foresee. This allows the child to make predictions which will be fairly accurate and so relieves eventual anxiety—although there may be a period of anxiety and depression while he adjusts to this view of himself with a chronic disease.

Children rarely ask outright if they are dying, or will die from their illness. More often they will make testing-out statements about death, or ask searching or leading questions about other people's illness. Just occasionally a junior member of hospital staff or a parent may be confronted directly with a statement like 'I'm going to die' or a question 'Am I going to die?' Then you have to be prepared with some comments to make so that you are not forced into an obviously defensive avoidance of the subject. First of all you have to take into account the child's age, for the younger ones may have a very different concept of death than yourself. So for young children it is often a good idea to counter their statement with a question about what they mean by dying. When you are satisfied you know what the young child means (and in the case of older children you may not need to enquire), it is probably wise to say something like:

'You must be very worried about your illness to start thinking about dying. I know a lot of children do worry at times. Things must have been happening which make you think you are not getting better. Obviously your illness is more serious than perhaps you thought at first. When we get ill most of us just expect we will have some medicine or some other treatment, and then in a week or two we will be better. But some illnesses do go on for a long time; and some aren't ever really over and you have to keep taking medicine from time to time to keep you well. You have got a disease a bit like that. Sometimes you will feel not too well and have to have treatment, and perhaps be in hospital. At other times you will be very well, at school and doing all your usual things. You must get very fed up about it and sometimes feel annoyed that the doctors are not getting you better quickly, and at times you probably feel a bit hopeless and can't imagine that soon you will be feeling much better again. That's probably how you feel now, isn't it?'

In order to avoid a general prescription of management measures for all children with fatal disorders, it is necessary to base one's own approach to the child, and any suggestions one wishes to make to other staff and parents, on an assessment and thorough knowledge of the particular child and his family. Such an individual approach means that the child must be seen regularly, so that one gets to know him very well and establishes a personal rapport with him. This goes beyond the usual sympathetic and kindly manner which most people have towards sick children, and implies that the doctor develops a respect for the child as a person, a knowledge of his temperamental characteristics, and his reaction to previous experiences, so that it becomes possible to predict how he will react to similar or new events.

The day-to-day practical implications of this individual approach are that one is taking an interest in things of importance to the child, his pets, hobbies, school activities and friends; and remembering his birthday or other important events. But more importantly, one is constantly trying to see events and experiences from the child's point of view and keeping alert to the child's ways of expressing feelings of unhappiness, discomfort or anxiety. Let the child know you understand how he feels and give him the chance to talk about it if he wants to. For example, you might say 'You seem a bit down-in-the-dumps today' or to the child who is obviously anxious in hospital 'It's sometimes a bit scaring at first when you come into hospital—you wonder what's going to happen'. He may go on to say what is particularly worrying him—or it may be necessary to talk clearly and simply about what you know of his treatment as far as the immediate future is concerned. Anticipation helps prevent undue anxiety and distressing misconception and fantasies. This can be achieved by telling children about changes in their medication and other treatments, or the need to come into hospital, or in preparation for specific surgical procedures.

Discomfort or pain should not be denied; do not say 'Don't cry, it doesn't (or won't) hurt', or 'Big boys don't cry', or 'It's only a prick'—But rather 'I know it hurts a bit—I'll try to make it quick and hurt as little as possible' or 'We are going to do—such and such—nothing more—sometimes children think we are going to do much more (or keep doing it for a long time)—but we are not'.

Some children are clearly anxious about intravenous transfusions and it may be necessary before or during the transfusion to search out their particular worry—'Many children get upset when they have to have a blood drip—and sometimes they tell me its because they think it will hurt all the time'. The child may agree, and he can be given some reassurance that if it is uncomfortable he can say, so that someone will relieve the pain. He may say that is not the reason and give some other reason for his anxiety—like worrying where all the blood goes to, or not wanting other people's blood in him, or may mention that 'Johnny (who died) had a blood transfusion, didn't he?' You may have to say 'Many children, with all sorts of illnesses have transfusions, and you are not like Johnny'—or discuss the other anxieties in a simple, truthful and realistic way.

If you suspect that a child has some worry about his illness or treatment which he cannot talk about, it is sometimes useful to describe to him a boy or girl of about the same age telling him of the feelings this child had about similar symptoms or procedures, and what the doctors and nurses did about it. This may help the sick child to acknowledge openly that he has been feeling like the child referred to and enable him to ask further questions about his own specific situation.

If by these means a child begins to make sense of what is happening to him, especially if he feels he has some say in, and control over, what goes on, the anxiety is usually alleviated. However, the mixed feelings of anger and dependency which he has been feeling towards those who have seemed to impose their will on him may still be expressed in some way, and may disturb his relationship with his parents and hospital staff. These emotions need to be accepted by someone who is able to discuss them with the child while showing that he is neither put off by the anger, nor over-involved because of the dependency.

The nature of the predicament of these children, who are likely to die before even the minimal fulfilment of their life, is such that some degree of denial of the information they receive about the seriousness of their state is probably inevitable in order to continue to cope with their remaining life. For those who have grown to know these patients without being blinkered by cold detachment or blinded by an emotional over-involvement, it is possible to see where denial should sometimes actively be encouraged in order to maintain mental as well as physical comfort.

Part IV

Helping the family

12 An interdisciplinary approach to the dying child and his family

Bianca Gordon

Hospital personnel and the dying child

Death has always been an enigma to human beings; it is a mystery with which everyone is inevitably confronted. When the loss is that of a child, there is, in addition, a deep sense of sadness and regret about the incompleteness of the life and the many things that will remain for ever undone. Whatever the age, duration of illness or cause of death, the ending of a young person's life is not only a shattering tragedy for the parents but an acutely distressing event for the physicians and nurses who have looked after him in hospital.

The care of the fatally ill child is one of the most difficult tasks for the hospital staff. It has an immediate, powerful and often lasting impact on their work. In many respects the reactions of the staff are similar to those of the parents. They too are anxious about death; they may have feared, or experienced, the fatal illness of a close relative or friend. Indeed some may have chosen their profession because of a similar event in earlier life. One of the fundamental and most widespread responses to dying and death is the fear of loss and of being abandoned. It is based on the deep-rooted fear of pain, separation and the unknown. Those caring for the dying child are in no way immune from these anxieties and unless they know how to handle their own, it will be difficult for them to deal with those of their patients.

The purpose of this chapter is to discuss the problems which face hospital personnel in their efforts to help the dying child and his family.

The views are based on interdisciplinary work within Well-Baby clinics, paediatric and obstetric departments and multi-disciplinary and inter-hospital study groups[1] on the effect of illness and hospitalisation on children.

The common aim of these undertakings was to help provide for the needs of sick children and their parents and to help staff towards a better psychological understanding of their day-to-day tasks. These undertakings emphasised the essential need for discussion and co-operation among the various professional disciplines involved in the care of the patient, so that the widely adopted practice of treating body and mind as separate entities should be replaced by the recognition of the patient as a whole person. In particular, we were concerned that the physical and emotional needs of the sick child and his family be met by joint interdisciplinary efforts of total care.

Clearly the work of those entrusted with the care of a sick child depends for its effectiveness on the extent to which the mind and personality of the young patient and its interrelationship with his physical health is understood.

Unfortunately, present-day medical and nursing training tends to see this task as relating only to the care of the body. Yet, sick and dying children are extremely dependent on emotional support based on sustained contact. It is a terrible shock for them to find that suddenly their body is not their mother's concern, but that of a stranger, and that at a time when their emotional need for her is greatest. The child cannot understand why his body has to be looked at, handled and sometimes hurt, when a sympathetic personal relationship with those who are to care for him has not first been established.

When thinking about the difficulties encountered in the care of children during terminal illness, one starts with the realisation that hospital is a highly organised structure orientated towards saving life and curing. Roles and responsibilities are well defined to maximise success in these life-saving efforts by the hospital team. Any encounter with death is therefore experienced as the antithesis of this orientation and frequently evokes a sense of personal inadequacy and defeat. As a paediatric ward sister said:

'The most difficult part of the management is the actual dying of the child, from the point at which active treatment ceases, because this is when you know that you have lost the battle. The process of dying is often long, and the nurses feel utterly helpless, particularly when they can see the child is frightened. You suffer with him when he is coughing and gasping; you know what is happening and you feel that you are prolonging an agonising life.'

Unfortunately most of those whose main aim it is to treat and cure are here confronted with problems for which their vocational training has not adequately prepared them. Death therefore is too often regarded as a battle lost. The accepted roles of nurses and doctors have lost their clear definition at a moment when it is most necessary that their function during this final phase is clear and seen as an integral part of their professional activity, that is that it extends beyond the purely medical function, and that the end of physical treatment should not be the end of their involvement with the patient and his family. Staff will be better able to accept this wider role if they are helped to recognise that their despondency and frustration when active treatment is terminated result largely from feelings of inadequacy, loneliness and isolation in a situation in which all of them tend to search on their own for a solution, instead of drawing together within the unit, which at other times would, as a matter of course, act in collaboration and share responsibility. The stronger their sympathy and concern for the child, the more painful are their feelings.

A death in the ward often brings to a head tensions among the staff. When these reach crisis point and are discussed, it frequently emerges that the death of the child was not the real cause of these tensions, but was the trigger to some other problem of long standing. It helps in these situations to realise that it often proves too difficult to contain the tensions, anxieties and frustrations arising from the care of the dying child. The risk of a crisis occurs at this point, because of a temporary breakdown in the structure of the roles and responsibilities, caused by a situation in which everyone feels greatly affected by the loss of a child, without at the same time knowing what he can and is required to do.

Open discussions in which all concerned can give vent to their feelings should ideally take place as a routine after every death. When through these discussions a mutual understanding has been achieved it is less likely that refuge will be taken in staff conflicts and recrimination. These discussions must be democratic and include all staff. Going over the whole case in its entirety is a most valuable and constructive task.

The problem of caring for the dying child is such that it cannot be managed by individual workers on their own. It must be shared by the team as a whole. Only from collective responsibility will staff members derive the emotional support necessary to cope with the demands of the family and also with their own guilt and self-reproach arising from what they regard as their inadequate endeavours. The sharing of difficulties and anxieties with others at such critical times minimises the build-up of personal and team stresses, and creates an atmosphere in which the individual worker

143

can give the greatest measure of conflict-free energy to the task in hand.

Ideally, a practice of patient allocation should be developed in our hospitals, with the corollary that one or two members of the team should be given responsibility for sustained contact with the child and his family. Those who undertake this role will need additional time to spend with the family and additional skills for this task, which is made more difficult by the absence of guidelines and prescriptions. Further training in dealing with people under stress will have to be offered, with emphasis on the uniqueness of each family. In addition, a colleague with psychological training should be available for consultation. Such training is essential in modern hospitals with their emphasis on specialisation, division of functions and tendency towards an impersonalised service with all its inherent hazards. As it is, such training is sadly lacking in the great majority of our medical and nursing schools, where for some extraordinary reason, it is widely assumed that these skills develop of their own accord.

Staff shortage and frequent changes of personnel make it difficult to put this ideal of patient allocation into practice, although without it there is little chance for the creation of a relationship of trust and security so essential for the dying child and his family. However, not all staff are capable of working in a sustained way with patients suffering from terminal conditions. This has to be recognised and respected. One must also realise that not everybody is able to express sympathy in other than practical ways.

It is generally agreed that the nurses have the hardest task. They become very attached to the children under their care. It is therefore natural that they should suffer considerable distress. Young nurses frequently need to protect themselves against this distress. They may therefore shy away from facing the reality of the child's situation, and will therefore be unable to help him face up to it himself. They are likely to plead that 'they are only children, they would not understand and only be frightened'. Denial may also result in unconscious avoidance of the dying child, and, essential though privacy and quiet are for such a child, care must be taken that these conditions do not cause him to feel abandoned.

That this danger exists is brought out by the comments of a ward sister: 'Junior nurses are often so distressed that they will no longer go into the child's cubicle. In this way they reject the child because they cannot bear to see him suffering.'

Another ward sister expressed much the same thoughts when she said: 'Junior nurses need a great deal of support. They are naturally very frightened of death, and because of their fear they will stay away from the child if they have a chance. They are afraid of the contact.'

A play specialist's remarks show that this problem is not confined to nurses: 'I find that being with the dying child is a terrible strain. You are trying to be natural, but it is hard and needs a great effort. One is sometimes worried and tends to keep away, although I try not to avoid the child.'

One doctor said: 'Dealing with a dying child is even harder than dealing with an adult. You tend to identify more. With an older person you have more distance....When a death occurs the doctor finds he is just a human being.'

One doctor recalled her distress during ward rounds when a dying patient was 'geographically ignored'. 'In terms of the ward rounds', she said, 'the patient was already dead'.

Clearly, there should never be a point during a child's life, however near to death, when it is thought that nothing more can be done for him. When active treatment has ceased, there must be continuing activity around the child, regular efforts to make him comfortable, and friendly words so that he is encouraged to talk when he wishes. During the routine services of the ward, his bed should never be excluded. On the contrary, more time should be spent with him so that he has no sense of isolation.

Privacy and quiet are further needs of the dying child. It is often difficult to provide for these in our modern paediatric wards, which have changed from institutions where life was very restricted to an environment almost too free to give the emotional support and security needed by the very sick child. Often there is too much noise and too many comings and goings. The child's confusion may be heightened in wards where some staff no longer wear uniform.

While there is now growing awareness of the need for continued care after cessation of treatment, the nature of this care is ill-defined, so that it is very often not clear who should be responsible for it. 'Everybody looks upon it as someone else's responsibility....' It seems that there is an almost desperate wish for someone with near magic powers to take over and in this way absolve the staff from the painful and seemingly frightening task.

More research is needed to throw light on children's concept of death. There are vital areas of emotions and mental processes which remain to be explored. However, it is certain that children associate death with sadness, separation and pain. The older ones may actually ask whether they are going to die. It is such direct questions which nurses and doctors naturally find hardest to deal with. Every attempt should be made to avoid fostering uncertainty, as this will only add to the child's bewilderment and fear. He should be

145

encouraged first of all to express what he thinks and feels so that the nature of his specific fantasies and anxieties can be understood.

Often we shall find that his preoccupation is not with death in general, but with fears relating to parts of his body and his environment. They may be very specific. He may be terrified of certain conditions: pain, operations, suffocation. Whatever his questions, much can be accomplished by reassuring the child that everything is being done to make him better. It will help him to be told in some detail about the medical and nursing procedures to which he is being submitted, adding: 'We all work together. We do what we can, and your body does what it can.' In this way the child will be brought to look upon our concern and support as an all-out fight against his disease.

An honest approach to the dying child is a first principle. This cannot, however, be implemented without the consent of the parents. When they oppose the notion that the child should be encouraged to express his worries and that he should be given truthful answers to his questions, the team is faced with a real dilemma.

In the case of twelve-year-old Colin, who was suffering from terminal cancer, the hospital personnel were convinced that he was preoccupied with the fear of dying and felt that he should be given a chance to express his anxieties. His parents, however, refused to discuss the possibility of death with him and insisted that no one else should do so. Concerned about the boy's anguish, the paediatrician considered that the hospital had a moral obligation to take over the responsibility of helping him talk about his fears. Although the staff agreed, their reluctance to act accordingly was striking. All thought that their intervention might widen the gulf between the parents and their son, and each member gave reasons why he should not be the one to take on this responsibility.

Sustained contact with the parents is of paramount importance since it would be insensitive and ineffectual to attempt to impose on them an alien approach to their own child. The aim should be to help these parents to an awareness of their own feelings through their relationship with a member of the staff. They will then be better able to accept what had previously seemed strange and frightening and to establish a relationship to their son which is not affected by their need to deny the reality of his condition.

Sometimes children have confessed that they pretend to be cheerful for their parent's sake because they do not wish to add to their distress. What course should be taken when the child's wish to comfort and protect his parents is perceived? He should then be reassured that he can express his feelings freely to the staff, that they

146

are not afraid of anything he might reveal and that he has their sympathy and support. Given a sustained relationship with one or two trusted members of the team, many children will express their fears.

Such reassurance is as important to the dying child now as it was when, as an infant, he needed an environment that would contain his anxieties and tempers, and provide for his needs without his having to put them into words. While it is natural that parents and staff are anxious to avoid worrying or burdening a fatally ill child, those who deal frankly with questions and anxieties of young patients find that they show a considerable improvement after an honest discussion, and co-operate more in the treatment. Even if the child cries, his initial distress should not be taken as being harmful, but as a healthy response to the encouragement not to suppress his feelings. The stiff upper lip tradition which is so much a part of our culture not only inhibits the show of emotions but also deprives the sufferer of the sympathy he needs.

As hospital staff have not generally been trained to attend to the emotional needs of the dying child, their reactions to this task are entirely natural and must be appreciated. In-service training designed to help them understand the dying child's needs will have to concern itself also with reactions to loss of ego functions during the terminal phase of his illness. In the past he has been proud of his bodily controls; to be in charge of functions such as eating, urination, defecation or washing marked important milestones in his life. Having to surrender the control over these functions to others is experienced as a most painful backward step. Children naturally differ in their reactions to this change. One child may submit without any apparent difficulty; another may fight against his helplessness and suffer from the agonising shame of such physical weakness as incontinence. He is then in urgent need of gentle treatment and reassurance, especially because he may be enabled by these means to retain the self-image of the active and controlled child he used to be. Associated with this is the possibility that when his motor activity is curtailed he may become anxious, angry and aggressive. In his normal life he had adequate opportunities for the necessary discharge of energy. When deprived of mobility he must be provided with outlets for his frustrations through verbal expressions, and — as long as practicable — through suitable play material. The nurse who is called upon to adjust to the child's regression must take on the maternal role of caring for the dependent baby he now is. If she does not understand his changed emotional state, she may take his 'going into a shell' as a wish to be left alone, and withdraw from him. If,

147

however, she is able to appreciate the child's position, she will interpret his lack of verbal communication as an expression of his need for the undemanding love he had been given as a helpless infant. He may want to be talked to without having to answer in words, and be handled lovingly without having to reciprocate. Children, and especially young children, do not readily give verbal expression to their thoughts and feelings, and this is particularly true when they are very ill. It will often be extremely hard for the young nurse to respond with selfless devotion to the needs of the dying child, but it must help her to know that her warm-hearted handling gives him the sense of security he desperately needs.

As his state deteriorates, the child may display anger and hostility towards his parents. Staff are often puzzled and distressed by apparently resentful and aggressive behaviour of the child towards his parents, particularly when there has been evidence of a good family relationship.

Seven-year-old Stephen, who suffered badly during the last stages of his illness, became aggressive and hostile to his loving and gentle parents. They were broken-hearted. When they visited him, he told them to go away: but when they left, he wanted them back. Eleven-year-old Jane was dying of leukaemia. She was a beautiful and intelligent girl with a devoted family and a mother who scarcely left her bedside during the last phase of her illness. Just before her death, Jane leaned forward, looked scornfully at her mother and said: 'I hate you'. She fell back and died without speaking again. Her father collected the death certificate, and that was the last contact between the ward and this family.

The distressed parents could have been helped to bear the shock of their child's hostility had there been someone to explain to them that such uncharacteristic behaviour was the result of pain, fear, frustration and disillusionment with their inability to protect and cure. It would have consoled them to know that it was their love which had made it possible for their child to express these seemingly negative feelings.

If a child patient seldom vents his anger and hostility against the staff, it is because he is less sure of them, frightened of being punished for his temper and petulance and afraid of being abandoned by the very people on whose help he so desperately depends. Had such understanding been conveyed to the parents, their immediate distress might have been alleviated and they would have been spared the haunting agony of imagining that their child died feeling unloved and full of hate towards them. As it was we shall never know what Jane's words meant to her mother, or how they affected her life and that of her other children. Surely, after an occurrence of this kind, the issuing of the death certificate should never be the last contact with the family.

Parents also need sustained emotional support before their child dies. Often this entails a humble admission that in the area of bereavement there are more unanswerable questions than in any other spheres of work. A tacit acknowledgment of this at the outset provides the right basis for our contact with the bereaved.

One of the most important functions of the staff is that of listening sympathetically and of encouraging parents to express their thoughts, feelings and fears freely. Yet, the ability to listen, particularly in these circumstances, is very rare. As an experienced sister put it:

'One of the real problems is that we are not taught to listen to what patients and their relatives say. People find it easier to talk, somehow they find listening hard to manage. We must help the staff to realise that patients and their families do need and want to talk to us.'

Similarly, nurses and doctors frequently find that they are at a loss to know what to say to mothers and fathers.

'We doctors feel useless, at the time of crisis words of sympathy are barren. What I find hardest to take is watching each such situation developing as a separate, unique experience, and not having any stock answers, or standard reponses. A great deal has been written about the stages that the dying and the bereaved go through. Though it may be instructive to know about these, it does not help you when you have to deal with parents at these times.'

A paediatric ward sister said:

'I find it extremely hard to deal with the weight of sorrow imposed on the parents. You know you must be available to them, but this can be an ordeal from which it is natural to retreat when you, too, feel shattered. It is so hard to know what to say to them, once there is no hope.'

Like their child, parents also need continuous contact over this sad period with a minimum number of staff, for an effective personal relationship cannot be established with a large number of people. Parents simply do not have the strength to discuss their child's history and condition with members of the staff who do not already know the facts.

149

Only sustained contact allows them to feel free to ask the numerous questions that preoccupy them, and they must have sufficient confidence in the honesty of the replies to feel secure in revealing their thoughts and worries. Furthermore, some parents may turn against the helping figures, voicing antagonism to the hospital, or criticism of the professional competence of the staff. However wounding this may be, such reaction must be both tolerated and actively encouraged as it signifies an important effort to cope with their problem. As one doctor said: 'The relationship with the parents has to continue even if the doctor is rejected, because it is he who has told the truth about the nature of the illness'.

It is vital that the situation be seen entirely from the parents' point of view, and that no attempt be made to put their remarks into a wider perspective. The helping figure should not attempt to convince them that their grief is excessive or disproportionate to the circumstances. Neither must there be an attempt to comfort the bereaved by asking them to count their blessings, to be soothed by memories of the past, or to take stock of their hopes for the future. A mother who has lost her eldest son aptly said, 'We have our other two children and they are wonderful, and I know there are families who have lost an only child. But what can I do? Each finger that is cut off hurts unbearably.'

At this time parents are too distraught to feel that they can possibly be helped to cope with their grave loss. Rarely do they, therefore, ask for psychological help at this early stage. Occasionally their apathy and wish to withdraw make them even resentful of such an offer. Nevertheless, staff must be available to them in a tactfully unobtrusive manner.

While some families appear to have their own resources to deal with the problem and prefer not to discuss their feelings with outsiders, it is of value to them that help is available, should they wish to make use of it. It has been our experience that most families eventually appreciate the opportunity for such a contact.

The Society of Compassionate Friends was founded precisely because bereaved parents want contact with and support from the community. Their postbag bears witness to the fact that many people are not getting the information and support that they need from professionals. In one group of hospitals[2] parents of dying children are able to see the consultant paediatrician[3] and the psychoanalyst in a special clinic.[4] Priority is given to specific problems, on which bereavement is one. Some mothers and fathers who have attended this clinic commented:

We are trying to avoid self-pity over our loss, yet we have appreciated that our meetings with you gave us not just sympathy, but the co-operation we needed to understand and argue out our sorrow. This is the true meaning of sympathy, and sympathy in this sense is rare.

One couple who had lost their daughter wrote:

The common impression is that at the point of a patient's death, the doctor immediately transfers his attention to the living. It was very comforting at that time to realise that this was a somewhat false impression and that your interest was still maintained even after defeat.

And from another husband and wife:

Of all groups needing help, bereaved parents must be just about the most difficult and very nearly impossible to help. Yet the great value of your work lies in getting parents to talk about their loss, to express their grief properly, and to come to terms with it.

And another mother:

You are of help to parents in getting them to express their grief openly and in encouraging them to talk about their loss, especially to their surviving children, thereby helping them to come to terms with their own grief.

One couple, who continued to vist the clinic for two years after the death of their child wrote:

It was very important to our peace of mind to be able to talk about the tragedy because most people find the situation embarrassing and deliberately avoid you or the subject. It was particularly helpful, therefore, to have discussions such as we had with you, without any such embarrassment, and in the knowledge that we had something in common in that we had worked together as a team during Nicola's illness.... There is no doubt that the special clinic is carrying out a very necessary function and it is of particular comfort to those who, like ourselves, cannot make use of religion to share the burden of their grief.

When considering the needs of families who have lost a child, it is essential to include stillbirths, neo-natal and cot-deaths. These deaths come without warning and are therefore particularly difficult to cope with by mothers who are at that time in a most vulnerable emotional state.

Overwhelmed by grief, they show considerable guilt reactions. 'Why has my baby died? Is it anything I have done? Any infection I have had? Is it because I smoked or because I drank? Have I made him wrong?' They keep hearing their baby cry and complain of a feeling of emptiness. One mother expressed her reaction in these words: 'I feel as if a piece of me had been chopped off, and I have an incessant craving for another baby. Until I have another child, I shall not feel complete.' Another mother developed fainting attacks, the first of which occurred at the cremation of her child.

A mother who lost her twin-daughters felt soon after their death that if only she had had an opportunity to touch them, she could have stood their death more easily. For months she suffered from nightmares in which she saw herself next to the incubators, but unable to get close to her babies.

These early deaths are often treated as though they have not occurred. Here too denial is the most common method by which the staff cope with their own shock and distress. It takes on the form of accepting the prevalent view that the loss will be easier to bear because a relationship between the mother and her baby had not yet developed. Reactions of mothers show, however, that this assumption is entirely incorrect. Staff in maternity units are frequently aware of their lack of training in dealing with these situations. When management problems are discussed a need for guidance is often reflected by the many questions raised.

Who should tell the mother about the death of her baby? When should the news be broken? Should she be given an opportunity to see and touch her dead baby? Should she be put in a room of her own, or will she be helped more by the normal life of the maternity ward?

While it is understandable that guidance is desired on these points, it is not possible to prescribe one single pattern of behaviour and treatment, since this would not take into account important emotional and character differences between mothers. It may well be helpful for one to see her stillborn baby, when another mother may feel persecuted by the guilt-arousing suggestion that she ought to look at her dead infant.

It is vital that in all cases the mother's own wishes should be respected once they are understood to reflect a real inner need, rather than an immediate reaction to the traumatic experience.

As in the paediatric ward, so here, all members of the team can make their contribution through understanding and sympathetic behaviour at a general level, but it should be the specific task of one member of the staff to establish a rapport with the mother,

152

sufficiently sustained, to permit her to express freely her intimate thoughts, feelings and needs. We clearly have a long way to go before such service will be standard practice for all mothers who have lost a baby. If facilities in paediatric wards for giving individual help to parents of dying children are inadequate, those offered to mourning mothers in maternity wards are practically non-existent. As it is, parents are seen in order to discuss the cause of the baby's death and the question of future pregnancies. But there is a sad lack of adequate provision of psychological help for mothers in these circumstances, as well as for the staff who feel that they are not equipped to deal with the psychological problems encountered in their work.

Yet it is widely recognised that unexpressed grief almost invariably has a harmful effect on the future life of the bereaved. It is therefore important for the parents and for their children that they should be able to mourn in the full knowledge of what has happened to them. This aspect of the contact with the child-mourning family is crucial and most difficult to handle.

Parents may require assistance in overcoming their deeply rooted aversion to showing emotion. From early childhood they may have been taught to mask pain, fear, sadness and anger. They were enjoined: 'Don't cry; never mind the pain; don't worry; don't be afraid'. They will have been praised for bravery when suppressing emotional reactions to falls and injuries, being told it was good to be brave, and bad to show weakness and helplessness. The person brought up in the 'stiff upper lip' tradition which applauds the suppression of emotion even within the family, is ill-equipped to cope with the shock, grief and sense of helplessness he feels as a bereaved parent. The effect of such an upbringing seen already to be harmful to the child is equally unhelpful to bereaved adults. It is not uncommon for parents to hide their grief from one another, either because each believes they feel the hurt more deeply: 'It's different for me. I'm his mother', or because each is unwilling to add to the distress of the partner.

People need to be made aware of the therapeutic value of 'a good cry', by which is meant full uninhibited weeping. It is interesting that the importance of giving rein to grief was understood long before modern psychology emphasised its value.

People in acute stress, as during bereavement, tend to bring to the fore earlier traumata or failures. In helping parents to work through the immediate ordeal, it is often possible to help also with the unresolved aspects of earlier happenings.

When prolonged depressive states are encountered or when there is an avoidance of mourning, more intensive psychiatric help is needed.

The degree of eventual adjustment and recovery from the shock of losing a child will depend very largely on parents' freedom to express and to work out their grief and anguish.

The needs of siblings

After the death of a child parents may for some time have no wish to live. This period can be most hazardous for other children in the family. Any help given to parents will naturally extend to their surviving children, whose response to the death, and ultimate recovery from it, will depend on the parent's ability to give them the opportunity to express their feelings about the tragedy.

Some parents are initially reluctant to accept the fact that the mental and emotional welfare of their surviving children should be discussed, and often even show irritation at the staff's concern. While their fatally ill child is still alive, their attitude is: 'Do everything you can for him and don't concern yourself with our healthy children'. They are clearly afraid that the staff's concern will take away attention from the dying child. Moreover, our concern may suggest to them that their other children are also thought to be at risk, and that professional scrutiny may reveal that this is so. Their resistance stems from their own underlying anxiety about the physical and mental well-being of their surviving children. This often comes to the fore after the initial shock of the child's death has been overcome. It manifests itself in an exaggerated concern with even trivial symptoms of their other children, and a tendency to live in fear lest further tragedies might occur. Lacking confidence in their own judgment, they tend to ask for check-ups, and hospital staff must patiently and sympathetically comply with these requests, always bearing in mind the emotional stimulus for their anxiety.

Of greater concern, however, than the physical health is the mental and emotional welfare of siblings, for the effects of bereavement are less obvious, more complex and frequently more far reaching. Manifestations of acute disturbances in siblings can also be seen after stillbirth or neo-natal death. What has happened to the baby the parents had promised to bring home? Why has it happened? Did the child's resentful feelings about his mother's pregnancy and departure lead to this? If these questions remain unexpressed and unanswered, they work to the detriment of the emotional development of the child. Therefore in the wider context of preventive work with the family, it is necessary to consider its needs as an entity.

Much evidence has emerged from psychiatric work with child and adult patients of the destructive and permanently scarring effect of confused and unresolved mourning experiences in childhood. The loss of a sibling or a parent in early childhood is particularly damaging to the development of the bereaved person. This can even apply to a brother or sister who has died before his own birth and who will often continue to be part of the family as a powerful ghost sibling. Indeed, the experience of early loss of a sibling, if left un-resolved, can be revived painfully at critical times in later life—when becoming a parent, during early child rearing, the illness of a child, or the death of a close relative. It is because the inescapable effect of the death of a child can be transmitted by the parents to surviving siblings that it is imperative to take a long-term view when assessing the needs of a child-mourning family.

Notes

1 This work is a contribution by the Hampstead Child-Therapy Clinic, London, to preventive work in community services and is supported by the Grant Foundation, New York.
2 The Woolwich Group of Hospitals, London.
3 Dr David Norris, Consultant Paediatrician.
4 Bianca Gordan 'A Psycho-analytic contribution to paediatrics', *Psycho-Analytic Study of the Child*, vol. 22, pp. 521-43.

George A. Edelstyn

Caring for a child with malignant disease is possibly one of the most exacting tasks facing a doctor. Not only are treatments growing in complexity and scope, requiring constant updating of medical skills, but also the emotional impact upon the patient, his family, and, to a lesser extent, attendant medical personnel requires a sensitivity of handling which does not come easily.

Despite continuing interest in this field, only gradually have I come to appreciate the emotional and psychological problems involved. An unwillingness to intrude, the parents' fears when faced with an apparently non-communicative, remote doctor, the pressures and lack of opportunity for meaningful relationships inherent in the Health Service, combined with the resentment displayed by ward staff when faced with parents needing reassurance, all limited comprehension of the inherent stresses. Once aware of their existence, to continue to regard the disease as the principal problem, and to neglect the coexisting emotional situation, is a restrictive view of medicine quite out of keeping with professional responsibility. It is a withdrawal, or refusal to help, in the greatest tragedy afflicting a family unit.

The situation presents a challenge initially to understand the inherent personal problems and subsequently to evolve a definite psycho-therapeutic role. It is not enough merely to make oneself available for interview—though this is essential. Rather must the doctor decide how best to use the interview to meet the needs, expressed and otherwise, of the parents.

At the outset of treatment the prime need is for reassurance. Both parents must be given the feeling that the doctor is genuinely concerned for their child, that his welfare will be given maximum attention.

To facilitate such feelings the parents should be seen privately in peaceful surroundings. Wards, corridors, or busy waiting rooms are inadequate for such an exchange, as is an atmosphere of noise and bustle, clock watching, a ringing phone, comings and goings. Time must be set aside for the interview, which should be given top priority. Only then can the parents truly believe that they have the doctor's undivided attention, and only then can they be certain that their child, in turn, will receive such interest.

Some previous knowledge of the child, his first name, school, hobbies, brothers and sisters is helpful. Should the doctor have children, this fact can be brought up—that he is a parent implies comprehension of how they feel, and suggests that he will strive the harder for their child.

Obviously the doctor's enthusiasm will be best conveyed, and the initial interview of maximum value to the parents, if it is held at the earliest opportunity, and certainly before definite anti-cancer therapy is commenced. Then the parents' permission can be sought for the ensuing procedures and they can be made to feel collaborators, rather than useless puppets standing by whilst others perform the necessary tasks.

It would seem essential from the outset that parents and child both have total confidence in the doctor's competence, and, whilst the initial interview may take place before all investigations are complete, it serves no purpose to allow the parents to share in medical speculation. Equally it is disadvantageous to convey any lack of information about the individual case, or shortcomings in experience of similar cases. Parents need to feel that their adviser is not only conversant with their child's case, but also with similar occurrences; an aura of competence and self-confidence must be projected.

But not only do parents need to trust their doctor, they must also have hope. Frequently religious faith is tested, if not broken, by the diagnosis, and, as this trust declines, the doctor may have to assume responsibility for maintaining the 'will' to continue. An attitude of optimism compatible with the diagnosis must be projected. Certain reassurances can be given. Cancer is not always fatal, a substantial number of children are treated successfully, and the quality of subsequent life may be indistinguishable from normal.

If parents are given some hope, and are reassured that they have the doctor's total interest, it may be possible for them to grasp something of their child's disease. The magnitude of grief at this point precludes any real comprehension, nevertheless some basic facts must be explained, and always in simple language. Treatment pro-

157

cedures, their discomforts, all the complications must be discussed fully, as must the prognosis. The doctor will do well to remember that every word, gesture, and nuance of expression may be reflected upon, analysed and misinterpreted pessimistically, and miserably, unless abundantly clear. Much unnecessary suffering will be avoided by careful choice of words and a sensitive approach.

Much of what transpires at this first meeting will go unappreciated no matter how carefully explained. Emotional disturbance is such that simple comprehension may prove too much. This is not a reflection of parental stupidity and patience is needed. Questions will be repeated over and over, and yet the answers will not sink in. It is therefore important to have frequent meetings during which the doctor probes to discover just what has been appreciated, and indeed whether such facts are correctly understood.

In addition it is essential to search for other information— evidence of feelings of self-blame and personal responsibility. So many parents believe that the child has been afflicted because of a sin committed by them, either singly or together. The illness may be viewed as the result of something they failed to do for the child, or the end product of some punishment or maltreatment. This point, rarely raised spontaneously, figures largely in the parents' thoughts. It must be brought to the surface early, and reassurance given, or it will burn deep and poison relationships when they should be strongest. Apart from allaying needless stress, such questioning may also bring to light, and reverse, misunderstanding.

One example is that of a four-year-old whose parents noted an abdominal swelling. The specialist considered this a pancreatic cyst and so informed the parents. The word 'cyst' was remembered and, when subsequently a tumour was diagnosed, a cyst became synonymous with syphilis. The impact in terms of marital dissension, suspected infidelity, and consequent responsibility for the child's ultimately fatal disease needs no elaboration. Direct questioning made apparent this misapprehension, but only after weeks of needless pain.

Frequently parents feel guilt for not appreciating the significance of symptoms at an earlier stage, thus believing they have prejudiced their child's chances of recovery. Again, such feelings are usually unexpressed. Early diagnosis is a byword in cancer, and often the child has symptoms common to many a simple condition for weeks or months prior to diagnosis. This bogey must be searched for and settled. Blame may be attached to the family doctor, and indeed even to the hospital, for failure to act with sufficient speed. It must be made clear that childhood cancer is rare, that the average GP in the United Kingdom sees only one new case every twenty years, and that often the symptoms are those of more common complaints. An over-frank, unsympathetic, exposure of possible culpability will not contribute to the situation, nor ease the burden.

Parents may wish to know whether the disease is hereditary, and whether their other children, born or yet to come, are at risk. Again reassurance on this common, but infrequently expressed, anxiety can help, as can explanation about its non-infectious nature. Pain is another worry. No one should suffer continuously, and continued pain constitutes a reflection upon the attention received.

Emphasis has so far been placed on the parents' requirements. But the child also has needs, and as one evolves a philosophy for the parents, so must one consider and devise a method of approaching and supporting the child. 'Common sense' alone is not enough.

What does one say to the child? A difficult question to which there are as many answers as there are children. As Dr Howarth has already outlined (see chapter 11, p. 132) one starts off just by chatting, admiring his toys or hobbies, asking about school, home, brothers and sisters, friends, and any subjects considered appropriate. This preliminary talk should, where possible, take place either prior to admission or immediately thereupon. If before admission the child feels there is at least one friend who knows him, expects his arrival, and will, in all senses, look after him, he will be more at ease.

Once the initial feeling-out process is past both participants are better able to relate. The doctor can then draw out the child, gently and easily. Why does he think he is in hospital, what caused the illness, what does he anticipate in the way of treatment, and, most sensitive area of all, what does he think about the future? Many misconceptions, usually worse than the facts, will emerge. Fears and childhood fantasies can be terrifying enough when there is no reason for their existence. In the setting of a cancer clinic the scope for fantasy is considerable. Such fears can be so easily dispelled by a few words of comforting reassurance, but often no thought is given to the matter, and the unspoken questions remain unanswered.

The young child, possibly up to three years of age, has little concept of the specificities of his illness, and whilst he has clearly defined emotional needs, they are of a more general nature and merely accentuated by hospitalisation. Nevertheless, even some very young children show an unexpected appreciation of aspects of their disease.

Thus, Cluney, four years old, attended hospital weekly as an outpatient for chemotherapeutic injections. Regular admission for planned intensive treatment was necessary. At one stage, although

159

he was reasonably well, glands enlarged at his jaw. Knowing this, he told his parents that he hoped these would be gone before the next treatment day as otherwise he might be kept in—as indeed occurred, despite concerted efforts on Cluney's part to disguise the glands by blowing out his cheeks, hamster-like. Neither parents nor doctor had considered his grasp of the situation to be so well developed. This little boy, incidentally, a lively, talkative member of a large family when at home, during all the time spent in hospital steadfastly refused to communicate with any member of staff, though obediently collaborating with all instructions. In this way he undoubtedly preserved his independence in a strange environment, something earning respect. 'Jocular' remarks by a senior nurse on a ward round to the effect that if he continued his refusal to communicate Mummy would not be permitted to visit reflect an attitude not unique, and which often finds subtle expression in the placing of obstacles in the way of parental visiting and child care. Parents may tend to disrupt normal ward routine and so occasion nursing resentment but this is to the emotional detriment of the patient.

Cluney appreciated the significance of much that went on around him. In this he was not unusual, and great care must be exercised in discussions held within the child's earshot. Much of what is said may be appreciated notwithstanding age, and an appearance of non-comprehension or disinterest. Despite this, facts which would, or should, not be discussed before an adult patient are often freely expressed within the hearing of a child, and great fear or doubt may result. Children expect adults, particularly hospital figures, whom they imbue with considerable authority, to know everything, and the uncertainty which besets any doctor with insight must never be transmitted. Unnecessary preventable dismay is engendered by needless, and confusing, talk of possible emergencies, therapeutic eventualities, and prognosis. Such talk may be misconstrued, and indeed anxiety enhances this probability, so feeding childhood fantasies. Remarks unrelated to the child may cause untold suffering, and every contact must be considered from his standpoint. Knowledgeable discussion with long words should be avoided. The child's intelligence and imagination should never be underestimated, nor his intuition, and powers of deduction.

Hospital admission is disturbing for an adult, despite comprehension of the need for it, and knowledge that life and relationships will normally resume. How much greater is this upset for a small child, who, understanding none of these things, and being accustomed to an emotionally and physically comfortable existence, develops the discomfort of illness and the transference to a hostile environment. How else can he comprehend the needles, operations and immobilisations?

Equally he may fear separation from those upon whom he has grown to depend. Distress so occasioned is often misunderstood by hospital staff and parents, yet comprehension could obviate this very real cause of immediate unhappiness, and prevent later problems.

The first symptom of such fear—protest behaviour—now so well documented, commences upon admission, being characterised by the tears and tantrums of acute dismay. This phase can last up to ten days. Gradually a sense of hopelessness develops, and distress behaviour becomes less obvious. At this point the child's interest in his surroundings, his increasing contacts with hospital staff, his play with toys, are interpreted as recovery, but this is not so. The child is still mourning the loss of his loved ones. Sometimes an element of attachment, often to a nurse, takes place, and, whilst this is to be welcomed in most cases, should staff changes lead to further separations, the child may progressively reject external relationships, becoming absorbed in material comforts. Such a child, often superficially content, is not readily upset by farewells, because he is now more interested in the objects his visitors bring rather than in the people themselves.

Less information is available about parental response to separation from the child at such times. Guilt, arising from feelings of responsibility, allied to helplessness in the face of the child's great nee, compounds the expected reactions within the situation (discussed in more detail by Mrs Gibbons, chapter 9, p. 116).

Much can be done to offset these problems. The greater time the parents can spend with the child, the better for both; the more the parents do for the child, the better for both. Ideally this takes expression in the provision of parent-child units. Not only may the mother or father sleep there, but kitchen facilities enable performance of some domestic duties, thereby creating a semblance of normality. Tasks such as bed-making, administration of medicines, even performance of simple dressings, all constitute good therapy for both partners in the situation, and these activities should be actively encouraged.

Many emotional problems can be avoided by treating the child on an outpatient basis. This may not be possible because of distance, illness, or therapy requirements. Often, however, hospital admission occurs because of thoughtlessness, medical tradition, reluctance to undertake the more complex arrangements, or a desire on the doctor's part to keep his beds occupied, and thereby preserve his status.

Therefore, prior to admission, it is important to critically evaluate all these factors.

When hospital procedures are required, thought must be given to the approach most likely to be accepted, and, if possible, understood by the child. Whatever system be followed, the presence of a parent close by does much to reduce the impact of the ominous towering white-coated strangers.

Whilst it may be preferable to exclude parents from certain diagnostic or therapeutic procedures, in many instances this is unnecessary, unfeeling, and, in the final event, shortsighted, for the child's trustful co-operation is less speedily obtained.

Preliminary explanations concerning procedures should never be omitted or minimised, because the child seems too small or terrified to understand. Whilst this may be the case, so often these reasons are used as excuses by staff, who thereby pursue a technical, rather than an empathetic responsibility. In any case anxious parents will always welcome explanations in comprehensible terms.

In radiotherapy some form of skin markings are common. To the adult such a simple procedure seems to need no explanation, but from the child's standpoint the instrument to be used could be a sharp knife, a pricky needle, or some instrument vicious to an unimaginable degree. Similarly, several shiny steel instruments are used to measure up the child. Whilst they have no sinister purpose, they can look dreadful to the uninitiated, and especially to anyone who has suffered from the depredations of apparently similar weapons.

A simple, and quite convincing method of reassuring the child about the marking-up is to allow him to use the gentian violet stick to draw upon the doctor. They can then play 'noughts and crosses', with the young patient winning! Similarly, one can demonstrate the usefulness of the measuring calipers by allowing the child to determine which staff member has the largest head. Such measures will go a long way towards easing any anxiety the child may have, and thereby greatly assist the staff in fulfilling their roles.

These treatment procedures, without subjective unpleasantness, demand little more than an appreciation of the child's point of view. Others are less pleasant and do involve discomfort, if not actual pain. Despite considerate efforts of staff, this may be impossible to avoid. Yet something may still be retrieved from the situation. None are more acquisitive than junior members of society. A carrot helps. One scheme is to award redeemable tokens—say, one for an injection, two for the taking of blood, three for a difficult dressing, and so on. Regularly during the week an adult, whose responsibility it is to look after 'the shop', exchanges tokens for tiny toys. A 'lucky dip' is a useful alternative. So successful is this scheme that several children on regular courses of intravenous injections (an approach becoming much more popular, and sometimes requiring light general anaesthesia for administration), now submit to their therapy, if not enthusiastically, at least without struggling. Not only is the child easier, and the parents not so upset, but medical staff find the experience much less of a strain and the sometimes difficult problem of placing the needle accurately in a vein is simplified by this lack of protest. Other more obstreperous children are seen, shortly after prolonged shrieking resistance, to be enthusiastically rummaging in the box, to emerge triumphant with their prize.

Incidentally one recalls the seven-year-old, who on being asked what he most wanted replied 'a new set of veins for Christmas'—a gift which would have been appreciated by all.

There is great satisfaction in helping a child to regain life. The medical team achieves a sense of purpose and reward when things run well, even if this is only in the short term. There is pleasure in visiting the leukaemic patient in remission, or examining a rapidly disappearing abdominal mass. Should matters deteriorate, and further attempts at therapy fail, a different situation prevails.

A dying child fills us with dismay. Many factors—the inherent wasteful tragedy of young life lost, the inability of the doctor to live up to trusting expectation, exposure of his professional inadequacy, identification with his own children—produce a failure to visit the child, or to cutting his visit short. It is easy to miss the bed—because the child is asleep, is receiving nursing attention, the parents are there, or what have you. There is real difficulty for many doctors and nurses in overcoming such a situation, but such evasion of responsibility must not happen. Normal routine must not be abandoned, for children are creatures of habit, and rapidly adapt to the hospital patterns. Significant or even trivial alterations are noted, and often correctly interpreted. Whoever else may realise the inevitability of death, the child, I believe, must be spared this final terrible realisation for as long as possible.

Again the approach must be studied, and all staff apprised of the situation. An ill-considered philosophy can jeopardise everything and add to unnecessary irreversible suffering.

Activities in which other children partake such as the hospital school should not be interrupted because of purely practical problems. This aid, discussed elsewhere (chapter 8), is not solely a preparation for the child's future, but carries the implicit suggestion that there will indeed be such a future.

Thus, if it becomes difficult to take the child to the school, then the teacher, and as much of the apparatus as possible, should come to the child.

Everyone, including parents, must co-operate at this difficult time, if the dying child is to spend his last days with as much tranquillity as the situation allows. One three-year-old, whose mother could no longer contain herself, was very disturbed by her uncontrollable bedside weeping. He appreciated something fearful was about, and his anxiety for himself, and for her, was manifest in his repeated questions after she had departed.

An alternative response, the result of anticipatory mourning (discussed in chapter 2), leading to a detachment from the child, must be prevented where possible by counselling the parents early as to the dangers.

If this pattern is established, informed ward staff, alert to the hazard, should draw the doctor's attention to the matter. Indeed, he ought already to be aware through his regular contacts with the family unit. No simple formula can be proposed to help.

Careful, sympathetic, and detailed explanations of the processes are essential, and just what is happening must be made clear.

Implications for the child are considerable in terms of lack of real support at a time of probable physical distress and a growing mental awareness of realities. Thus, at a time when the child's needs are perhaps greatest, parental grief may not only block the possibility of a last significant contribution but actually heighten distress. Even where parental reaction is less extreme, the effect on the parents may be long lasting and profound. If in the final event they feel they have failed the child in his hour of need, how much worse, and how much longer will be the period of their readjustment to reality.

In conclusion, this area of medicine carries a responsibility comparable, if not greater, to that encountered elsewhere. Rapid progress in detail and protraction of therapeutic techniques poses many problems for the doctor who wishes to give optimal treatment. Emotional problems experienced by the patient can be profound and require a studied empathy if they are to be reduced, and distress minimised, both during and after treatment. Interactions within the total family unit can be difficult to detect, potentially destructive, and most awkward to handle. Nevertheless the possibility of long-term negative consequences for the family makes such an effort essential. Attention must be directed towards ensuring that supporting staff are equally aware of the problems, that facilities such as activity rooms, teaching provision, mother and child units, and free visiting are all available. These will not be wasted. Just as important as ensuring the presence of these facilities, is continually ascertaining that restrictive hospital attitudes—which may be encountered in unexpected quarters—do not interfere with their intended use.

In short, therefore, caring for a child with a potentially fatal disease creates for the physician a situation with wide and far reaching ramifications, difficult to manage, but one in which a most important role can be fulfilled, a role which can be discharged with distressing ineptitude, or a remarkable and rewarding insight.

Parents' groups and associations

Mary P. Patten

The mother of a little boy killed at Aberfan wrote that for eighteen months after the ordeal she lived as if in a dream. She was then asked to join with other parents to work for the new community centre. In the midst of this work she found happiness. Before her son's death, her life was centred round her husband and children; now, a new dimension was open for her, that of service to the community.

Many of the associations concerned with the welfare of sick or handicapped children have been founded by parents. In this chapter we look at what these groups have to offer. We discuss some of the practical aspects of setting up a group or running a local branch, so that it is a source of help and meaning to all who work within it. When our little girl was ill, there was an overwhelming feeling of being cut off. Parents were coming and going to the big ward, laughing and talking, and making plans for their children to go home. My brother's son was top of the class, my niece was in the Christmas play, even our youngest child, cared for by a grandparent, seemed more her child than ours, lively, growing, successful. The mother of a spina bifida child called into our side ward on summer afternoons. I could talk to her, because hers was a waiting game as well, and she had already put behind her the major dreams. We talked about such things as hairstyles for little girls who are confined to bed.

Most parents of an ill or handicapped child will gain a great deal from getting to know other parents in the same position. There is a wide range of associations which offer help to parents of children with such illnesses as muscular dystrophy, cystic fibrosis, spina bifida and leukaemia. There are also associations which welcome both relatives and patients since they cater for people who become ill or handicapped in adolescence or maturity. These include the Diabetic Association, cardiac groups, and groups for patients with multiple sclerosis, and those with rheumatic diseases. Some associations are concerned with a range of conditions rather than with one particular illness. These are such organisations as the Council for Orthopaedic Development, or local Associations for the Handicapped, or the young chronic sick. We are not attempting to offer a list of voluntary organisations, because such groups grow, flourish or disappear according to local interest. The people who, normally, can give up to date knowledge of what exists locally, are the consultant who is treating the child, the ward sister, or the social worker attached to the hospital. Perhaps the child is attending hospital a long way from home, and the people who know what is available in his own community are the staff of the social services department, the health visitor and the Citizens Advice Bureau.

The primary function

In the Parents' Association one can talk about one's child and one's own feelings, and other parents will understand and will accept because it is something that they know. The paths of grieving are all too familiar. The torturing doubts about what one should have done, the focusing of anxiety on a detail such as the child's loss of hair, the complete dependence on the physician. During periods of extreme anxiety many parents are afraid that they are becoming mentally ill. After solitary periods of watching a sick child it is not uncommon for the mind to play tricks. It is a great relief to know that other parents have had such experiences and have come through. The courage of other parents is something that one holds on to in difficult times. Jeanette's three-year-old daughter has leukaemia, and she was finding it very difficult to be with the child on the ward without breaking down into tears. She met Anne, a single girl, at the Parents' Association, and she seemed to be able to draw strength from the fact that Anne was faced with the same situation as herself, and yet coped cheerfully without the support of husband and family. Later in the year a new member came in whose daughter was undergoing the same treatment as Jeanette's had undergone, and Jeanette was a great help to her. The opportunity to assist this mother became a time of growing. The primary function of the Parents' Association is to bring together parents with a common experience to satisfy their need to talk about what is happening, and to find comfort in helping each other.

MARY P. PATTEN
The programme

Many parents' groups which have small beginnings in an evening spent together in the home of one set of parents reach the stage of adopting a formal structure of a committee, and arranging regular meetings in such places as a room in the hospital, or in a school. It is quite common to invite a speaker, such as a dietician, or the manufacturer of children's clothes or toys. Experienced secretaries vary the formal programme to control and direct the amount of emotion, so that on one occasion a psychologist may talk about the frustrations of the handicapped child, but before the evening is over the group will be planning for a puppet show by their children for the next occasion. Such persons as a children's librarian, and occupational therapist, or a peripatetic teacher, are usually happy to come, but it is wise to approach the speaker well in advance and find out if the permission of his employing authority is necessary. Most speakers prefer to ask permission themselves, but if you will, request that the secretary of the Association writes a formal letter to the employer. Some social service departments and health authorities prefer to use a particular member of staff for all speaking engagements. In this case, it is correct to write in the first instance to the director of the service. Some speakers have a set fee, others will accept a small honorarium from the group. Many do not accept a fee, but should be offered expenses. It is appropriate to discuss this matter in writing when the initial approach is made to the speaker. It is practical, as well as courteous, for the secretary of the group to meet the speaker some time before the engagement, and brief him on the membership of the group. Most speakers like to know the size and composition of their audience, such features as whether it is likely to be mothers only, or mainly fathers, or a combination of fathers and interested businessmen, as when a group attracts outsiders. The speaker will probably want to know at what level to pitch his talk, and it will help him if the experience of the members is outlined, with a brief resume of their social and educational background. He should be told of particular aspects of the subject that the group would like to hear covered, and, in some instances, should be advised of areas to avoid. Practical details, such as the exact location, the size of the room, the name of the chairman, and the usual length of the talk, are included in this briefing.

Films may provide an acceptable alternative to a talk. These may be hired from a central distributor, or from the headquarters of some charitable associations. Advice about relevant films may be available from the tutor in the school of nursing in the area, from the training officer in the social services department, or from staff engaged in teaching social work, nursing, or other similar courses in a polytechnic, training college, or university. Ideally, films should be reviewed before ordering. If a film is being offered as an alternative to a speaker, one member of the group might be asked to guide the discussion, and be given the opportunity of seeing the film before it is shown to the whole group.

The chairman

Occasionally, it is an advantage to elect a non-parent as chairman to the group, or a parent whose experiences are now past, and who has had an interval of some years to build a new life. The health visitor or social worker may accept the position of chairman, or may offer to lead the discussion at certain sessions at which the subject matter is likely to evoke deep response. Such a person, who has not immediate needs of his own to be met in the group, may be better able to help parents to express their feelings, whether these be anger, guilt, anxiety or sorrow, and yet bring the group forward.

Each child shows his own physical and psychological response to the disease process, but so too each parent has his own way of living with his child. One father forbade all discussion of the child's condition, yet came to a group, and then became angry with other members whom he could not control as he controlled his own family. In another situation, two sets of parents whose children were showing excellent response to treatment, were in turn forced to withdraw because of the hostility directed at them by a very dominant member of the group. Parents have the capacity, both to help, and to hurt each other. Ideally, there should be some informal screening before members join the group. If most members come through a consultant or ward sister, such a person should be invited to have close links so that the primary function of the group is understood, and appropriate persons invited. Occasionally, one finds an association being treated as a repository for all personal problems, and general practitioners, who are short of other resources, refer to it parents with marital problems, economic, and housing problems, and in all too many cases, intractable personality difficulties. Healthy parents who have much to contribute, and who are coping well, are not informed about the group, because it is seen as a one way process to help those only who are in trouble. For this reason, it is perhaps preferable to start a group with the assistance of a health visitor or social worker, or ward sister, who will suggest the stable parents who will form the core or nucleus. Some groups are started

169

by putting an advertisement in the newspaper, and while this has the advantage of drawing in those who are not directly in touch with statutory services, one may end up by helping no one if persons with pathological needs are attracted.

In a small number of instances, a parent becomes ill with depression. He or she is listless and apathetic, or, more rarely, agitated. Most parents feel like this at times for short periods, but the sick parent shows a constancy of mood, a continuing state of hopelessness or anxiety, which is not modified by the help or comfort offered by the group. Depression is an illness which usually responds well to medical treatment, and such a parent will normally return to the group when he is well. A good chairman identifies parents who need a more specialised type of help than is available in the group.

Activities

Some groups develop specialised services to assist members, such as baby-sitting, a library of toys or books, exchange of recipes relevant to the child's diet, a second-hand store of equipment and modified clothing, or a rota of car drivers. An additional advantage of making close links with a health visitor or social worker is that the group can be kept in touch with new developments available in equipment or facilities from the health authorities, or inform the group about statutory benefits such as constant attendance allowance. The financial strain of having a child with a long-term illness is considerable, and one of the real benefits of group membership is the better information service, and the pooling of some resources.

Fund raising

The primary function of the Parents' Association is that it gives the parent strength to go on loving and caring for her sick child. It also prepares the parent, so that when the caring is over, and the work of mourning is finished, she should be ready to invest her love in new areas of life. Some parents return to the Association to work for other people's children. The two major areas of activity are fund raising and political pressure groups. Most parents' groups combine their educational programme with fund raising, or with pressure group tactics, but the care of a sick child leaves little time or energy for this type of involvement. A successful compromise is the formation of a friends or associates group which some parents will later join, and which will carry the major responsibility for fund raising.

Many parents feel bewildered and resentful when they are faced with the apparent lack of money for research, or for facilities and comforts for the sick child. It is difficult to appreciate that costs have risen very much faster than knowledge of what can be done in the Health Service, and all types of sick people are in competition for the scarce resources. The demand for care in all sectors has increased, and there are new expensive problems such as the rising proportion of elderly in the population, and the increasing number of persons who survive major road accidents and require intensive care. Some parents' groups devote their entire activities to collecting money for research. Some research fellowships endowed in this way may later be taken over by university authorities, or by larger trusts. Parents' groups work to build nursery schools, commission swimming baths, equip playrooms and holiday homes, furnish parents' rooms in the hospital, and, on a smaller scale, provide a range of improvements and comforts for the child.

The fund raising committee

It is usually necessary to set up a small committee, appoint a secretary and treasurer, and open a bank account. It is wise to invite outside people to the initial meetings, such as a member of the administrative or professional staff from the hospital. Sometimes when a project is fully discussed, the money is found to be forth-coming from other sources. One group wished to pay for the services of a teacher in a small hospital, and then found from an outside member that this payment could be made by the education authority. In another instance, a group invited a hospital secretary to discuss the plans to furnish a new playroom. He was able to arrange for the major cost of this to be included in the hospital rebuilding plan. On other occasions a compromise is reached, whereby the group finds part of the money and qualifies for a grant. The second reason for inviting professional staff is so that they can discuss their feelings about the scheme. A Parents' Association wished to provide toys for a particular ward, but did not appreciate that the sister had no place to store these. After discussion, it was decided that some of the money should be spent on toy boxes on castors. In another instance, sand trays and finger paints were to be bought, but it became obvious that the ward was not sufficiently well staffed to cope with the extra work, and puppets were chosen as an alternative.

Methods of fund raising

Fund raising can be undertaken in a variety of ways, and there are many factors to be considered in the selection of a method. These

171

include not only the target to be achieved, but also the length of time available, the potential help, the type of area, and the likely effect of the appeal. Some fund raising activities are linked with educational programmes, others have an important, secondary, social function.

The quickest, surest way to obtain relatively small sums of money, for example £200, is a jumble sale. It may be advisable to take out fire insurance and to put a notice on the door to the effect that no liability is admitted for accidents or thefts occurring on the premises. In some areas jumble sales attract professional buyers who pay low prices. This is particularly likely to happen if a public hall, such as a market hall, is rented. In other areas, it is essential to take precautions against theft of articles for sale, or the loss of takings.

Custom is the best guide to what will be acceptable in a community. In a small country town, stalls or shops with nearly new clothes might prove a failure as everyone may know the wearer. In a country area, home baked teas at 4.30, with an auction sale of produce, bring in much support. In the suburbs, a coffee party with a bring and buy sale may be well attended. One society ran both a hot pot supper and a cheese and wine evening, and there was very little overlap of customers. These last two ventures require initial financial outlay, and it is common to make sure that one does more than cover costs by some form of raffle competition or tombola. In some instances, firms may be willing to supply such items as cheese or sausages as an advertising venture. Other firms may donate tombola items if prizes carry the words 'donated by'. Joint sponsorship between commercial firms and charities is quite common. Sometimes this takes the form of a mannequin parade, but one intrepid Parents' Association ran a pet show under the umbrella of the makers of a brand of pet food.

Handicap, long-term illness and death in childhood are now such rare events that people are embarrassed because they have no experience in dealing with their own reactions to these problems. Some of the best fund raising has a secondary educational aim. Scouts, guides, school-children, members of a youth club or women's association, learn a great deal by helping at garden fetes or assisting the parents' group in the organisation of projects. It is sometimes acceptable and appropriate for the sick child himself to make some contribution, as in the making of goods for a stall. It is occasionally possible for handicapped and non-handicapped children to work together as in the PHAB clubs (Physically Handicapped and Able Bodied). It is important, however, to avoid any occasion in which the child might feel even more set apart or an object of charity. A young person may gain dignity and meaning from taking part in a

172

wheelchair rally for DIG (Disablement Income Group) to campaign for what he feels to be his legitimate rights, and yet be acutely unhappy if asked to sell flags.

Flag days and house to house collections must be organised well in advance. It is not uncommon for bookings to be made with a town clerk two years ahead. The same problem applies also to a radio appeal, even on a local station. To the parents, the charity for which they work appears to be more important than any other cause, but in the last few years we have seen a profusion of charities, and some attempt at co-ordination or federation of charities may be necessary, particularly in relation to fund raising and pressure group activity. In some areas councils of social service act as a convenient umbrella. In others, there is a committee of representatives of children's groups. Where there is no co-ordinating machinery it is very necessary before planning any fund raising event to contact the other charities, and so avoid the distress of overlap or apparent competition.

Pressure group activity

A few parents may feel less than satisfied with the care available for their child, and they will work for improvement by putting pressure on the appropriate statutory authorities. Some voluntary societies, such as the Association for the Welfare of Children in Hospitals, have this as their primary aim, although they may also raise money and pilot experimental services such as the provision of a play leader, usually services which will be taken over by the hospital at a later stage.

Complaints against individual members of staff should not be a matter for a parents' pressure group, but should be forwarded discreetly to the hospital secretary. Complaints concerning the treatment of a particular child are not themselves appropriate subject matter. The parents of the child should seek an interview with the consultant in charge, with the matron if it is a nursing matter, or with a hospital secretary. It is useful to write a letter first, so that the person one is going to see has adequate opportunity to find out the full facts. Initial letters should be in the nature of requests for more information, or should be phrased in such a way that there is no destructive general statement about a named individual. Parents who are not happy about some particular aspect of a child's care should make their letter as precise and factual as possible, saying what incidents displeased them, and when and how often and in whose presence and in what circumstances these occurred. Copies

173

should be kept of all correspondence, and on occasion a discreet friend, preferably not another member of the parents' group, might be invited to accompany the parent to the interview. Individual complaints are usually dealt with courteously, and most problems resolve themselves at this stage. If a parent feels, however, that he has a legitimate grievance which the hospital has not dealt with adequately, various other channels are open to him. The best advice at this stage is that which may be offered locally by a Citizen's Advice Bureau or the local MP, or a solicitor. Most problems can be resolved quietly by people with knowledge of the community and local contacts, though in some cases further help might be sought from bodies such as the Patients' Association.

Areas of concern

Parents' groups work appropriately in matters of more common concern, such as the visiting facilities available to parents, the public transport to and from a hospital, the provision of introductory leaflets about a hospital, and the availability of a library of children's books. For the provision of such items as personal aids for the sick child at home, parents' groups can be very successful in matters of this kind. One group requested that a ramp for wheelchairs should be provided outside a children's library. Another group arranged that the learner's part of the swimming pool would be made available at certain times for disabled children. Negotiations by another group led to a new children's entrance being added to one hospital, whereas, previously, all children had waited in a general casualty department.

Method

The most successful projects are those which will be seen to bring benefit to all concerned, children, parents, professional and administrative staff. The first stage is usually a small and informal meeting between a few of the parents, and friends with relevant expertise concerning town planning, education, nursing or from the local council. Such friends must not be asked to commit themselves as members of their own departments or hospitals (and for this reason a meeting in a private house is best), but they may be asked to offer advice on the preferred way of working with their own employing authorities. It may be useful for a parents' group, for instance, to know something about the preparation and timing of the agenda for the meeting of a Health and Social Services Board, so that the

174

request for consideration of their object may be sent at the best possible time. Sound advice is often forthcoming from people who have had the benefit of working in statutory authorities. One parents' group is at the moment putting pressure on an authority to supply two sets of built-up shoes to disabled children, so that such children will not be denied outings when the single pair is being repaired. This group has reached the second stage of forming a formal committee, and has invited to this a recently retired Medical Officer of Health. The original intention of this group was to campaign for duplication of all personal medical aids, so that children whose braces or straps became wet would have a second pair available. They have been advised, however, by the Medical Officer, to work initially on one small definable part, such as the request for the second pair of shoes for school age children, and later, with hope, to use the success of this as a precedent for other items.

There is a lot of hard work attached to pressure group activity. It is necessary to become conversant with the appropriate existing legislation. An authority may be obliged to supply a particular type of service, and may not be doing so. An example of this is a large hospital catering for a number of children, which has no teacher. In this case the pressure group is in a strong position. In other situations the Ministry of Health and Social Services may have made certain recommendations to hospitals, such as the one that parents should be welcomed to visit the ward frequently and assist in the child's care. The hospital is not compelled to accept the Ministry's advice, but it is usually prudent to do so. In this instance the pressure group may collect information about the hospitals where this advice is being implemented and find out the best ways in which it can be made to work successfully. Staff who are unhappy about setting up a system of unrestricted visiting may accept an invitation to see another hospital and talk with the staff there, as well as parents, about the problems and the benefits.

In some cases there is no relevant administration, that is to say the authority is legally free to agree to or to refuse the proposal, but it is a project which comes low in their accepted list of priorities. An example of this is where adolescents with long-term illness are nursed in a geriatric ward, and the parents' group requests separate accommodation. Such a group may find that it is asked to canvas the support of each individual on the relevant committees, and of persons who carry weight within the hospital world and the community. Letters to the press, public meetings, radio and television broadcasts, are all useful, but care must be taken with their presentation. It is unfortunately too easy for the distressed parent to

175

be led into laying blame against individuals, or to present an uncontrolled emotional account. Most campaigns are won because the committees are offered a convincing case by a well informed group who seem to have worked with them rather than against them. Goodwill demonstrated in a tangible form by fund raising may make it possible for a committee to alter its decisions.

Summary and conclusion

In this chapter I have considered some of the ways in which parents may join together in a parents' group to work for themselves and for their children. The main areas of interest are group discussions, fund raising, and pressure group activity.

A parents' group should be regarded as one way of coming to terms with one's self, and finding a meaning in one's position as a parent of a terminally ill child. But there are other ways which are perhaps more difficult and from which the parents' group may be a refuge. It is tempting to withdraw from close friends, perhaps because they are the bridge to a normal life and it sometimes happens that people who are deeply hurt begin to avoid relationships in which this hurt cannot be disguised. Thus a parents' group with the business of fund raising may at times come between a husband and a wife or between parents and old friends. Similarly talk, and more talk about the child, the 'muscular dystrophy child, the leukaemia child, the cystic fibrosis child' may for some get in the way of deep quiet love that grows within one for this son or this daughter. There is perhaps a spiritual or philosophical level of being essentially private where some parents may find a sense of the continuation of life and this may not be found in a parents' group. Nevertheless membership of a parents' group, when balanced by other relationships and other resources, can be a very positive and creative experience for the parent of the child with a life-shortening illness.

15 Counselling the grieving parent[1]

Audrey T. McCollum

The brightening outlook for children with potentially fatal illnesses is cause for concern as well as rejoicing. Treading a tight-rope between hope and despair for the uncertain duration of the child's life, parents must accommodate to emotional, social and economic stresses of awesome duration and intensity. In a mobile, industrial society, traditionally supportive liaisons between parents and their relatives or clergymen are subject to weakening and interruption. Physicians, absorbed in the increasingly complex management of the physical aspects of disease, may lack the time, inclination or skill to ameliorate associated psychosocial stress. For these reasons, it is increasingly important for the social worker to provide family counselling directed towards relieving psychic stress as well as reality problems.

Family adaptation to the child's illness proceeds through four stages (dealt with at greater length in chapter 2): pre-diagnostic (in which the child's symptoms arouse concern and influence family life, but the underlying illness has not been identified); confrontational (in which the family is faced with the diagnosis and an anticipatory grief reaction is aroused); long-term adaptation (usually marked by fluctuation between anticipatory mourning and denial); terminal (which may replicate many aspects of the confrontational stage).

Family needs and accessibility to help vary in each stage. The confrontational stage is an optimal time for the introduction of the social worker as family counsellor, since the intensity of the crisis may diminish the effectiveness of existing patterns of coping behaviour in the family and motivate its members to accept help in modifying and strengthening their adaptive capacities. This chapter will, therefore, be focused upon this period, and will be limited to direct counselling of parents.

During the confrontational stage, parents face a threefold task: to

177

assimilate the reality (the child's illness); to master the anticipatory grief reaction aroused by that reality; to maintain need-fulfilling relationships within the family. In each area, contributions of the social worker can be delineated.

Assimilating the reality

Appraising defences An unendurable reality (and the emotions it arouses) can only be assimilated in manageable 'doses' over a period of time. Therefore, parents confronted by the possible loss of a child must be expected to ward off this threat by employing a variety of psychic defences such as denial, repression and isolation of affect. Such defences play a necessary role in protecting the parent from incapacitating despair, depression and anxiety. It would, therefore, be ill advised—and often futile—to attempt an abrupt penetration of defences.

A careful appraisal of the parents' defences can, however, help to ensure that their needs are adequately met. First, such an evaluation can safeguard relationships between parents and other significant persons. For example, physicians and nurses rather commonly respond to parental denial or repression with marked concern. They may feel frustration or annoyance that their communications seem to have been ineffective and their explanations seem not to have been understood. They may feel harassed by the parents' insistent questions and dread the necessity for imparting painful information repeatedly.

By listening attentively to the parents' communications, the social worker can appraise the extent to which a defence such as denial is operative. Is the diagnosis pervasively denied (if such were the case, would the parent permit the child to receive treatment?) or is there an intermingling of disbelief and acceptance? Is it perhaps not the diagnosis but only the prognosis which is denied? Are there, even so, signs of a dawning acceptance (does the parent say, '*When* Johnny goes to school' or '*If* Johnny goes to school'?)? It is often constructive to interpret the necessity for and appropriateness of the defences to medical personnel. Reassurance that his communications are indeed being gradually assimilated can aid the physician in accepting the parents' slow and uneven pace, and help him determine optimal timing and 'dosage' of information. It thus enhances physician-parent rapport.

Second, evaluation of defences helps to ensure that inapparent needs are not overlooked. For example, isolation of affect may facilitate the initial, intellectual assimilation of information about the

178

child's condition. It may permit the parent to act calmly and competently on behalf of the child in an urgent situation (coping with a bleeding episode, a seizure, a fainting spell). However, such a parent may appear so calm and competent to medical staff that his inner anguish is overlooked; he, as much as the distraught, volatile parent whose behaviour commands attention, must be afforded opportunity for emotional abreaction.

Third, evaluation of defences makes it possible to reassure parents themselves about the appropriateness of their responses. For example, a parent may be frightened by his sense of unreality about the diagnosis, his strange lack of feeling, his unaccustomed forgetfulness. Questions such as, 'How do other parents feel?', 'How should I behave?', 'Are my reactions normal?' are gravely troubling to grieving parents, perhaps particularly in a heterogeneous society such as the USA in which expectations concerning 'styles' of mourning behaviour are ambiguous. An understanding that his responses are expectable, understandable and prevalent among grieving parents can relieve his anxiety.

Seeking information constructively Parents can scarcely assimilate the reality of their child's illness unless they develop effective ways of gathering information. It is useful for the social worker to review with parents their understanding of the illness, perhaps initiating the review with a query such as, 'If you were explaining Johnny's illness to a relative or close friend, what might you say?' Such a review often reveals areas of confusion, distortion and forgetfulness which result from defensive 'warding off'; it also gives clues as to the parents' intellectual endowment and capacity to comprehend the medical and biological terminology frequently employed by physicians.

This review should also reveal what sources of information the parent has utilised. For example, a parent who has repressed significant information given by the physician may engage in frantic and random efforts to inform himself from inappropriate sources such as outdated medical texts in a neighbourhood library. A parent, who is likely to be keenly attentive to non-verbal clues in this period of heightened anxiety, may have reached erroneous conclusions from the facial expression, tone of voice or the posture and motility of professional staff.

It is constructive to encourage the parent to view information-gathering as a gradual process, not as an event. Supported in accepting his confusion and forgetfulness as understandable responses to stress (and not as signs of deficiency to be concealed), the parent may

179

feel more confident in requesting conferences with the physician as needed. He can be helped to make optimal use of such conferences by preparing his questions in advance. For example, information about the treatment regimen may be useless unless the parent is helped to accommodate the regimen to the developmental status of the child (e.g. how might postural drainage be carried out with a resistant, negativistic two-year-old to avoid a struggle in which the child perceives the 'clapping' as a variant of spanking?).

Mastering the affect

The anticipation of loss of a child arouses in parents a constellation of affect sometimes termed the 'anticipatory grief reaction'. The social worker can offer the parents significant help in gradually acknowledging and enduring their emotions, and in discharging the affect through non-destructive channels. Artificial as it is to separate the emotional components of the grief reaction, the counselling role of the social worker can best be illustrated by so doing.

The central emotion is, of course, sorrow. By offering a predictable time and a place for the release of sorrow, and by conveying—through sympathetic listening—that it is understood, the social worker may help parents contain and endure their sadness. Unfortunately, sorrow can be assuaged only to a limited degree. The social worker can, however, effectively help parents deal with their guilt, anger and anxiety.

Guilt Parents expect to nurture and protect their children themselves. Therefore, when a child is jeopardised by grave illness, most parents experience at least transient self-accusatory thoughts and guilty feelings. Unrelieved self-reproach and guilt constitute an important barrier to successful adaptation to the illness. A guilty parent experiences significant loss of self-esteem. Unable to value himself, he will have difficulty supporting the child's own sense of worth. He may, in a frantic effort to 'atone' for his guilt, become inappropriately indulgent towards the child. Therefore, the social worker's role in dispelling such feelings has preventive as well as therapeutic implications.

Self-reproach sometimes yields to reality testing. This process can often be initiated with a simple statement such as, 'Parents of sick children often blame themselves in some way'. The social worker can review with the parent his fantasies of omission or commission. Appropriate information can then be sought from the physician to help dispel such fantasies.

Self-accusation which does not readily give way to self-forgiveness may be rooted in ambivalence towards the child. Possibly the pregnancy was untimely and unwanted. Perhaps the child, prior to the onset of illness, was in a particularly negativistic, provocative or competitive phase of development. Perhaps the child's symptoms had been of a nature to arouse feelings of helplessness, frustration or disgust in the parent (e.g. failure to thrive, irritability, foul stools, etc.). Possibly the parent had the thought, 'If John is going to die in the end, maybe it would be best if it happened soon'. In any such instance, the parent may reproach himself bitterly for his negative attitudes towards the ill child, judging them to be 'bad' or 'unnatural'.

The social worker can often help the parent search out such guilt-laden thoughts and feelings. The exploration might be initiated with a comment such as, 'John must have been very hard to take care of (because of his irritability, stubbornness, night-time crying, vomiting, etc.)'. The social worker's understanding and acceptance supports the parent in acknowledging and verbalising the troublesome ideas and impulses. The parent can be helped to recognise that all parents have some negative feelings towards their children, that these are often appropriate responses to the child's behaviour, and that parental disapproval plays a necessary role in child-rearing.

Diana was admitted to hospital, gravely ill, at 3½ years of age. Her mother, who appeared defensive, agitated, and unable to control her tears, was referred to the social worker for evaluation. Mrs W. recounted that the night before admission, Diana had come to the parents' bed and fretfully demanded access. She crawled in between the parents, turning her back to mother and snuggling close to father. Unable to go back to sleep, Diana unaccountably lost control of bladder functions and soaked the the bed. Weary and on edge after a long day with an increasingly irritable and demanding child, Diana's mother allowed her own controls to loosen. Scolding furiously, she removed the child from the bed, smacked her buttocks and ordered her to return to her own bed and stop being a pest. When, in the morning, the child's illness was unmistakable, Mrs W. felt her own outburst to be unforgivable.

In a frenzy of self-recrimination, Mrs W. recounted many other incidents in which Diana's impudence or disobedience had aroused her anger. She recounted that, whenever Diana's beloved father came home, Diana boisterously claimed his attention, pleading to be kissed first, and treated mother like an unwelcome intruder. To her dismay, Mrs W. found herself responding to this rivalrous behaviour with momentary jealousy.

As the mother-child relationship was explored, however, Mrs W. was able also to recall the many times when Diana was loving towards her, happily helped with the housework, emulated her in play, and declared her wish to be 'just like mummy' when she grew up. Mrs W. began to acknowledge the affectionate and devoted care she had given the child much of the time.

It was relieving for her to be reassured that the opposing trends in Diana's feeling and behaviour towards her mother were expectable at her age, and that Mrs W.'s ambivalent responses were understandable and not uncommon. The acceptance of her feelings by the social worker and the tacit reassurance about her adequacy as a mother helped to restore Mrs W.'s self-esteem. Although she continued—understandably—to regret her nocturnal outburst, her bitter remorse gradually softened into mild regret. Mr W. later commented that after each of these interviews his wife had come home seeming 'somehow more at peace'.

An occasional parent will seem to experience the child's illness as deserved punishment and will engage in virtually intractable self-recrimination. He may manifest intense feelings of worthlessness, perhaps accompanied by symptoms of clinical depression. In such cases, psychiatric consultation should be sought to determine what therapeutic strategy would be most timely and appropriate.

Anger The massive threat and frustration of the child's illness arouses aggressive impulses and anger in most parents. Since few can tolerate undirected, free-floating anger, it tends to be directed towards a significant object (the choice of object, of course, having unconscious determinants as well as those in reality). The marital partner may become the target of anger, subject to blame for the child's illness or reproach for his response to the diagnosis and mode of coping with the stress. Siblings of the patient may become objects of the anger, perhaps readily selected because they manifest provocative, demanding behaviour in response to the family crisis. Anger may be directed towards doctors and nurses, perhaps superficially precipitated by an insensitive remark or a callous demeanour, but also reflecting underlying disappointment because they lack the omnipotence to cure the child. The clergy, the church and God may become targets of angry protest: 'I'm unable to continue believing in a God who could act as cruelly as this'.

Such anger can exert a destructive influence on necessary relationships, and may alienate the parent from significant sources of help and support. It can, therefore, have preventive as well as therapeutic import if the social worker can help the parent contain his anger by exploring and ventilating it within the counselling sessions, and by finding appropriate channels for discharge outside. For example, the purposeful use of motility—lamentably inhibited in a technologically sophisticated society—can be fostered. Housecleaning and gardening afford numerous opportunities for aggressive movements such as scouring, scrubbing, kneading, pounding, yanking, shoving. Many sports require physical attack such as hurling, walloping, kicking. Others engage the body in rhythmical, repetitive movements which are tranquillising.

Parents can constructively utilise aggressive energy in fighting on behalf of the child: mastering the treatment regimen, raising funds to support medical research, influencing social institutions (e.g. schools and hospitals) to accommodate more adequately to the needs of chronically ill children. However, support and guidance are needed in finding such outlets.

Apprehension and anxiety A child's illness constitutes a grave challenge to his parent's mastery of the protective role. This challenge is one source of the deep apprehension and anxiety usually experienced. Awareness that there is only a limited amount the parent can do to alter the outcome stimulates intense feelings of helplessness. Conversely, the responsibility for home treatment may seem overwhelming; the parent may feel as though the child's life is in his hands.

Anxiety may be generated by the intensity of the grief reaction. Parents experience fantasies of being engulfed by their emotions, losing control over their behaviour, and losing their capacity for continuing function under such stress.

The threat of losing the child may arouse intense separation anxiety in the parent. The normal progression through stages of detachment from the developing child (which parallels the child's progressive individuation and separation from the parent) is abruptly aborted. Indeed, the child's illness may result in regression in this process of mutual separation, with a return toward the symbiotic attachment characteristic of early infancy.

Confrontation with possible death in the child may arouse the parent's latent anxiety about his own death. If his inner stress has produced somatic symptoms, these may be interpreted by him as confirmation that he also is in peril (e.g. gastrointestinal dysfunction,

183

a common response to stress, may be interpreted as symptomatic of cancer, etc.).

Apprehension and anxiety can often be ameliorated if the parent is afforded opportunity to explore and verbalise his fears. Clarification of the fears subjects them to reality testing. The parent can be helped to recognise what information is needed to enable him to distinguish fact from fancy. The sense that his fears are understood is supportive (he is then no longer alone in his terror). Furthermore, direct reassurance can be offered that certain thoughts and emotions are prevalent among grieving parents and are not 'unnatural' or indications of being 'crazy'.

The parent's sense of mastery can be enhanced if he can be guided in adjusting his expectations of himself to a realistic level. The anticipatory grief reaction may temporarily impair function as thoroughly as, for example, influenza. The parent, already subject to a loss of self-esteem from the child's illness, may experience further self-deprecation as a consequence of this impairment. It is important, therefore, to reassure the parent that his altered functioning— e.g., forgetfulness, confusion, irritability, apathy, sleep or appetite disturbance, etc.—is an understandable response to massive stress (in a case of severe decompensation, psychiatric consultation should of course be sought).

Many grieving parents experience heightened dependency needs, and may long to be free of their painful responsibilities. If the parent expects too little of himself, and abdicates responsibility, there is risk that his existence will become a void filled only with despair (and thus unendurable); furthermore, he may begin to reproach himself bitterly for his 'abdication'. On the other hand, an unduly high level of expectation predisposes him to frustration and failure. The social worker can assist the parent in designing a realistic compromise by reviewing with him his tasks and responsibilities, and differentiating those which are essential from those which could be deferred or assigned to others. The social worker can guide him in utilising all available sources of support —for example, consulting his physician about medication to relieve tension or sleeplessness, arranging for home nursing supervision and procuring temporary household help.

Modulating the parent-child relationship

The grieving parent faces the awesome task of maintaining a need-fulfilling relationship with a child whose expected death he mourns.

Some parents show a remarkable capacity for this. Not infrequently, however, the illness sets in motion a regressive trend in the relationship in which parental protectiveness fosters undue helplessness and dependency in the child. The child may be kept home from school more often than his physical condition warrants and may be isolated from contact with his peers. The parents may become excessively indulgent and have difficulty setting limits on the child's behaviour. They may assume unnecessary responsibility for his bodily care. During hospitalisation, the parent-child relationship may assume a quasi-symbiotic nature, and efforts of the staff to establish rapport with the child may be resisted. Such an 'over-protective' trend may have muliple determinants, including the parent's separation anxiety or his need to relieve his guilt through atonement; it may also represent a reaction formation against unacceptable hostility towards the burdensome child. Although it affords the child certain gratifications, such parental behaviour also deprives the child of a sense of mastery and may arouse anxiety and resentment.

Alternatively, the illness may set in motion a loosening of the emotional bonds with the child (the 'decathexis of the object' which is a central task of mourning). Parents may strive to attain emotional distance and to avoid interaction with the child. Responsibility for his care may be turned over to other family members. During hospitalisation, the parent may either refrain from visiting or engage in cursory contacts with his own child while directing his attention towards the staff, other patients and their parents. In contrast to the 'overprotected' child, such a child may be expected to maintain an unattainable level of independence and self-mastery, and be deprived of needed support.

The social worker can sometimes significantly help the parent modulate his relationship to the ill child so that his own needs and those of the child are safeguarded. Such intervention requires an interplay between helping the parent understand and endure the emotions his child's illness arouses, supporting him in modifying his behavioural interactions with the child, and guiding him in utilising all available external resources.

In his tenth year of life Johnny E. was found to have an inoperable brain tumour which was expected to follow a slow but inexorably progressive course. The mother became known to a social worker when the desirability of Johnny's admission to a clinical research centre for palliative chemotherapy was being evaluated.

In response to the social worker's interest in the mother's own needs, Mrs E. confided that she found daily life with

185

Johnny unendurable. Because of deterioration of motor and language functions, school attendance had seemed inadvisable for several months. Johnny spent every hour of every day at home; his existence was unstructured, formless. He trailed his mother continuously through the house, fretfully demanding her attention. He was unable to initiate meaningful activities without guidance and he sustained only brief interest in any pursuit. Minimal frustration provoked outbursts of fury. Because of his clumsiness, he was prone to injury and to inflicting accidental damage upon his environment. He, therefore, seemed to require his mother's continuous supervision.

Mr E. dealt with his own anguish about the anticipated loss of his son—his only child—by becoming increasingly remote and spending longer periods away from the household. He was unable to offer emotional support to his wife or son and gave minimal practical help (such as staying with his son while his wife went shopping, rather grudgingly.

Mrs E. feared being engulfed by the rage and guilt which her continuous interaction with Johnny aroused. She feared that in a moment of intense anger she might inflict physical harm on the child. Furthermore, her despair was so intense that she had begun ruminating about suicide; at moments, this seemed the only available release.

A two-pronged strategy of intervention was indicated. With Mrs E's apprehensive but relieved consent, psychiatric consultation was arranged to appraise the risk associated with the homicidal and suicidal ideas. At the same time, Mrs E. was reassured that the pattern of daily life with Johnny did indeed need modification.

After an extensive search for appropriate resources within the E's own community, a rehabilitation centre willing to accept Johnny was located. Fully aware of the prognosis, the imaginative director expressed interest in designing a programme which would utilise Johnny's remaining capabilities, permit him some gratification, and relieve the mother of his care for predictable periods of time. The concurrence of Johnny's neurosurgeon with this plan was obtained.

It was the opinion of the consulting psychiatrist, after a diagnostic interview with Mrs E., that the prospect of realistic relief would diminish the urgency of her aggressive and suicidal impulses. She was referred back to the social worker for continued counselling.

Safeguarding family needs

The family of a child with life-shortening illness face a massive and multi-faceted challenge. Significant alterations of family 'life-style' may become necessary. For example, the family may need to move its residence in order to live closer to medical facilities. The wage-earner(s) may be required to change jobs. Recreational activities may be curtailed because available time and funds are limited. Educational or vocational plans for siblings of the patient may be compromised because financial resources become depleted. The success of the family in adapting to such stresses is significantly influenced by the success of its members in dealing with the apprehension and resentment which are inevitably aroused.

The marital relationship is subject to severe strain. There may be bitter recriminations concerning the cause of the illness. Differences in coping behaviour of each spouse may result in alienation between them. One parent may, for example, seek the comfort of closeness, wishing to share her grief in words and tears. The other parent, in contrast, may deal with his grief by withdrawing emotionally or physically. Aloof and inarticulate, this parent leaves the other feeling abandoned and alone. One parent (often the father) may be excluded from a meaningful role in the child's care and thus subject to intensification of his feelings of helplessness and guilt. The sexual relationship may be disrupted by fatigue, fear of another pregnancy or diminished time for intimate solitude.

Siblings of the patient need help in understanding the nature of the illness and in dealing with their questions and fears about its outcome. They need reassurance that the illness was in no way a result of their own earlier hostile thoughts and wishes towards the afflicted child (a common misapprehension), and that their resentment about the attention required by the ill child is understandable. They need reassurance that the alteration in their parents' moods and behaviour does not reflect a loss of love or interest in them. They need reassurance that they are not expected to grieve in the same fashion as do their parents. They need reassurance that they will not also develop the illness.

Because of this broad spectrum of alterations, stresses and needs, the family of the ill child is at risk. The illness may result in ever-widening circles of social and psychic pathology, or it may stimulate the family to develop effective coping behaviour and emotional bonds of enduring strength. Remaining sensitive to potential sources of stress, the social worker can help the parents maintain or re-establish constructive communication of needs, attitudes, worries and feelings

187

among family members. In so doing, she may make a preventive as well as therapeutic contribution to the family's mastery of the challenge of life-shortening illness.

Professional considerations

All professional persons who interact with the fatally ill child and his family are vulnerable to emotional responses which parallel those of parents. In some respects, the social worker is particularly vulnerable since she is trained to perceive and respond to the nuances of the client's emotional experience. Empathy is an essential component of the counselling relationship.

Too readily, however, empathy may merge into identification with the grieving parent. The social worker may begin to mourn as though it were her child who is fatally ill. She may experience unaccustomed anxiety about her own children. Latent anxiety about her own death may be aroused. Grief associated with significant losses in her past may be re-experienced.

To remain effective, the social worker must contain her emotional reponses within endurable limits, and must maintain clear psychic boundaries between herself and her client. Such processes are fostered by regular review of the work with a supervisor, experienced colleague or psychiatric consultant. Such review is helpful to the social worker in developing a high level of self-awareness concerning the nature of her reponses to the tragedy and the sources of her feelings and attitudes about it.

The social worker's sense of mastery is enhanced if she can maintain a clear sense of purpose in the family counselling, and if she avoids involvement with child or family which does not serve the therapeutic aims. It is important to structure the contacts with the family so that these painful encounters are predictable, so that they can be arranged for times of the day when the social worker's reserves are at a high level, and can be scheduled in thoughtful juxtaposition to less stressful activities. Prompt recording after an interview relieves the social worker of the charge to remember the material and introduces some psychic distance from it. No aspect of professional functioning is, in fact, unimportant if it influences the social worker's capacity to help the grieving parent master his profound anguish.

Note

1 This chapter is based in part on observations gathered in the Yale Children's Clinical Research Centre, supported by grant RR-00125, National Institutes of Health.

16 Caring for the brothers and sisters of a dying child*

Mary Lindsay
and
Dermod MacCarthy

There has been much interest and concern focused on the dying child and his parents and it is right that this should be so, for there are few situations more tragic for the parents to face than this. Much less concern has been shown for the child's brothers and sisters and yet these children are important, for it is they who, when they grow up and have their own families, are likely to have to cope with situations that in some way will remind them of this time. Equally some day they are certain to have further losses by death. Not only may bereavement in childhood affect the course and speed of their emotional development but it will certainly contribute to the way in which they cope with a similar crisis in the future.

There is a considerable gap in our knowledge concerning the severity of the problems facing the brothers and sisters of the dying child; likewise we know little of the way such problems can be prevented or treated. Those closest to the child and his parents are the doctors and nurses, competent to deal with physical illness but not necessarily aware of the emotional needs and reactions of physically well children whom they may not see. There is a limit to the amount of concern anyone can feel and most of it will naturally be for the ill and dying child and his parents. As mentioned previously (chapter 3) doctors and nurses may see death as a professional or even personal failure and this, along with their own fears of death, may contribute to

*The consultants in charge of the Paediatric unit at Stoke Mandeville Hospital are Dermod MacCarthy, M.D., F.R.C.P., D.C.H., J. A. Hadfield, T.D., F.R.C.S., M.S., M. A. Salmon, M.R.C.P., D.C.H. (Glas). D.C.H. (Eng). and C. J. Smallwood, F.R.C.S., M.S. We are grateful to our colleagues for permission to describe the wards, and for their comments. We also wish to acknowledge the help of the ward staff, in particular Miss E. Vernon, S.C.N., Miss R. Woodley, S.R.N., and Miss P. Masinin, S.R.N.,—ward sisters—who by their work with parents and children in hospital have contributed much to the ideas contained in this chapter.

their inhibitions about enquiring into the repercussions the illness and death may have on other people, especially children. For example, Welldon (1971) suggests doctors prefer not to know and for this reason Harrison (1967) points out the validity of accounts of children's bereavement reactions given by mourning adults—parents, doctors and nurses. Similarly during the fatal illness of a child the siblings may not know the nature of it and when death comes they may show a normal child's reaction to such a situation—that of denial—and so may not themselves present symptoms.

The illness

The family

During the illness or episodes of it the siblings are affected by the way in which the family group reacts to this particular stress. The illness itself may induce stark fear (Debuskey, 1970). There will be some family disruption due to it. Time, energy and money may have to be spent on treatment at home, as in fibrocystic disease, as well as visits to the hospital. Though the siblings may not know the outcome, the parents certainly will and there will therefore be more than the usual parental preoccupation with the sick child and this will be intensified at the time of the diagnosis and during the exacerbations of the illness.

The parents

Feelings aroused by the nature and prognosis of the sick child's illness are so overwhelming that the demands made by the other children on the parents may at times be resented. At the beginning and occasionally during the exacerbations of the illness, parents may find difficulties in looking after the house, the children and even themselves (Orbach, 1955). These feelings subside, but, as mentioned elsewhere (chapter 2, p. 16) anticipatory mourning makes parents feel depressed and they find, to their distress, a lack of warmth and an irritability towards everybody including their children. Then at other times when the sick child is better may feel quite cheerful and these mood swings may be unsettling for the siblings and even for the sick child.

At the time of the diagnosis there is usually denial of it, but often this is followed by anger, anger that this should happen to them. This is normal and natural but may at times be difficult to contain and it

190

was found in one series (Orbach, 1955) to be more marked with mothers anticipating the loss of a son than of a daughter. This anger is sometimes projected on to the doctor or the hospital or outside bodies but one of the children, either the sick child or his siblings, may also become a target. Some children because of their particular personalities, or because of the meaning that they have for the parent, are more vulnerable in this respect than others.

Other factors affect the way in which well children may be treated by their mourning parents, such as feelings of parental guilt and responsibility for the child's illness, inadequacy at producing an imperfect child, and occasionally fears of breakdown. These may contribute to the parents feeling less confident in their role so that they find it more difficult to contain and control their children. Turk (1964) found that some families with cystic fibrosis were caught in a 'web of silence'. This may occur because feelings are so overwhelming that the parents fear loss of control and so, increasingly, prefer not to speak of the illness; this silence may extend to all other aspects of family life. As can be envisaged various problems that the siblings may have are affected by it.

Marital difficulties occurring either before the child's illness or precipitated by it may greatly add to the complications. On the other hand the stress evoked by the illness often produces a deepening and consolidation of inter-family relationships (Turk, 1964).

The siblings

It is the parents' preoccupation with the dying child that is probably one of the most important aspects as far as the siblings are concerned. The children will respond in various ways to the pre-occupation and one of the most important determinants will be their age.

It is the baby who is the most vulnerable in this situation. Worried about the sick child and often depressed, the mother is less able to adapt herself to the baby, providing a relaxed awareness of his needs, picking up his cues and making sense of his environment. The younger the child the more potentially damaging this experience is, because of the urgency of his emotional needs. It is a time when the whole course of his development may be altered and irreversible damage may take place. The mother may very much want to give this time and devotion to the baby and will be distressed by her inability to do so.

The possibility of a change in the infant's development due to such factors has been illustrated by two studies of mothers and babies by Joyce Robertson (1965). For two weeks two mothers became preoccupied by family circumstances. In one case the child became much less active after he had failed to get his mother's usual responses and following this his development slowed down. The other child's physical needs were unsatisfied. He was often left hungry and this inner discomfort acted as a stimulation. He reached for his own bottle at nine weeks of age. This brought in its train other precocious development.

Davidson (1968) described a child 'following his mother into her depression' and produced evidence to show that the mother's moods contributed to the infant's emotional pattern and that these responses persisted into adult life.

The work of Bowlby and Spitz concerning the effects of maternal deprivation have been discussed in another chapter (chapter 2, p. 16). Prugh and Harlow (1962) have also described 'masked deprivation' in infants and young children brough up in intact homes where the mother/child interaction was inadequate. They describe this inadequacy as a potential trauma, a very complex process and influenced by many factors. They point out that each stage of development has its potentially vulnerable age.

If the mother is away for any length of time the baby may—because of its needs—become attached to somebody else. This will be upsetting to the mother on her return and if not understood, may lead to difficulties in the relationship between the mother and baby.

The toddler may well see his mother's preoccupation or absence as a rejection of himself (Freud, 1969) and feeling himself bad and unacceptable, he may regress in his development. He may become naughty or aggressive, he may develop sleeping or digestive disturbance, and he may feel lost and actually get lost.

Older children may 'understand' but still feel the parents' concern for the sick child as rejection of themselves. They may be resentful and angry that their needs are not met, and at the same time feel guilty about having these needs and therefore deny their existence.

Well siblings will have to cope with the general anxiety, the parental preoccupation with the dying child, and, if old enough, their own feelings of guilt towards the dying child. All this will cause emotional pain. This may vary in expression from a protesting, grumpy unacceptance to passive resignation. The former reaction will be more inconvenient—but at least the feelings will be externalised. Sandler and Joffe (1967) describe a 'depressive reaction' which can occur in any child over varying periods of time. The child looks unhappy, has little interest in his surroundings, appears withdrawn, bored or listless, has a feeling of discontent with what is offered to him and shows little capacity for pleasure, thus communicating a feeling of being rejected or unloved and not prepared to accept help or comfort. Various sleep disturbances are noted. A general feature is that there is more difficulty in making the same contact with the child than before.

However, the feelings of depression that brought on these symptoms are not easy to tolerate and so various defences are brought into play. Sad feelings may be inverted and obscured by excitement and clowning but the real feelings show up in the child's facial expression in unguarded moments. Seeing this it is tempting to believe the child is as happy as he seems. Children may recognise that the circus clown is fundamentally sad.

Regression may occur in this, as in any stressful situation— there may be a retreat to a previous phase in development and recently acquired achievements may be lost. The child may also retreat into day-dreaming. This, combined with anxiety, may contribute to his doing badly at school.

Psychosomatic symptoms may occur. This may be a child's preferred reaction to stress, e.g., by an exacerbation of asthma or eczema. The child may become vulnerable to infections, various aches and pains may occur, either of a hysterical or hypochondriacal nature. In any case he may feel either consciously or unconsciously that the only way to obtain his parents' concern is to become ill—but he may also be frightened of being like the sick child. Obsessional symptoms may also be brought up as a defence against painful anxiety.

Special mention should be made of siblings who have the same disease as that of the child who is ill—for they are quick to notice similarities between themselves and the child. For instance, an eight-year-old girl said, after she was told she was 'doing fine', 'that's what the doctor said about Mark and he died'.

The child's behaviour may look as if he is asking for punishment. He may easily have accidents. These may occur partly because he feels 'no good' and partly to get the interest he feels he needs. He may also show some form of delinquency, as a distraction from the feelings of depression.

Rutter (1970) using parental illness as an indication of family stress noted that boys became anti-social but girls did not. We would add from clinical impression that this is so until adolescence but after this girls can act out as much as boys.

Anxiety also abounds. It may show in vague fears. The normal anxiety shown by young children separated from their mothers may be heightened. Fears of getting ill have already been mentioned. In older children the anxiety about unacceptable angry feelings towards the parents contributes largely to their difficulty in leaving home and getting to school (so called 'school phobia').

Most of these symptoms have been described by Binger *et al.* (1969) in a retrospective study of twenty out of twenty-three families where a child had died of leukaemia. They found that in half the families one or more of the siblings was affected. Eneuresis, headache and abdominal pain, poor school progress, and school phobia are described, as also are guilt and feelings of rejection stemming from the parents' preoccupation.

Older girls are often given responsibility for looking after younger children. Identifying with their parents they may quite competently take on the task thus gaining their parents' approval. At the same time they are vicariously looking after their own needs. We know of one seven-year-old girl whose intense rivalry with her five-year-old brother had caused much family friction. When he developed leukaemia this hostility to him was turned by 'reaction-formation' into concern. Family relationships improved. The general practitioner's help contributed much to this. At the same time one wonders at what cost this girl was enabled to be aware of, and to tolerate, her own feelings of resentment about attention that her brother was given.

This sort of reaction would be more usual where there is a larger gap between the ages. We know of a ten-year-old girl referred because of various fears and phobias, not doing well at school, and tearfulness, whose parents found it difficult to get through to her. She was the eldest of three girls, the youngest had fibrocystic disease. She repeatedly asked her mother to allow her to look after this girl, but she admitted to the doctor, when alone, that she was frightened, something might go wrong whilst she was nursing her. She was not able to talk over these feelings at home, nor was she able to talk over the nightmares she had. She feared it would worry her parents, already so concerned with the sick child. Although she badly needed the concern and understanding she obtained from the child guidance clinic doctor, her attendances were erratic. This was because she felt so guilty about receiving such concern and interest for herself, and the parents themselves did not encourage attendance. When all this was discussed both she and the parents were able to see things more clearly. The conflict within her remained, however.

Feinberg (1970) treated two girls aged seven and nine because their six-year-old brother had leukaemia. Both girls knew this was the reason they were coming weekly to therapy. They were free from symptoms, but there were indications that the older girl might develop symptoms later. The whole family knew the diagnosis and prognosis. Feinberg points out the need for a readiness to tell the truth rather than actively 'tell' and that this helps to establish a climate of trust. While not threatening their defences he did not allow either child to maintain they did not know why they were coming. Discussions concerning the death of pets enabled the children to mourn at second hand and encouraged the older girl's understanding of the finality of death. They expressed their feelings about their mother's preoccupation with their sick brother, the older girl showed anger and resentment at this. The younger one was more concerned about guilt in relation to previous aggression towards her brother; the older one showed anxiety about whether her hostility had actually caused the illness but was able to arrive at an acceptance of this and was then able to understand the mixed feelings she had about her brother. Feinberg helped them both to increase their tolerance of painful feelings associated with loss and anger. The older girl felt the way to get her mother's attention was to get ill herself and this was discussed. They were able to remain in touch with the situation as it really was by describing their brother and his physical state so that they had an understanding of the disease and were able to clarify misconceptions. Feinberg hoped that if in future they needed to mourn a loss then clear memories of this illness might be more available. This was easier for the older girl than for the younger one. Induction of mourning was easier with the older girl and she was able to share sad feelings, and to say that it was not good to keep sad feelings inside or there would be an explosive discharge, but the younger girl's strong avoidance and suppression prevented her experiencing these feelings. When their brother died both children showed the tendency to replace him by requesting babies or pets rather than losed the relationship. Feinberg felt it had been a help to express feelings at a time of stress thus preventing behavioural complications or an outburst of neurotic symptoms, in a ten month follow-up there had been no overt mourning activities. Whether this is desirable or undesirable in a child we do not really know.

The sick child and his brothers and sisters

Sibling relationships are intense, complex and of infinite variety. Siblings usually share a common background and outlook but they also have to share their parents' time, interest and love; so that loyalty, companionship, rivalry, love and hate, jealousy and envy, may all be present in varying degrees at different times. The problems between siblings usually arise when one child's needs are met

195

at the expense of another's. When there is a sick or dying child it is very difficult for this to be avoided. The sick child may become irritating to others, and be very demanding to his parents, who themselves feel extreme tenderness for him and may tend to over-indulge him. The illness may restrict activities the siblings might otherwise enjoy. Finding themselves in these ways deprived they may 'take it out on' the child, feeling hostile and resentful towards him for his demands and to the parents for complying with them.

If the ill child is the younger, jealousies and rivalries originating at the time that this child was born may be reactivated. If the child is older, feelings about his privileges and accomplishments, previously envied, may be intensified. The siblings may well feel guilty at being well and at home, guilty about the resentment that they feel and they may wonder sometimes if the hostility they have felt for the sick child is in some way responsible for his illness. Occasionally they may even want to be rid of him and feel guilty about this too. At the same time there will also be much concern felt for the sick child. This will be real but it may become exaggerated in order to cover up and compensate for the negative or ambivalent feelings just described.

What should be told to the siblings of the nature and prognosis of the sick child's illness? This is a very controversial subject. A certain amount depends on how much the sick child knows. It seems that older siblings, say those over ten years old, should at some time be informed about the outlook, in spite of the difficulties this may give rise to, particularly when they are visiting the sick child in hospital, or when the sick child comes home because of a temporary improve-ment or to die. It is difficult enough for adults faced with people who are dying, but even more so for children, with their more intense relationships and their immaturity in dealing with difficult situa-tions. Occasionally we have found that siblings have not wanted to visit once they have been told. The parents may also fear, especially with the younger brothers and sisters, the possibility of casual remarks. Anxiety is felt that the siblings may comment on the approaching death and in one case because of this possibility visiting by siblings ceased after they were told.

On the other hand if the siblings can be helped to voice their worries or ask questions (the parents may be better able to do this if they themselves have had help) the fact that the sick child is going to die may emerge. A formal 'telling' would seem undesirable but the more honesty that can be achieved in family discussions the sooner will the siblings grasp reality without such formal telling and probably this will benefit them. Binger *et al.* (1969) in their retro-spective interviews of families in which a child had died of leukaemia found that 'most families would have told the older siblings of the diagnosis and prognosis'.

It has been said by Cecily Saunders (1969) that the dying child needs to have 'a climate of security' and indeed the siblings' need is just that. The parents too need much support in helping them with a situation of anguish for there must be everywhere a feeling of abandonment—the parents abandoned by their child, the dying child 'abandoned' by his parents and, at home, the brothers and sisters facing the universal fear of children—that of being abandoned.

The death

But when death comes, how do the children react? Though there are many similarities in the way a child may respond to a loss, there are also many differences and these may cause difficulties in the family if they are not understood. For an adult to mourn, everything is temporarily suspended, but this is not possible for the child in the course of his emotional development which has to proceed (Nahera, 1970).

There is a tendency for adults to protect children from death. Questions about the beginning of life are answered easily because we really know the answer, those about the end are less welcome and there is more hesitancy because we really do not know. Partly because of this, but mainly due to their intellectual immaturity, children under five are not able to grasp the full significance of death except fleetingly. This does not prevent them using the word appropriately thus making people think they understand more than they do. From around the age of five their intellectual understanding of death increases (Anthony, 1971). They see that death is caused by something and is not the result of their wishes, that it is universal and so may happen to them and that it is final. By the age of ten they usually can grasp the adult concept of death.

However, when a brother or sister dies it is different. This is painful and they do not have the emotional capacity to tolerate the pain, and can therefore only experience sadness for short periods. Also because of the pain they deny both facts and feelings and bring forward opposite thoughts and feelings. Rather than lose the relationship they substitute something (e.g., a fantasy relationship is kept going, the mother is asked to have another child, or a new friend may be endowed with the characteristics of the lost sibling). Finding the emotional pain too much to tolerate they may wait for a while, till it becomes easier to bear. At the time therefore they show no grief but later may do so under the cover of some other loss, or when something reminds them of it, and thus displace their feelings. When this happens they may over-react to the death of a pet, the loss of a friend, or their failure in some hoped-for achievement. By becoming unusually upset they are in fact enabling themselves to work on their feelings of loss and hopefully adjusting to it. Understanding and help at this time will be of great benefit to them.

Unable to express their feelings in any other way they may do so by developing various behaviour disturbances—these may include (more often in boys) some degree of delinquency.

Some writings on sibling loss in children

Though there have been a number of reports on the effect of parental death on children there have been only a few concerning the effect of sibling death.

Cain, Fast and Erickson (1964) describe reactions in children to the death of a sibling. The children were psychiatric patients and in each there was evidence that the symptoms were substantially related to the death of a sibling. The age at which the children were seen, the age at the time of death and details surrounding this are not mentioned, but those of chronic illness and sudden death are included. In about half the cases guilt was present and, in some, still active five years or more after the event. The children were sad and depressed, often feeling responsible for the death or that they should have died instead. Some had suicidal thoughts and impulses, wishing to join the dead sibling, and pondered on the good and bad thoughts, and actions, related to the dead sibling and became accident prone and presented punishment seeking behaviour. Poor progress at school seemed to confirm their feelings of worthlessness. Further guilt was often imposed on the child by the parents because he showed no regret, sadness or grief at the loss of his sibling. Distorted concepts of illness and death caused these children to fear that coughs, colds, high temperatures or bruises could lead to death. Parents became overprotective of the remaining child, sometimes even indulging one particular child to make up for feelings of guilt concerning the dead child. Overprotection made the children immature and dependent, feeling small, inadequate and vulnerable in a dangerous world.

There were also disturbed attitudes to doctors and nurses, doctors being perceived as being impotent in the face of illness and even somehow responsible for the death. The parents probably contributed to this, for they were distrustful of doctors and were subsequently reluctant to let the remaining children be admitted to hospital for necessary medical treatment. God was also seen as a destructive element and faith in Him was lost. In nearly half there was hysterical identification with the dead sibling's symptoms, live children were confused with the dead sibling and in a few cases the parents even changed the living child's name to that of the dead child.

Green and Solnit (1964) mentioned overprotection following the death of a child as one of the causes of the vulnerable child syndrome.

Rogers (1966) describing children's reaction to sibling death showed that no specific syndrome could be designated as a reaction to sibling death.

MacCarthy (1969) described some phenomena encountered in paediatric practice and how mourning in children may present as physical symptoms. Though other members of the family had got over the loss, there might be one child who was still suffering from the effects. Feelings of guilt in the parents following the death of one child may mar relationships either with other children of those born after, so that they are unable to commit themselves to their living children. He presented a case to show how the ghost of the child who died may become an important factor in family relationships.

He points out the need for further consultations with the family after the death and that these should be taken by someone who had the responsibility for the child at the time of death and was with them during their distress.

Binger *et al.* (1969) described sibling reactions to death in families where a child died of leukaemia. Some childen cried and verbalised their grief, others worked it out in play activities, some apparently unconcerned at the time overreacted to subsequent loss or showed marked behavioural changes. The children felt responsible for the death—or thought they would die too. During the general turmoil parents were not able to deal effectively with their feelings.

Rosenblatt (1969) described the brief psychotherapy given to a six-year-old boy following the sudden death of his two-and-a-half-year-old sister. The boy was referred because he was preoccupied with the thought that he would soon die. Rosenblatt was not sure that, though the treatment resulted in symptomatic improvement, it would prevent neurosis later on.

Replacement children

These children merit special discussion. Cain and Cain (1964) describe a syndrome concerning children specifically procreated to replace one that had died. They found phobias specially centred upon death, fears of abandonment and castration, and having a special need to stay near their parents lest 'something' should happen. The result was that the children were infantile, immature and passive with regressions in all spheres. There was hysterical identification with the dead child's physical symptoms. As the children approached the age at which their sibling had died they might announce that they did not want to have any more birthdays and morbid preoccupations were frequent. Identity problems were common because parents compelled them to be like their dead sibling, but at the same time indicated that they could never be as good. Such parents were found to be depressed and to have suffered a surprising number of family losses in their own childhood. They had been unable to mourn the loss of the child.

Effects in adult age of sibling loss in childhood

It often happens that children may present with problems at the same age as the parents were at the time of a family crisis, e.g., a sibling death. Any situation that may remind parents of upsetting experiences in their childhood can precipitate disturbances.

Hilgard (1969) describes this situation, giving some examples. In one case a mother had a psychotic reaction when her son was admitted to hospital which brought back unresolved conflicts originating at the time her brother died in hospital. In another, a father committed suicide when his son was twelve years one day—the age he was when his brother died.

There appears to be a connection between sibling death and subsequent development of schizophrenia. Rosenzweig and Bray (1943) found that in patients with schizophrenia (as opposed to those with other diagnosis) there was a larger than expected number who had suffered from sibling death in childhood. Difficulty in mourning that occurs in families where there is a schizophrenic patient is further discribed by Welldon (1971).

Pollock (1962) found in patients referred to him that a number had experienced a sibling death. What is interesting is that the women had lost older brothers and the men younger brothers. He postulates (1972) that it was the loss of two sisters that contributed to the pathological mourning shown by Bertha Poppenheim (Anna O), a famous case treated by Bruer.

It seems that the effect of the death of a brother or sister may continue in one way for many years.

200

Ways in which the paediatric ward can help the family

During the diagnostic period, the consultant will have been able to make some assessment as to how well the family functions. Further information concerning previous stresses and how well the family have coped with them, may be obtainable from the general practitioner. The oncoming death will reawaken feelings associated with other deaths. A good paediatric history will have brought to light other deaths in the family, and how they are seen. (It will not have brought out deaths the parents themselves experienced in their childhood.)

All this will enable the consultant to have some idea as to how the parents and children will be able to cope with this tragedy, and thus some idea of what the possible effects on the children will be. It will enable him and the ward staff to provide help that is appropriate, so that as far as possible the effect on the children may be mitigated. Because of the special relationship that is built up in the care of the sick child, the staff have a unique opportunity of helping in this.

It is interesting to reflect that when we know what to do, as in the case of infection following contact with physical illness, practical steps are taken for prevention. For instance, if tuberculosis is found in the family, active steps are taken to find contacts, to investigate them and inoculate them if necessary. And we now vaccinate against measles to diminish the occurrence of encephalitis. Much less effort is put into the emotional repercussions following the death of a child in the family, even though the consequences may be just as severe in a different way (e.g. suicide, to take an extreme example).

These are some of the ways whereby the paediatric staff can be of particular help.

Understanding of the physical illness is important. This will start when the doctor sees the parents following the diagnosis (it is important that both parents are available at this stage). The shock the parents feel will prevent understanding of the illness at the time. Opportunities for further discussions should be encouraged. The doctor has to realise that there may have to be many of these repetitions and must be patient. It has been suggested that the siblings of the child should be included in these talks (Green and Solnit, 1964; Binger *et al.* 1969). If this is practical, and it is felt that the siblings are old enough to understand, with reservations, this seems a good plan; for the more they can understand directly from the parents and from the doctor, the less likely they are to have misconceptions about illness (Cain *et al.*, 1964). But the desire for information can get out of hand.

201

Participation in the nursing of their child will also enable the parents to gain understanding and they will also gain confidence in themselves by looking after their child but this is apt to be badly undermined by the initial shock of the diagnosis of a fatal prognosis.

Encouragement of visiting by siblings is important in order that they shall not build up fantasies about the ill child. It also enables them to see the hospital in a rather better perspective, and to ask questions themselves of the doctors and the nurses.

Parents should be encouraged both to discuss ways and means whereby they, and the other children, can enjoy the rest of his life. The memories they build up together may be a comfort during the mourning period. If they can enjoy life, feelings about the death will be easier to manage. But they do need to have help in looking at the death. They need to talk about him who is dying and what he has meant to them, so that when he dies he is not too much idolised though it is impossible for this not to happen to a certain extent. They must realise that their hopes and aspirations are truly lost, rather than be left looking for a successor or a substitute in the form of one of the other children or a replacement child.

Discussion of the needs of brothers and sisters is necessary but it is very difficult sometimes for the parents to be aware of the needs of their children as well as their own, and they may need support in this. Frequent visiting by the siblings of the sick child will give the parents a chance to bring up any problems that they may have. The parents should be made aware that help is available if they become concerned about their children. Discussion increases awareness of the other children's needs, and it is very important that this takes place. A child disturbance is often a very good indication as to whether the family are coping with this stress or not.

In order that the parents can help their children, they themselves need to express their feelings and have them accepted and understood. The way this is done and the feelings aroused in those who are the recipients is discussed in another chapter (chapter 15, p. 177). It is important that, as far as possible, there should not be a scapegoat for these feelings, for it is not good for the siblings to see either themselves or the medical staff used in this way.

Mutual trust between members of the staff is essential and ideally everyone should be aware of how they feel. Feelings evoked by the death of a child are strange. The staff may bring anxieties about their own death into the situation. Feelings of frustration, disappointment and anger are common to everyone, but this is easily left out of account in the understanding of difficulties in relationships between staff who normally work well together. No person or institution is without its faults, and feelings may be difficult to contain and look for a place to land. It might be tempting sometimes to collude with the parents in this respect. It is tiring for anyone who does this work, and it may bring up memories of deaths they themselves have experienced and not worked through.

The following description of a paediatric unit may serve as a guide to ways and means of helping the brothers and sisters of a dying child. For many years, unrestricted visiting of parents and siblings has been part of the normal routine of the paediatric (medical and surgical) unit. It is also routine that mothers of young children are asked on the child's admission if they have come prepared to stay. The needs of the child patient, as opposed to the needs of the young children at home, are discussed (MacCarthy, Lindsay and Morris, 1962). The decision is always left to the mothers themselves who obviously know the situation better. If for some reason they cannnot stay, they are encouraged to come back as often as is convenient. They belong to the life of the ward, participate in any nursing that they feel they are able to do. Again, they usually know what they can manage. Staff relationships with them are as important as those with the children. Mothers are well supported, both by the staff and by other mothers (Robertson, 1958). There is a sitting room for those who are resident, and they have their meals from a hot trolley. The non-resident mothers can go to the hospital canteen.

There is also very active encouragement for parents to bring up other children if they wish during the day. There is a play-lady and these children are often included in her activities in the ward, or out of doors when the weather is all right. Children enjoy the toys and also the pets that are on the ward. Older siblings may not be able to get there during the week because of homework, but they make up for this at weekends. Siblings in fact sometimes become so much a part of the ward that on one or two occasions they have got bathed and put into pyjamas by mistake.

There is a great deal of interest and concern by the staff for all members. The sister always points out that it is 'part of our way of life'. Parents do not always have to leave children at home while they visit, or to put it another way, they can visit more easily when they know they can bring other children. Without sibling visiting some patients would not be visited.

The psychiatrist is available for both formal and informal discussions with the staff. There is a weekly ward meeting which is taken by the paediatrician and which the child psychiatrist may attend when these sort of situations are discussed so that conflicts in the family will less often produce conflicts between the staff. There is

also a weekly seminar taken by the psychiatrist for nurses in training. Informal discussions also take place. All these are opportunities
for learning and for supporting the staff, thus enabling the staff to
'take' more from the parents, that is to say, accept the expression of
strong feelings by parents without feeling personally attacked.

In addition, the psychiatrist needs to be available for staff to
discuss the mental state of the parents, for occasionally psychiatric
help is needed both during the illness and at the time of the death.
For some parents, the strain will be too much and breakdowns which
have been known to include suicide or attempted suicides, will be an
added hazard for the children.

Involvement of a psychiatrist may be seen as alarming; for people
do not see normal grief and mourning as a psychiatric problem.
However, both a psychiatrist and a social worker may be seen as
understanding and neutral persons standing beside parents and
doctor. If the parents or siblings become upset, it is easier for someone not directly involved in the physical care of the child to help the
family than for the doctor or nurse, who may feel they have to justify
themselves, both to themselves as well as to the family. Even so, this
could seem an intrusion and it needs to be understood and discussed
beforehand.

The child psychiatrist can always be available to the parents to
help them with their children and in this context is seen simply as
someone who has specialised knowledge of how normal children
react to stress and in particular over illness and death. The children
themselves may be seen at the parents' request.

As often as possible the child psychiatrist is present when the
paediatrician tells the parents the diagnosis and prognosis so that
should they wish later on to discuss any aspect of the family, this
painful experience is one they will have shared.

From past experience on the ward, we are becoming increasingly
aware that the time of dying is not a time to sit back and do nothing.
It is a time when a lot of hard work needs to be done.

Illness and death is a family crisis. When the family is in a state of
turmoil and change, feelings and anxieties that go back many years
can be expressed and consequently may be resolved. The family are
more available for therapeutic intervention than at any other time.
The work that can be done may be of great benefit to brothers and
sisters who are left.

Everyone dealing with a family where a child is going to die
sometime—or is dying—should be aware of this, for it is an
opportunity that should not be missed. The work that can be
done may be of great value to the children who will go on living—

the brothers and sisters of the child for whom they have been caring.

References

ANTHONY, S. (1971), *The Discovery of Death in Childhood and After*, Allen Lane, London.

BINGER, C. M., ABLIN, A. R., FEUERSTEIN, R. C., KUSHNER, J. H., ZOGER, S. and MIKKELSEN, C. (1969), 'Childhood leukaemia—emotional impact on patient and family', *New England Journal of Medicine*, vol. 280 (8).

CAIN, A. C. and CAIN, B. S. (1964), 'On replacing a child', *Journal of the American Academy of Child Psychiatry*, vol. 3, pp. 443-56.

CAIN, A. C., FAST, I. and ERICKSON, M. E. (1964), 'Children's disturbed reactions to the death of a sibling', *American Journal of Orthopsychiatry*, vol. 34, pp. 741-52.

DAVIDSON, J. (1968), 'Infantile depression in a normal child', *Journal of the American Academy of Child Psychiatry*, vol. 7, p. 522.

DEBUSKEY, M. (ed.) (1970), *The Chronically Ill Child and his Family*, Charles Thomas, Illinois.

FEINBERG, D. (1970), 'Preventive therapy with siblings of a dying child', *Journal of the American Academy of Child Psychiatrists*, vol. 9, pp. 664-8.

FREUD, A. (1969), 'The concept of the rejecting mother', in Freud A., *Indications for Child Analysis and Other Papers*, Hogarth Press, London.

GREEN, M. and SOLNIT, A. J. (1964), 'Reactions to the threatened loss of a child. A vulnerable child syndrome. Paediatric management of the dying child', *Paediatrics*, vol. 37, pp. 53-66.

HARRISON, S. I., DAVENPORT, C. W. and MCDERMOTT, J. F. (1967), 'Children's reaction to bereavement', *Archives of General Psychiatry*, vol. 17, pp. 593-8.

HILGARD, J. (1969), 'Depressive and psychotic states on anniversaries of sibling death in childhood', in 'Aspects of Depression', eds. Edwin Shneidman and J. Magio Ortegg, *Internal Psychiatry Clinics*, vol. 6(2), pp. 197-211.

MACCARTHY, D. (1969), 'The repercussions of the death of a child', *Proceedings of the Royal Society of Medicine*, vol. 62, pp. 553-4.

MACCARTHY, D., LINDSAY, M. and MORRIS, I. (1962), 'Children in hospital with mothers', *Lancet*, 1, pp. 603-8.

NAHERA, A. (1970), 'Children's reaction to death', *Psychoanalytic Studies of the Child*, vol. 25, pp. 360-400.

ORBACH, C. E., SUTHERLAND, A. M. and BOZEMANN, M. (1955), 'Psychological impact of cancer and its treatment. III. The adaptation of mothers to the threatened loss of their children through leukaemia', *Cancer*, vol. 8, pp. 1-33.

POLLOCK, G. H. (1962), 'Childhood parent and sibling loss in adult patients', *Archives of General Psychiatry*, vol. 7, pp. 295-305.

POLLOCK, G. H. (1972), 'Bertha Pappenheim's pathological mourning—possible effects of sibling loss', *Archives of General Psychiatry*, vol. 70, pp. 476-93.

PRUGH, D. G. and HARLOW, R. G. (1962), '*Masked deprivation*' *in infants and young Children. Deprivation of maternal care*, Public Health Papers no. 14, World Health Organization.

ROBERTSON, J. (1958), 'Going to hospital with mother', Film, Tavistock Child Development Research Unit, London.

ROBERTSON, J. (1965), 'Mother-infant Interaction from Birth to Twelve Months. Two Case Studies', in Foss, B. M. (ed.), *Determinants of Infant Behaviour*, III, Methuen, London.

ROGERS, R. (1966), 'Children's reaction to sibling death', *Psychosomatic Medicine: Proceedings of the First International Congress of the Academy of Psychosomatic Medicine, Spain Excerpta Medica*, International Congress Series, no. 134.

ROSENBLATT, B. (1969), 'A young boy's reaction to the death of his sister', *Journal of the American Academy of Child Psychiatrists*, vol. 8 (2), pp. 321-5.

ROSENZWEIG, S. and BRAY, D. (1943), 'Sibling death in anamnesis of schizophrenic patients', *Archives of Neurology and Psychiatry*, vol. 49 (1), pp. 71-92.

RUTTER, M. (1970), 'Sex differences in children's response to family stress', in Koupernik, C. (ed.), *International Year Book of Child Psychiatry*, vol. I, *The Child and his Family*, Wiley, New York.

SANDLER, J. and JOFFE, W. G. (1965), 'Notes on childhood depression', *International Journal of Psychoanalysis*, vol. 46, pp. 80-96.

SAUNDERS, C. (1969), 'The management of fatal illness in childhood', *Proceedings of the Royal Society of Medicine*, vol. 62 (6), pp. 550-3.

SOLNIT, A. J. and GREEN, M. (1959), 'Psychologic considerations in the management of deaths on paediatric hospital services. 1. The doctor and the child's family', *Paediatrics*, vol. 24, pp. 106-12.

TURK, J. (1964), 'Impact of cystic fibrosis on family functioning', *Paediatrics*, vol. 34, pp. 67-71.

WELLDON, R. M. C. (1971), 'The shadow of death and its implications in 4 families, each with a hospitalised schizophrenic member', *Family Process*, vol. 10 (3), pp. 281-300.

206

Bereavement and the rebuilding of family life

Rev. Simon Stephens

'In your service of others you will feel, you will care, you will be hurt, you will have your heart broken. And it is doubtful if any of us can do anything at all until we have been very much hurt and until our hearts have been very much broken.'
Michael Ramsey Archbishop of Canterbury.

'For months after our son's death, I felt a physical pain such as I should imagine having an arm or leg amputated must feel. And how my arms ached with emptiness!'

'His death left a terrible gap.'

'Please help us! We so often hear people advising us to pull ourselves together...but no one has given us any helpful suggestions.'

'The house seems so lonely and quiet.'

'My grief is still as keen as ever, mainly because no one has ever let me talk about it, not even a minister or doctor.'

'We cannot resume a normal life.'

'I felt like a leper in those first months, though I realised that my neighbours only avoided me because they couldn't cope with the situation. They didn't know what to say!'

'My husband thinks it is "best to forget".'

'The main aim of my relatives and friends is to distract and cheer me.'

'What is wanted is a compassionate listener who will let the bereaved talk about their loss from every angle and be prepared to let them cry and to cry with them.'

'Not even one's nearest friends want to talk about it and this is one of the worst parts to bear.'

'To us his parents, it has been a heart breaking journey through a strange land of very often faltering faith in God and humanity.'

I make no excuse in introducing this final chapter on 'bereavement and the rebuilding of family life' with quotations from just a very few of the hundreds of letters which I have received from bereaved parents in recent years. Their words contain, I believe, the key to our understanding the nature of the taboo which surrounds the subject of death and bereavement in contemporary society. Furthermore, what they have written comes from their hearts and, because it does so, we should be able to pinpoint those areas in the 'bereavement crisis' which can be most effectively helped if the bereaved are to readjust satisfactorily to the reality of their loss. But to understand the 'state' of bereavement presupposes that we understand the nature of death. Indeed, if we are to be of any real help to the bereaved not only must we have explored the presence of death in our midst, but, even more important, wse must come to terms with our own dying. For only when faced with death in others do we truly discover our ability, or the lack of it, to cope with death within ourselves.

For many people death is synonymous with darkness and the unknown and for many thousands of years it has challenged the world's greatest philosophers. Different civilisations and different cultures have interpreted and reinterpreted the meaning and implications of death and from this exercise some of the world's great religions have been spawned. Peculiar to Western civilisation has been the concept of dying and death as a crisis situation in which all the participants come before God to be judged. Indeed, the concept of the world's end as the 'Last Assize' with God as judge, and homo-sapiens as the defendant, is a familiar one to those who have studied the tomes of Victorian theologians. Perhaps it was this unspoken fear of divine retribution for past mistakes and failures that prompted the association of death with darkness and spiritual damnation. In the last century, this association of death with judgment and punishment became the breeding ground of fear. And fuel was added to the flames (if I may be permitted to use the pun) when contemporary illustrators of children's books depicted death as some wretched skeletal vision wrapped in chains and uttering unrepeatable curses in the night air. In her endeavour to 'frighten' her children into good behaviour, the Church painted such a horrendous picture of death, that, one hundred years later, we have been left with a legacy of fear surrounding this topic which has permeated all levels of contemporary society. The taboo, the conspiracy of silence which tries to conceal contemporary man's fear of death and bereavement, is to be directly attributed to the hell-fire zeal of our Victorian forefathers. Subconsciously each one of us is caught up in this conspiracy, but it is essential that we break with it if we are to minister adequately and effectively to the bereaved. Death seems remote in an age which has sacrificed so much for materialistic gain. Meanwhile, the traditional trappings of British funerary are gradually being eased out by a society which regards dying and death as indecent and demands the disposal of the corpse with expediency and with the minimum of ceremonial.

This retreat from a realistic approach to death has influenced adversely two groups of people within our society who traditionally cared for the bereaved. The first is the wider community of relatives and friends. As vast impersonal conurbations have swallowed up the intimate cellular life of English villages and townships, so loneliness and insularity have become the hallmarks of much of today's living. People are possessed by their own problems. Only a very few are prepared to share those of others. Centuries ago, the care of the bereaved—whether widow, widower or orphan—was a corporate responsibility. Family and friends were then able to identify themselves with the sorrow in their midst and in their corporate expression of grief lay the key to healing of both body and mind. Today, however, society would deny that any such problem exists and those who are unable to cope with their loss alone are advised to seek professional guidance.

Traditionally, this second group of people, comprising doctors and the clergy, have always led the community to a corporate sense of responsibility for all those in any kind of need. Such leadership was both possible and influential until urban encroachment finally swept away that intimate pattern of community living of which England had been proud for so many centuries. But the lack of leadership today in this important field of pastoral care can be attributed not only to the strength of the taboo which surrounds death, but also to very serious omissions in the training of student doctors and clergy. For the ability to be a leader in a crisis situation such as bereavement is dependent not only on the man's strength of character but also upon the training he has received, either at medical school or theological college. The care of the bereaved should not be included in the student's curriculum as an optional extra. It is a must! And those who would become doctors and clergy must be provided with adequate opportunity through group discussion to come to terms with their own dying. Only when this lesson has been mastered by these two important groups within our society will the bereaved receive adequate care. Meanwhile those who mourn the loss of the object of their love will have to depend on the very few voluntary agencies who are trying to meet their needs.

But what is bereavement? There are always two parties to a death; the person who dies and the survivor who is bereaved. In his book *Man's Concern with Death* (1968) Arnold Toynbee reminds us that 'the capital fact about the relation between the living and the dying is that there are two parties to the suffering that death inflicts; and in the apportionment of this suffering, the survivor takes the brunt'. This is especially true, I believe, in all cases of parental grief, and although it is dangerous to generalise when talking about the 28,000 homes which in Great Britain annually mourn the death of a child, it would seem that the suffering of a considerable number of this important minority group is actually increased by society's inability to help. Words such as 'leper', 'social outcast', and haunting phrases such as 'a heart breaking journey through a strange land', are indicative of that feeling of rejection and alienation which so many parents experience following the death of their child. But if we are to be effective in our care of such parents, perhaps we should examine the nature of their grief—for grief is that emotion which we experience when we lose the object of our love. Again the exact nature or pattern of the grief experienced will be dependent on the circumstances in which the child died. A traumatic, sudden death may well have serious and far-reaching repercussions in the mental health of both parents and surviving siblings—whereas an anticipated death, such as that resulting from a malignant growth, may well have provided the family with an opportunity for anticipatory grief.

According to Lindemann (1944) grief is a definite syndrome with psychological and somatic symptomatology—for this reason I shall divide my study of parental grief reactions into the normal and the abnormal, and then into the physical and the psychological.

Normal reactions

Physical symptoms

(a) Shock and numbness This is felt in the initial stage of grief when the majority of parents are unable to comprehend the reality of their loss. Looking back at this stage in their bereavement, many parents found that they were unable to accept the news of their

child's death. It is a time of disbelief, which some parents have compared to a nightmare, through which one struggles and fights in a desperate attempt to reach the light of day... in the hope that the reality of the situation will prove to be a fantasy. Tears are difficult to shed and the bereaved parent will search the faces of those around him in the vain hope that they will support his subconscious denial of the gravity of the news.

(b) Sleeplessness, loss of appetite, general apathy As the days go past the bereaved parents will slowly accept the truth of their loss. They will cease to have an interest in themselves and their immediate dependants. Mealtimes will be forgotten, the house will go un-cleaned, clothes may remain unwashed for weeks at a time. As the shock and numbness begin to wear off, the parents will begin to pine for the deceased child. Sedatives will only delay this very painful but necessary stage in grief through which every parent must work— and alone—towards readjustment to his loss. The sense of mutila-tion, the feeling of being disabled is very strong. It is no exaggeration when parents compare this phase in their bereavement to the imagined pain accompanying the loss of a limb (Murray Parkes, 1972). Special attention should be given at this time to the needs of the surviving siblings, who either experience a feeling of rejection because their parents are preoccupied with their own grief, or else temporarily lose their freedom through reactive over-possession. The use of sedatives and tranquillisers during this painful transition from denial to acceptance of the loss is common, but in no way replaces the 'compassionate listener', who has the key to grief's lock, and in his sharing of it enables the bereaved to come to terms with his loss.

Psychological symptoms

(a) Guilt Irrespective of the circumstances in which the child died there is always a tendency among parents towards self-recrimina-tion. If the father had tested the brakes on his son's bicycle perhaps... if the family had pooled their resources and engaged a London specialist then possibly...these doubts and inner question-ings seem to haunt the mind of every bereaved parent, and, unless he or she is able to share them, the resulting guilt complex may well require specialist treatment if it is to be resolved successfully.

(b) Idealisation It has been said that death erases from the human mind those faults and imperfections of the deceased which might mar the memory of those who outlive them. This can be true of some

bereaved parents, who, at the emotional expense of their remaining child or children, either idealise, or even deify, the dead child. All those people concerned with the welfare of the bereaved family, especially the family doctor and the local school teacher must be alerted to the possible dangers here for the child who feels rejected by his parents because of the death of a sibling and who may, at a later date, become anti-social and manifest serious behavioural disorders.

(c) Identification with the deceased child   Another method of dealing with the emotional complications of ambivalence is the adoption of the peculiarities of speech or gesture which were features of the personality of the deceased. To my knowledge this is a rare occurrence in parental grief, but sometimes a change in mannerism in either parent or sibling may be correctly attributed to this.

(d) Preoccupation with the deceased child's image   'It is thirty-four years since our child died and I do not think there is a waking hour when she is not in my thoughts', writes a mother from the North of England. It is not uncommon for recently bereaved parents to spend hours scanning shopping-day crowds for a glimpse of the dead child. Sometimes so strong is their preoccupation with the deceased that the bereaved will actually pursue the deceased's image into a crowd only to discover that a very painful and embarrassing mistake has been made.

Abnormal reactions

It has been suggested by psychiatrists that abnormal reactions to the death of a child are the result of either an exaggeration or a prolongation of those symptoms mentioned earlier. It would seem that they occur when grief has either been postponed or delayed following the death. They are also closely linked with the bereaved parent's inability to share his or her sorrow with a sympathetic community. Of course it is difficult to classify all those reactions to grief which community medicine might describe as abnormal. However, the following list may act as a guide to those involved in this specialist field of care:

(1)   Over-activity without a sense of loss. The subconscious denies the reality of the loss. The bereaved parent may well throw himself into a frenzy of activity in a desperate attempt to avoid being confronted with his child's death.

212

(2)   The acquisition of symptoms belonging to the last illness of the child. It is not uncommon for recently bereaved parents to experience some of the pain and discomfort which was associated with the child's illness. Such symptoms not infrequently occur at the time of an anniversary—perhaps a birthday but more often near to the anniversary of the child's death.

(3)   A recognised medical disease, namely a group of psychosomatic conditions—predominantly ulcerative colitis, rheumatoid arthritis and asthma.

(4)   Changed relationships to relatives and friends. As a result of abnormal grief reactions a previously gregarious person may give up all social contact and live the life of a recluse.

(5)   Furious hostility against specific persons is not uncommon amongst bereaved parents. Frequently the clergy, seen by the bereaved as God's representatives, come under harsh criticism...'You talk about a God of love, but he did not help my child!', as indeed do members of the medical profession at whose feet the responsibility for the child's death is sometimes placed.

(6)   On some occasions the child's death overwhelms the parents with a wave of apathy. All initiative and drive disappear and the bereaved find it extremely difficult to make even the smallest decision.

(7)   Finally, severe depression with insomnia is also characteristic of an abnormal reaction to grief and if unchecked may result in a suicide attempt—that final desperate plea for attention and help.

If we are to avert such serious repercussions in the lives of those recently bereft of their children, we need to examine the exact nature of our ministry to the bereaved. Such a ministry should follow the general principles of a ministry to those in crisis. These include the provision of material aid, comfort and moral support whilst the sufferer does his hard work of grieving. There is no use in telling the recently bereaved father that he must 'pull himself together', and 'forget the past', nor is a bereaved mother helped by being told that her child's painless death was 'a blessing in disguise', or that with time the 'wound will heal'. For the wound will only heal when it has been purged of its bitterness, and, even so, a scar will always remain. It will always be extremely sensitive. Likewise no bereaved father will ever come to terms with the years behind him until somebody is prepared to help him look to the future.

The major task in the care of the bereaved and the rebuilding of a family's shattered life—to which all others are subsidiary—is that of enabling and encouraging the mourner to face the reality of his situation. 'The terrible gap' must be faced and arms must 'ache with emptiness' if the bereaved are to work through their grief to-

wards readjustment and rehabilitation. But those who would help
the bereaved through the 'strange land of very often faltering faith
in God and humanity' must be prepared to share the burden of
sorrow, and, because bereavement is something which they will have
to experience subjectively, the helpers,,irrespective of profession, will
have to make an effort of imaginative sympathy. They will have to
try in some degree to enter into the other person's experience while
controlling their own emotional involvement. As Archbishop
Ramsey suggests (quoted earlier in this chapter) this is necessarily a
painful process, but, in the sharing of those tears upon which contemporary society frowns, healing is to be found. And let us not
imagine that those who would care for bereaved parents must be
gifted with words! Words are inadequate! Quite simply a 'compassionate listener' is wanted. Somebody who will let the bereaved
talk about their loss at length and from every angle. Somebody who
is prepared to let them cry and to cry with them without fear of
embarrassment.

It was upon this tenet that the Society of the Compassionate
Friends was founded in 1969 to offer help and understanding to
bereaved parents without regard to their colour or creed. This
growing international society was the 'brain-child' of a small group
of Warwickshire parents, all of whom had been bereft of a child,
and, as a result of their bereavement, had suffered ostracism at the
hands of the community. Concerned about society's apparent unwillingness to become involved in the much needed care of bereaved
parents, the Coventry group set about caring for one another, and, in
so doing, they found they were helping themselves. Grief and its tears
were shared, and in its sharing came not only peace of mind and
deliverance from guilt but a new zest for life. The ability to laugh or
simply to smile was rediscovered and the men folk recovered their
confidence not only on the factory floor but also in their ability to
cope with other children. Women who had lost all interest in their
appearance began to take a new interest in cosmetics, and a lorry
driver, who had abandoned his job on the day his son died in a road
accident, was taught to grasp the wheel once more. The privacy of
the individual was respected at all times but the Coventry group
emphasised that they were available day and night to help recently
bereaved parents work through their grief in sympathetic company.
Within four years, and with the help of publicity in many parts of the
English speaking world, this society has grown into a vast international organisation, with self-help groups of bereaved parents
meeting in places as far apart as Malvern and Miami, and Boston
and Birmingham!

But those who are closely associated with the work of the Society of the Compassionate Friends would express the hope that a day will arrive when the services of such an organisation are no longer needed. For although primarily the Society is dedicated to the care of the bereaved, it is also determined to remobilise the wider community to its responsibilities in the field of parental grief. Indeed its work has already excited considerable interest amongst those professional bodies mentioned elsewhere in this chapter. But it is only with team effort that the community will be able to care adequately for the bereaved parent. Of whom then, you may ask, does the team comprise?

The care of bereaved parents—a team responsibility

(a) Relatives and close friends At a time of crisis, the bereaved turn instinctively to members of their own family and to close personal friends for help. These are the only people who will have known the strength of the bond linking the survivor to the deceased. Only friends or close relatives will be able to understand fully the gravity of the loss sustained and should be able and willing to share the sorrow of the bereaved.

If positive help is not forthcoming from this group, then the consequences to the mental health of the bereaved may be extremely grave.

(b) The family doctor Tranquillisers and sedatives can never be a substitute for the compassionate listener, whether in the guise of a close relative, or the general practitioner. They can be of help to parents in the initial state of shock and numbness following the child's death, but if they are over-prescribed by a doctor who is unable to cope with the bereavement crisis, they may act as delaying agents in the path to recovery. Apart from his obvious medical skill and intimate knowledge of the family's history, the family doctor is in a position to alert the allied professions, both statutory and voluntary, to the specific needs of the parents in question. And, although doctors may well contend this suggestion because of the pressures under which they work, they might wish to co-ordinate the work of those agencies involved in the care of their patient(s).

(c) The social worker Armed with a considerable knowledge of local authority services and the working of voluntary agencies, the social worker is well able to apply his understanding of psychology to the needs of bereaved parents. If he thinks it necessary, he may enlist

215

the help of a local branch of the Society of the Compassionate Friends and encourage the immediate neighbourhood to take a special interest in grieving siblings. The neighbourhood in all probability will include the deceased child's school. The child's teacher and his peers, apart from being called on by the social worker to 'fill that terrible gap', may well have their own unresolved grief problems relating to the deceased child. These 'problems', which sometimes manifest themselves as behavioural disorders in those youngsters closest to the deceased, need to be understood by the sympathetic social worker.

[d] *The district nurse*   Wither her knowledge of the family, having tended the sick child, the district nurse should be able to pinpoint any abnormal reactions in the grieving family. As a friend she should encourage the parents to share their feelings with her. She should discuss the deceased child, with his gifts and his failings, openly with them. The parents should be encouraged to share their grief with one another, and, in so doing, avert either unnecessary marital stress or a complete breakdown in the marriage. But the success of this ministry is dependent upon the sensitivity of the helper.

(e) The parish clergy   In common with the family doctor, the parochial clergy will find their ministry to bereaved parents an extremely difficult one. No words can adequately express one's sorrow, but 'actions speak louder than words'. The clergyman will not always be remembered by the family for the prayers he used or for the homily he delivered at the burial service. But he will have made his mark if, in a quiet and unobtrusive way, he has shared the family's tears and mobilised his parishioners to be sensitive to the family's needs. How many times have bereaved parents expressed the wish to get away from it all—perhaps just for an evening—in order that they can 'sort themselves out', in the hope that their lives can be pieced together. So much depends upon the neighbourhood in which they live. And that neighbourhood is dependent in its care of bereaved parents upon the quality of its leadership.

Upon this team of doctor and clergyman, district nurse and social worker, relatives and friends, a great deal depends. If the professional workers through their training have come to accept the reality of death, they will be able to share their insight with the wider community upon whose hesitant shoulders the burden of corporate responsibility rests. This team, if well trained, can transform contemporary society's whole approach to dying and death in their midst. The taboo surrounding death will be finally broken down, and bereavement will no longer be thought contagious—rather a creative experience through which the human personality passes on the road to perfection.

But let us not imagine that the family who has lost a child through death will ever be quite the same again. In time and with care the wound will heal, but the scar on the family's soul will always remain. And so it should! For that sense of loss is not only a memorial to a well-loved child but also a tribute to all those who, throughout the entirety of his life, cared for him in both health and sickness. To forget is no path to a true cure. Only in remembering is healing and peace of mind to be found. The scar remains but with team effort and community participation its pain is transformed into the elixir of life.

They that love beyond the world cannot be separated by it. Death cannot kill what never dies. Nor can spirits ever be divided, they love and live in the same divine principle; the root and record of their friendship.

William Penn 1644-1718 (from Union of Friends)

Note

1 The National Secretary, Society of the Compassionate Friends, 8 Westfield Rd., Rugby, Warwickshire.

References

LINDEMANN, E. (1944), 'Symptomatology and management of acute grief', *American Journal of Psychiatry*, vol. 101, p. 141.

MURRAY PARKES, C. (1972), 'Components of the reaction to the loss of a limb, spouse or home', *Journal of Psychosomatic Research*, vol. 16, pp. 00-00.

MURRAY PARKES, C. (1972), 'Components of the reaction to the loss of a limb, spouse or home', *Journal of Psychosomatic Research*, vol. 16, pp. 343-9.

STEPHENS, S. (1972), *Death Comes Home*, Mowbray, Oxford.

TOYNBEE, A. (1968), *Man's Concern with Death*, Hodder & Stoughton, London.

217

Author index

Subject index

221